CONSENSUS IN THEOLOGY?
A Dialogue with Hans Küng and Edward Schillebeeckx

CONSENSUS IN THEOLOGY?

A Dialogue
with Hans Küng and Edward Schillebeeckx

by
HANS KÜNG, EDWARD SCHILLEBEECKX,

and

David Tracy, Avery Dulles, Gerard Sloyan, Leonard Swidler,
Rosemary Radford Ruether, Bernard Cooke, Arthur B. Crabtree,
George Lindbeck, David Willis, Paul M. van Buren,
Nikos A. Nissiotis, Jacob B. Agus, Seyyed Hossein Nasr,
Kana Mitra, John Nijenhuis, Werner H. Kelber, Karl-Josef Kuschel

Edited by
LEONARD SWIDLER

THE WESTMINSTER PRESS
Philadelphia

Originally published as *Journal of Ecumenical Studies* 17, No. 1 (Winter 1980)

Copyright © 1980 Journal of Ecumenical Studies

"Why I Remain a Catholic" copyright © 1980 Hans Küng. From *The Church —
Maintained in Truth*. Reprinted by permission of The Seabury Press.

The present volume has been revised and enlarged to include from earlier issues of
Journal of Ecumenical Studies reviews by Werner H. Kelber (Summer 1977),
Karl-Josef Kuschel (Spring 1979), and Leonard Swidler (Spring 1979).

First edition

Published by The Westminster Press ®
Philadelphia, Pennsylvania

Printed in the United States of America
9 8 7 6 5 4 3 2 1

Library of Congress Catalog Card Number 80-65385

CONTENTS

Contributors   i

Introduction
  Dialogue: The Way toward Consensus — *Leonard Swidler*   iii

Essays in Affirmation

  Toward a New Consensus in Catholic
    (and Ecumenical) Theology — *Hans Küng*   1

  I Believe in Jesus of Nazareth: The Christ,
    the Son of God, the Lord — *Edward Schillebeeckx*   18

Essays in Response

Roman Catholic

Particular Questions within General Consensus — *David Tracy*   33

Ecumenism and Theological Method — *Avery Dulles*   40

Jesus of Nazareth: Today's Way to God — *Gerard Sloyan*   49

History, Sociology and Dialogue: Elements in Contemporary
  Theological Method — *Leonard Swidler*   57

Is a New Christian Consensus Possible? — *Rosemary Radford Ruether*   63

The Experiential "Word of God" — *Bernard Cooke*   69

Protestant — Episcopal — Orthodox

Methodological Consensus? A Protestant Perspective
  — *Arthur B. Crabtree*   75

The Bible as Realistic Narrative — *George Lindbeck*   81

Catholic-Ecumenical Theological Consensus?
  A Reformed Perspective — *David Willis*   86

Historical Thinking and Dogmatics — *Paul M. van Buren*   94

An Orthodox Contribution to Consensus — *Nikos A. Nissiotis*   100

Jewish — Muslim — Hindu

Six Jewish Thoughts — *Jacob B. Agus*   110

A Muslim Reflection on Religion and Theology — *Seyyed Hossein Nasr* 112

A Hindu Self-Reflection — *Kana Mitra*   121

Schillebeeckx's and Küng's Recent Works

Christology without Jesus of Nazareth Is Ideology:
   A Monumental Work by Schillebeeckx on Jesus — *John Nijenhuis*   125

ON BEING A CHRISTIAN — *Reviewed by Werner H. Kelber*   141

DOES GOD EXIST? — *Reviewed by Leonard Swidler*   144

EXISTIERT GOTT? — *Reviewed by Karl-Josef Kuschel*   152

Final Statement

Why I Remain a Catholic — *Hans Küng*   159

CONTRIBUTORS

Jacob B. Agus (Jewish) was born in Poland, was ordained a rabbi from the Theological Seminary of Yeshiva University, and studied at Harvard University, where he received a Ph.D. in history and philosophy of religion. He has taught at Temple University, the Reconstructionist Rabbinical College, and at present teaches at Dropsie University. He is an Associate Editor of the *Journal of Ecumenical Studies*.

Bernard Cooke (Roman Catholic) studied at St. Louis University, St. Mary's College, from which he received a licentiate in theology, and the Institut Catholique in Paris, where he received a doctorate in theology. He has taught at Marquette University, the University of Windsor, University of Santa Clara, and at present is Professor of Religion at the University of Calgary. He is an Associate Editor of the *Journal of Ecumenical Studies*.

Arthur B. Crabtree (American Baptist) was born in England, studied at the University of Manchester and the University of Zurich, from which he received a Dr. Theol. He is Professor of Religious Studies at Villanova University and is an Associate Editor of the *Journal of Ecumenical Studies*.

Avery Dulles (Roman Catholic) became a Jesuit, was ordained a priest, and studied at Harvard University, Woodstock College, and the Gregorian University in Rome, from which he received an S.T.D. He is a past president of the Catholic Theological Society of America and is Professor of Theology at the Catholic University of America, Washington, DC.

Werner H. Kelber (Lutheran) was born in Germany, studied theology at the Universities of Munich, Tübingen, Erlangen, Princeton, and Chicago, where he received a Ph.D. in New Testament studies. He is on the faculty of Rice University, Houston.

Karl-Joseph Kuschel (Roman Catholic) was born in Germany, studied at the University of Tübingen, from which he received a doctorate in Catholic Theology. He is Research Fellow at the Institute for Ecumenical Research of the University of Tübingen.

Hans Küng (Roman Catholic) was born in Switzerland, ordained a diocesan priest, and studied at the Gregorian University in Rome, from which he received a licentiate in theology, and the Institut Catholique and the Sorbonne in Paris, from which he received a doctorate in theology. He is Professor of Dogmatic and Ecumenical Theology and Director of the Institute of Ecumenical Research of the University of Tübingen and an Associate Editor of the *Journal of Ecumenical Studies*.

George Lindbeck (Lutheran) studied at Gustavus Adolphus College and Yale University, from which he received a Ph.D. He was an official observer at the Second Vatican Council and is Professor of Theology at the Yale Divinity School. He is an Associate Editor of the *Journal of Ecumenical Studies*.

Kana Mitra (Hindu) was born in Dacca, India, studied philosophy at the University of Calcutta, receiving a B.A. (Honors) and M.A. She received the Ph.D. in Religion from Temple University with a dissertation on the bridge-building thought between Christianity and Hinduism by Raimundo Panikkar. She is on the faculty of LaSalle College, Philadelphia.

Seyyed Hossein Nasr (Muslim) was born in Iran, received a B.A. (with honors) in physics from Massachusetts Institute of Technology, an M.A. and Ph.D. in the Department of the History and Philosophy of Science of Harvard University. He is the former Chancellor of the Aryamehr University, Teheran, and President of the Iranian Academy of Philosophy, and at present is Professor of Islamics at Temple University, Philadelphia.

John Nijenhuis (Roman Catholic) was born in the Netherlands, became a Carmelite, was ordained a priest, and received a Ph.D. from the Angelicum University in Rome. He has taught philosophy and theology in Portugal, the Netherlands, Great Britain, Australia, and the U.S.A., and has just accepted a call to teach in Salisbury, Zimbabwe.

Nikos Nissiotis (Greek Orthodox) was born in Greece, studied at the universities of Zurich, Basel, Louvain, where he received a licentiate in Thomistic philosophy, and Athens, where he received a doctorate in theology. He was the Director of the Ecumenical Institute, Bossey, Switzerland, and at present is Professor of Theology at Athens University. He is an Associate Editor of the *Journal of Ecumenical Studies*.

Rosemary Ruether (Roman Catholic) studied at the Graduate School of Claremont where she received a Ph.D. in classical and early Christian history and thought. She has taught at Howard University, Harvard University, and at present teaches at Garrett-Evangelical Theological Seminary, Evanston, Illinois.

Edward Schillebeeckx (Roman Catholic) was born in Antwerp, Belgium, became a Dominican, was ordained a priest, and pursued higher theological studies at the Ecole des Hautes Etudes and the Collège de France in Paris and Le Saulchoir, where he received his doctorate in theology. Since 1957 he has been Professor of Dogmatics and History of Theology at the University of Nijmegen, Netherlands.

Gerard Sloyan (Roman Catholic) is a diocesan priest; he studied at Seton Hall University and the Catholic University of America, where he received the Ph.D. He is the editor of the New Testament of the New American Bible, Professor of Religion at Temple University, and an Associate Editor of the *Journal of Ecumenical Studies*.

Leonard Swidler (Roman Catholic) studied at St. Norbert College, Marquette University, and the University of Wisconsin, from which he received a Ph.D. in history and philosophy, and the universities of Munich and Tübingen, from which he received a licentiate in Catholic theology. He is Professor of Catholic Thought and Interreligious Dialogue at Temple University, Philadelphia, and co-founder and Editor of the *Journal of Ecumenical Studies*.

David Tracy (Roman Catholic) is a diocesan priest, former President of the Catholic Theological Society of America, author of *Blessed Rage for Order*, and at present is on the faculty of the Divinity School of the University of Chicago.

Paul M. van Buren (Episcopalian) studied at Harvard College, the Episcopal Theological School, and the University of Basel, where he received a D. Theol. He has taught at the Episcopal Theological Seminary of the Southwest, and at Temple University where he is presently a Professor of Religion.

David Willis (United Presbyterian) is Professor of Systematic Theology at Princeton Theological Seminary, and was the co-chairperson of the 1970-77 dialogue between the Vatican Secretariat for Promoting Christian Unity and the World Alliance of Reformed Churches.

INTRODUCTION

DIALOGUE: THE WAY TOWARD CONSENSUS

Leonard Swidler

The conception of this book took place in June, 1979, long before the calling of Edward Schillebeeckx to Rome for interrogation and the censure of Hans Küng. Schillebeeckx had been to Tübingen early in 1979 for an extended seminar, in the process of which the fundamental consensus on how to do theology between Küng and Schillebeeckx—as particularly exemplified in their recent "Jesus books"—became dramatically apparent to Küng. Küng then wondered whether the basic theological method employed by Schillebeeckx, himself, and others might provide the basis on which a new consensus on how to do theology could be formed among contemporary Catholic, and perhaps even non-Catholic, theologians. To this end Küng wrote an essay outlining this theological method as he employs it and as he perceived Schillebeeckx to also use it. The plan was then laid to solicit for a special issue of the *Journal of Ecumenical Studies* major essays responsive to Küng's by Schillebeeckx and leading Catholic and non-Catholic theologians from North America. Then Küng was in dialogical fashion to write a concluding essay, taking up the major points of the responsive essays.

However, Roman developments in the late Fall of 1979 prevented the complete carrying out of the original plans. As the pressure from Rome on Schillebeeckx mounted his health sagged so badly that he collapsed and was told by his physician that he had to cease all work for an extended period of time lest he bring on a heart attack. Hence, he had to forego the writing of a fresh essay commenting on Küng's, as planned. However, he fortunately had just completed a new essay on Christology, the focus of the current investigation by the Vatican and also the major exemplification of the theological method employed by him and Küng. Since it was written in French, the language chosen to be used in the December 13-15, 1979, Roman interrogation, it may well have been a kind of preparation for it. That essay was offered by Schillebeeckx as a substitute for the planned responsive essay. Hence it sees here the first light of day.*

The unexpected Vatican action against Küng on December 18, 1979, unleashed such a fury of turbulence and activity that continues even as this volume goes to press, and promises to continue for a long time to come, that it became impossible for Küng to find the time and calm needed to write the

---

*Because the male gender references are so imbedded in the French text that it would at times require major rewriting to eliminate them, and because Schillebeeckx is not available to undertake such work at present, the full application of *Journal of Ecumenical Studies* linguistic sexism guidelines has been suspended for this essay.

creative final response essay that was planned. Rather than delay this book indefinitely it was tentatively decided to proceed without it. The subject matter and authors involved made the making of this book available even without the planned Küng response as soon as possible extremely pressing.

On January 11, 1980, one more attempt was made by phone to see whether Küng thought it possible to write at least a brief final responding essay. Sadly it was learned that that very day Küng's health had suffered a serious setback, such that he too was told by his physician that he had to immediately reduce his activity to a minimum to avoid precipitating an even more serious condition. However, Küng had just completed an essay on "Why I Remain a Catholic," which he offered for publication at the end of this volume. Thus, we have here the latest substantive writings on the controverted subjects by both Küng and Schillebeeckx.

This volume is an example of how theologizing in the Church and the wider world should be carried on—not by juridical decision but by judicious dialogue. There is no prefabricated consensus here on consensus. The reactions to Küng's proposal and various aspects of his essay range over an extremely large spectrum. But the ideas proposed by Küng are taken seriously. The dialogue is engaged and sustained. When that is done there is solid hope, even expectation, that eventually better, more helpful conceptualizations and formulations will slowly and continually emerge. When the dialogue is not entered into or is broken off there is certitude that thought patterns will freeze, and that the passage of time and the accompanying changes in the world will quickly lead to a growing distortion, or at least irrelevance, of the Gospel, the Good News. The Church will less and less be able to speak to the world with effectiveness. Contrary to the old adage, in that case no news will *not* be Good News.

Dialogue, then, is the model that is recommended and exemplified by this book for doing theology, that is, reasoned reflection on one's beliefs about God and the meaning of human life. It is a model that is distinctively different from a defensive, or even explanatory, model—the second is really just a less abrasive, kindlier form of the first. They both assume that the first party has the truth which either must be defended against the attacks of assumedly evil-willed others, or explained to ignorant others. The dialogue model assumes a commitment to truth on the part of *all* participants, but also a realization that no one partner has an exclusive or complete hold on that truth. In the words of the Vatican Secretariat for Unbelievers, the purpose of dialogue is to attain "a greater grasp of truth . . . to liberate those engaged in discussion from their solitude and their mutual distrust . . . to reach an agreement, to be established in the realm of truth . . . and the achievement by common effort of a better grasp of truth and an extension of knowledge."[1]

---

[1]Secretariat for Unbelievers, *Humanae Personae Dignitatem*, August 28, 1968, in *Acta Apostolicae Sedis* 60 (1968), pp. 692-704; English in Austin Flannery, *Vatican Council II* (Collegeville, MN: Liturgical Press, 1975), p. 1005.

Various other elements of the central authority of the Roman Catholic Church have also in recent years publicly recognized the propriety of pursuing the truth by dialogue. For example, Pope Paul VI in 1964, in his very first encyclical, focussed on dialogue, stating that, "dialogue is *demanded* nowadays. . . . It is *demanded* by the dynamic course of action which is changing the face of modern society. It is *demanded* by the pluralism of society and by the maturity man has reached in this day and age. Be he religious or not, his secular education has enabled him to think and speak and conduct a dialogue with dignity."[2]

Ten years later the Vatican Committee for Religious Relations with the Jews wrote, "From now on real dialogue must be established."[3] Years earlier (in 1968), the Vatican Secretariat for Unbelievers forcefully expressed the idea that "all Christians should do their best to promote dialogue . . . as a duty of fraternal charity suited to our progressive and adult age."[4] This impressive document (is there a certain irony in the fact that—with its spirit of openness and generosity—it was issued by a Vatican agency for relations with unbelievers, and not from one for relations with Catholics, like the Congregation for the Doctrine of the Faith?) goes on to essentially link a commitment to dialogue with a commitment to Church renewal: "The willingness to engage in dialogue is the measure and the strength of that general renewal which must be carried out in the Church, which implies a still greater appreciation of liberty."[5] That being the case, such renewal-related dialogue should be pursued not only when the various views are moderately close together, but rather, "dialogue is of *greater* importance . . . when it takes place between people of different and even sometimes opposing opinions. They try to dispel each other's prejudiced opinions and to increase, as much as they are able, consensus between themselves."[6]

Thus dialogic "search for truth," as all the Catholic bishops of the world taught at Vatican II, "must be carried out in a manner that is appropriate to the dignity of the human person and his social nature, namely by free inquiry with the help of teaching or instruction, communication and *dialogue*."[7] According to at least one Vatican curial agency this dialogic search for truth is by no means limited to "practical" matters, but in a central way is to focus on theology and doctrine, and to do so without hesitation or trepidation: "Doctrinal dialogue should be initiated with courage and sincerity, with the greatest of freedom and with reverence. It focuses on doctrinal questions which are of concern to the parties to dialogue. They have different opinions but by common effort they

---

[2]Pope Paul VI, *Ecclesiam suam*, no. 79. Emphasis added.
[3]Committee for Religious Relations with the Jews, *Guidelines on Religious Relations with the Jews*, December 1, 1974, in Flannery, *Vatican Council II*, p. 744.
[4]*Humanae Personae Dignitatem*, ibid., p. 1003.
[5]Ibid.
[6]Ibid., p. 1005. Emphasis added.
[7]*Declaration on Religious Liberty*, December 7, 1965, no. 2, ibid., p. 801. Emphasis added.

strive to improve mutual understanding, to clarify matters on which they agree, and if possible to enlarge the areas of agreement. In this way the parties to dialogue can enrich each other."[8]

However, "If dialogue is to achieve its aims, it must obey the rules of truth and liberty. It needs sincere truth, thus excluding manipulated doctrinal discussion, discussion which is undertaken for political ends. . . . in discussion the truth will prevail by no other means than by the truth itself. Therefore the liberty of the participants must be ensured by law and reverence in practice."[9]

To be sure, there is risk involved in dialogue—if one is really open to what the partner says one has to reckon with the possibility that s/he will prove to be persuasive on any particular issue: "Doctrinal discussion requires perceptiveness, both in honestly setting out one's own opinion and in recognizing the truth everywhere, even if the truth demolishes one so that one is forced to reconsider one's own position, in theory and in practice, at least in part."[10]

We of course never will know for certain what the attitude of Albino Luciani would have been as Pope John I toward doing theology on the dialogue model, but we do know that he wrote a complimentary letter to Hans Küng on his 1974 book *On Being a Christian*,[11] which on the other hand was the object of a bitter, protracted attack by several German hierarchs[12] and the Congregation for the Doctrine of the Faith on December 18, 1979.[13]

Even though there has been an extraordinary return to the pre-Vatican II defensive model by the Congregation for the Doctrine of the Faith in 1979,[14] there still are public verbal commitments by Pope John Paul II to intellectual freedom of inquiry, which is the foundation of the dialogic model: "The Church needs her theologians, particularly in this time and age. . . . The Bishops of the Church . . . all need your [theologians'] work, your dedication and the fruits of your reflection. We desire to listen to you and we are eager to receive the valued assistance of your responsible scholarship. . . . We will never tire of insisting on the eminent role of the university . . . a place of scientific research which must

---

[8]*Humanae Personae Dignitatem*, ibid., p. 1007.

[9]Ibid., p. 1010.

[10]Ibid.

[11]Cf. Jason Petosa, "Inside NCR," *National Catholic Reporter* (Kansas City), January 18, 1980.

[12]Cf. Walter Jens, ed., *Um Nichts als die Wahrheit* (Munich: Piper Verlag, 1977).

[13]For the text of the Declaration, see the *New York Times*, December 19, 1979.

[14]The public facts of the restrictive actions by the Congregation for the Doctrine of the Faith (CDF) were reported widely in the press. In summary fashion they include the following: a) in Spring, 1979, Father Jacques Pohier was silenced by the CDF for his book *When I Speak of God*; b) in July, 1979, the CDF issued a condemnation of a book on sexuality by a team of American theologians headed by Father Anthony Kosnik; c) on December 13-15, 1979, Father Edward Schillebeeckx of Holland was interrogated by the CDF concerning alleged heretical opinions; d) on December 18, 1979, the CDF issued a Declaration stating that Hans Küng "has departed from the integral truth of Catholic faith, and therefore he can no longer be considered a Catholic theologian nor function as such in a teaching role"; e) in late December, 1979, the CDF "condemned" some of the writings of the liberation theologian Father Leonardo boff of Brazil.

apply the highest standards of scientific research, constantly updating its methods and working instruments . . . *in freedom of investigation.*[15] He even went so far as to comment that, "Truth is the power of peace. . . . What should one say of the practice of combatting or silencing those who do not share the same views?"[16] However, that statement was released by the Vatican on December 18, 1979, three days after the Vatican mandatory interrogation of Schillebeeckx and the same day the Vatican, with Pope John Paul II's explicit approval, censured Küng, "who did not share the same views" as the Congregation for the Doctrine of the Faith. Is the dialogic model to be used by the Vatican only *ad extra*, while the defensive model is to be used *ad intra*?[17] If such is the aim of some in the Curia, they are deluding themselves. All credibility in the necessary honesty and sincerity of the Roman Catholic partner is automatically shattered by such a double standard. This can be seen by the immediate, uniformly negative outpouring of protests by an extraordinarily wide range of Protestant and Orthodox Christians, starting with the World Council of Churches in Geneva:

December 19, 1979

Geneva (EPS) A Spokesman for the World Council of Churches (WCC) made the following statement today on the dispute between the Roman Catholic Curia and Professor Hans Küng:

"The dispute is in essence concerned with the issue of authority in the Church which has become the most sensitive point in ecumenical theological discussion. The action taken against Professor Küng, therefore, cannot be regarded simply as an internal affair of the Roman Catholic Church but has immediate ecumenical repercussions.

"Already in 1973 when the Sacred Congregation for the Doctrine of the Faith published a 'Declaration in Defence of the Catholic Doctrine on the Church against Certain Errors of the Present Day' (Mysterium ecclesiae), the General Secretary of the World Council of Churches, Dr. Philip A. Potter, said, in his report to Central Committee: 'I regret the publication of this Declaration which seems, in its basic intention, to limit the search for new ways of understanding and expressing the Church's faith and life in the post-Vatican 2 climate and in a rapidly changing world. It will now be necessary to discover how far and in what manner we can together pursue theological discussions whether bilaterally or multilaterally.'

---

[15]Pope John Paul II, "Address to Catholic Theologians and Scholars at the Catholic University of America," October 7, 1979. Emphasis added.

[16]Reported in the *Washington Post*, December 19, 1979.

[17]Cf. Thomas Sheehan, "Quo Vadis, Wojtyla?" *New York Review of Books*, vol. 27, no. 1 (February 7, 1980), pp. 38-44, for a detailed and documented analysis of what appears to be a widespread pattern of the application of the defensive model *ad intra*.

"The decision against Professor Küng highlights the urgent need for
the WCC, and in all likelihood for the Churches which are in official
dialogue with the Roman Catholic Church, to raise this fundamental
issue with the Secretariat for Promoting Christian Unity of the
Roman Curia."

In any case, Küng, Schillebeeckx, and the other Roman Catholic, Protestant, Orthodox and non-Christian scholars do here proceed to do theology
according to the dialogic model, which, as noted above, at least part of the
Vatican Curia insisted "is the measure and strength of that general renewal
which *must* be carried out in the Church, which implies a still greater appreciation of liberty. . . . Doctrinal dialogue should be initiated with courage and
sincerity, with the greatest freedom and with reverence,"[18] remembering that
2500 bishops at Vatican II stated that, "*all* are led . . . wherever necessary, to
undertake with vigor the task of renewal and reform," that all Catholics'
"primary duty is to make a careful and honest appraisal of whatever needs to be
renewed and done in the Catholic household itself," in working for the "continual reformation of which the Church always has need."[19]

---

[18]*Humanae Personae Dignitatem*, in Flannery, *Vatican Council II*, p. 1007. Emphasis
added.
[19]*Decree on Ecumenism*, November 21, 1964, ibid., pp. 457, 459. Emphasis added.

TOWARD A NEW CONSENSUS IN CATHOLIC
(AND ECUMENICAL) THEOLOGY

Hans Küng

In the recent past Catholic theology has experienced some stormy times. The Second Vatican Council turned out to be a more decisive theological turning-point than many observers initially assumed. The First Vatican Council brought on the virtually complete triumph of neo-scholastic theology. More precisely, it marked the victory of that brand of Vatican Denzinger theology that was almost entirely supported by the Church's Magisterium which culminated in those addresses of Pius XII, produced by Roman professors, and issued from the Vatican practically on a daily basis. However, the Second Vatican Council demonstrated that this theology was unable to deal effectively with the contemporary problems of humanity, the Church, and society. Although it did not result in the disappearance of the theology that dominated the scene between the First and Second Vatican Councils, it nonetheless did spell the end of its absolute theological hegemony. As a result there emerged once again the ancient Catholic theological pluralism which had been repressed with every possible means during the interim period in question. However, a concomitant development was the undermining of that no doubt artificial, yet nonetheless actual, consensus in Catholic theology that previously existed. Moreover, at that time it was not clear how any kind of consensus could be established.

On the surface Vatican II appeared to grapple only with intra-church problems and very constricted areas of theological concern. It touched upon the relationship between Scripture and tradition (however still within a Tridentine frame of reference). The Council dealt primarily with ecclesiology and the related issues of ecumenism, Judaism, world religions and religious freedom. Finally, it concerned itself with the question of the "Church in the Modern World." However, in the meantime, it was not generally noticed that all the other areas of theology were affected by the new orientation. What was only intimated in the debate about such topics as the Church, apostolic succession, the structure of offices and the celebration of the Eucharist became clearly evident to everyone in the debate over infallibility. That meant that the very foundations of the prevalent theology were under attack and apparently neither the defensive, positivist Vatican theology nor the newer patristic or speculative mediating theology could secure them. Was, in fact, a consensus in Catholic theology no longer possible?

It should be noted that those who have called attention to the problem were not its creators. Radical, fundamental questions had arisen since the Reformation and especially since the Enlightenment. However, the prevalent "Theologie der Vorzeit" (J. Kleutgen) did everything within its power to forestall them—at least until the next crisis. The numerous theological arguments prior to Vatican I

1

and the "Syllabus of Errors" of Pius IX 1864, the Modernist crisis and the encyclical "Pascendi" of Pius X (1907), the "Nouvelle Theologie" and the encyclical "Humani generis" of Pius XII (1950) along with the attendant purges represented the widely visible outbreak of an underground rumbling that had now surfaced.

Thus, in Vatican II, despite all the difficulties, much was accomplished theologically. It took place in the area of inner-church reform, especially worship, and in the relationship to other churches, the Jews and the other religions of the world, and finally in the Church's stance vis-à-vis contemporary society in general. However, a genuine reflection on theological foundations could not take place because of the domination of the Council by the curial apparatus, especially the theological commission under Cardinal Ottaviani. As a result there were no decisive contributions from the domains of critical exegesis or the history of dogma nor above all from Protestant and Orthodox theology. The foundation appeared once again to be given in defined or undefined traditional doctrinal elements. To be sure, even a not particularly sensitive observer could perceive a dangerous dampness on the arches and corrosion on the walls of the great traditional doctrinal edifice. However, instead of a radical restoration of the foundations, what one found was an attempt to cover over the elements under attack with new paint. Little wonder then that after the Council the critical defects were soon visible again and the corrosion threatened the stability of the entire edifice of traditional doctrine.

There was a double movement evident in the post-Conciliar theology. On one hand the movement was centripetal. Critical research proceeded from the secondary areas of research of ecclesiology and ecumenism to a quest for sure foundations necessary to the primary areas of Christology and the theology of God. Exegesis had effected preparatory work in this domain for decades with its quest for the historical Jesus. The demand to integrate the results of this work into a benumbed neo-scholastic dogmatics became ever more imperative. And since modern exegesis was generally neglected in otherwise productive movements of theological renewal, such as the patristics-oriented "ressourcement" (H. DeLubac, J. Danielou, H. U. Von Balthasar) as well as the speculative-transcendental mediation of Karl Rahner, their insufficiency became more and more apparent.

On the other hand the movement was centrifugal. "The Modern World," introduced into the Church during the Council, desired not only abstract and general theological recognition but as serious a consideration as possible in all its multi-layeredness and ambivalence. Reading the "signs of the times" proved to be an endlessly more difficult and complex task than had been assumed in the Council. The societal upheavals of the late sixties gave rise directly to "political theology" and then in Latin America to a "Theology of Liberation."

In our current decade it has become increasingly evident that the only theology (primarily systematic and especially dogmatic theology) that could survive the future would be one that was daringly able to blend two vital elements in a nontraditional and highly convincing manner. These two elements are a "return to the sources" and a "venturing forth on to uncharted waters," or to put the matter less poetically, *a theology of Christian origins and center enunciated within the horizon of the contemporary world.*

Is all this self-evident? No, such a theology is essentially different from those which envision Church dogmas as the *terminus a quo* and *terminus ad quem* of systematic theology. Such theologies reiterate in positivistic fashion dogmas that have become questionable while attempting to demonstrate their validity on the basis of Scripture and tradition, attempting to make them more palatable to contemporary humanity by the use of transcendental or other speculative methodologies. On the other hand, a theology which attempts to reflect out of the Christian origins and center within the horizon of the contemporary world will not view Church dogmas, despite all necessary critiques, as unnecessary or even impossible. Rather, these dogmas will retain their function, or better, they will recover their original function. Unlike the various forms of Denzinger theology, dogmas will not be equated with the Christian message: rather they will be viewed as originally formulated, as official aids, guides and warning signs in the course of the centuries that are intended to protect the Church, the individual, and of course theologians, from misunderstanding the Christian message.

A Possibly Useful Comparison

In both Edward Schillebeeckx's books on Jesus, *Jezus, het verhaal van een levende* (1974) (*Jesus, an Experiment in Christology*, 1979), and *Gerechtigheid en liefde: Genade en bevrijding* (1977) ("Justice and Love: Grace and Liberation"), and in my recent books, *Christ sein* (1974) (*On Being a Christian*, 1976), and *Existiert Gott? Antwort auf die Gottesfrage der Neuzeit* (1978) ("Does God Exist?"), an attempt was made to develop a theology of origins for the benefit of the present. It would thus be appropriate in accordance with a desire expressed by many to attempt a comparison of these two theologies, not in a detailed fashion but only in their main features, primarily in the area of hermeneutics and methodology. This comparison will be effected on the basis of Schillebeeckx's *Tussentijds verhaal over twee Jezusboeken* (1978) ("Interim Report Concerning Two Jesus Books") in which he presents the interpretive principles which guide both his Jesus books.[1] Such a comparison is all the more interesting since we were both theologians at Vatican II and have been active in the direction of the international theological publication *Concilium*. Although

---

[1]Unfortunately, the report was published in German under the completely misleading title: *Die Auferstehung Jesu als Grund der Erlösung* ("The Resurrection of Jesus as the Basis of Salvation").

our books were contemporaneous, they were written completely independently of one another.

Nevertheless, a comparison of these books is not an easy matter because their thematic structure is in no way identical. For example, in *On Being a Christian* there are only brief sections concerning grace and justification, whereas Schillebeeckx developed in the second volume a wide-ranging theology of grace from the New Testament.[2] In addition, Schillebeeckx handles the problem of God in the context of Christology, whereas I dealt with this theme in a separate volume in the light of modern philosophy and theology. Also, while Schillebeeckx provides a thorough treatment of hermeneutical-methodological issues, I have done so only where absolutely necessary. As a result Schillebeeckx envisions his two volumes as prolegomena to a future third volume that will actually treat of Christology. On the other hand, I hope to take up the question of *Justification* (1957) once again in the context of a treatise on "grace."

Nonetheless, if seen in the context of interpretive principles, despite their differences, there appears to emerge from these books *a fundamental hermeneutical agreement* which is shared not only by most Catholic exegetes but also by an increasing number of younger Catholic systematicians more adequately trained in exegesis. Perhaps this development will form the basis for a new fundamental consensus in Catholic (and possibly not only Catholic) theology, despite legitimate methodological and factual differences. The fundamental hermeneutical agreement primarily concerns what Schillebeeckx terms the "two sources" upon which contemporary scientific theology can draw, namely, the "traditional experience of the great Judeo-Christian movement on the one hand, and on the other the contemporary human experiences of Christians and non-Christians" (p. 13).[3]

Without engaging in the kind of semantic debate so common in theology, I would rather speak of the "two poles" of theology. I do so in order to highlight more vividly the tension within, as it were, the elliptical movement of our theologizing, more than would be the case in using an image of two sources or streams flowing together. Let us attempt to work out on the basis of Schillebeeckx's *Interim Report* a fundamental consensus that, despite the not to be overlooked distinctions, will possibly point the way for Catholic, and might I say for ecumenical, theology of the future. We will treat the first and second poles in separate sections and, in addition to pointing to fundamental agreements, we will also raise some critical questions.

---

[2]For this reason, the title in Dutch is most appropriate: *Gerechtigheid en liefde. Genade en bevrijding.*

[3]Unless otherwise indicated, quotations stem from Schillebeeckx's *Interim Report* that capsulizes and explicates the basics in his Jesus books, as well as responds to criticisms thereof.

The First "Source," Pole, and Standard of Christian Theology Is God's
Revelational Address in the History of Israel and the History of Jesus

The following points of agreement stand out:

1. *Divine revelation and human experience are not simply antithetical.*
Rather, divine revelation is only accessible through human experience. Schillebeeckx affirms quite rightly that revelation to be sure "does not originate in
subjective human experience and reflection" but "can only be perceived *in* and
through human experiences" (p. 20). God speaks through humans. God's revelation is not a human product or project, yet it embraces human projects,
experiences, events and interpretations. Human experience is not the ground of
God's revelation, rather God's revelation is the ground of the human faith
response. However, revelation is not directly and immediately the Word of God
but the human word engendered in an interpreted context from the experience
of the Word of God.

In this sense there is no revelation outside of human experience. And
without the specific experience of Jesus of Nazareth, who provides sense, a
meaning, and a direction to human existence, there would be no Christianity.
For the Christian faith, Jesus is the definitive revelation of God in the history of
Israel because he was so experienced by his first disciples (subjectively) and he
was such for them (objectively). The subjective and objective moments belong
together. "The interpretive experience is an essential element in the concept of
revelation" (p. 20f.). Certainly the faith of Jesus' disciples does not constitute
God's revelation, salvation and grace. However, without their experience of faith
they could proclaim nothing about Jesus as God's revelation, salvation and grace.
Thus revelation comes about "in a lengthy process of events, experiences and
interpretations," and "not as a supernatural 'intrusion' or, so to speak, a magical
trick, although it is nonetheless not a human product" (p. 21). Thus we have the
image of revelation coming "from above," from God but continually experienced, interpreted, verified and then made the object of theological reflection
"from below" by humanity. This leads us to our second point.

2. *The human experience of revelation is not interpreted after the fact.*
Rather it is always given from the outset through the medium of human
interpretation. Again, Schillebeeckx quite rightly affirms "the interpretive
explication is an inner moment of the experience itself, at first unexpressed and
known later upon reflection" (p. 22). No experience—of love, but also of
revelation, salvation and grace—is ever "pure," but only interpretively given,
even if this is not a matter of reflection from the outset. Every experience is
already accompanied by elements of interpretation. At the same time this
experience is enriched by further interpretive elements and finally verbalized in
specific conceptual or figurative statements of the interpretation (interpreta-
ment), which can affect the original experience by deepening or leveling it.

However, beyond all concepts and images there are general interpretive
frameworks or theoretical models of understanding (paradigms) of which we are

more or less conscious. It is from the perspective which they provide that we attempt to comprehend, order and synthesize our varying experiences. No experience, even in the instance of biblical or ecclesiastical expressions of faith, is without an interpretive framework, model of understanding or implicit theory. The influence of experience and theory is reciprocal.

Thus, not only the experiences from the history of Israel but also the experiences of Jesus were from the outset interpreted differently by the biblical authors. The basic common experience of salvation from God in Jesus was depicted in the Synoptics, in the Pauline and Johannine writings, in very distinct sets of questions and conceptual forms utilizing varying patterns of thought and speech. They wrote within the interpretive frameworks of their environment and the socio-cultural milieu of their age. These figurative and conceptual models and descriptions stem from a completely different world of experience that no longer speaks directly to us today, but which we must interpret anew.

At times the reality of Christian salvation was confused with certain time- and culture-bound images, concepts and frames of reference taken from popular experience (for example, release from slavery, bloody cultic sacrifice, world ruler). This occurred to the detriment of the Christian faith itself. "We cannot truly make it incumbent upon Christians throughout the ages who have believed in the salvific worth of the life and death of Jesus simply to give credence to all these 'interpretaments' or explanations. Once meaningful and suggestive images and interpretations can become irrelevant in another culture" (p. 25).

In the New Testament different interpretaments were utilized with great freedom. "This also affords us the liberty to depict anew our experience of salvation with Jesus in key terms that are taken from our own contemporary culture with its own problems, needs and expectations. These latter, of course, must also undergo the scrutiny of the expectation of Israel as it was fulfilled in Jesus. Even more, this must be done if we are to remain faithful to the experience of salvation in Jesus which New Testament Christians encountered, preached, and therefore promised to us" (p. 25). This leads us to the third point.

3. *The source, standard and criterion of Christian faith is the living Jesus of history.* Through historical-critical research into the life of Jesus the Christian faith is historically responsible in the light of the contemporary consciousness of problems and is protected from faulty interpretations arising from within or outside the Church. Schillebeeckx is correct in affirming that, "It is not the historical image of Jesus but rather the living Jesus of history who stands at the beginning and is the source, standard and criterion of that which the first Christians interpretively encountered in him. It is precisely by considering the structure of primitive Christian belief that historical critical research can clarify for us the manner in which the actual content of this original Christian belief was fulfilled by the Jesus of history" (p. 44).

Further historical inquiry into the Jesus of history is not only possible on the basis of the New Testament sources but also necessary in the light of the advanced state of the contemporary consciousness of problems. Christianity is not founded on myths, legends or tales, nor solely on a doctrine (for it is not a religion of a book). Rather, it is based primarily on the historical personality of Jesus of Nazareth who was seen as the Christ of God. The New Testament witness—kerygmatic reports—does not enable us to reconstruct Jesus' biographical or psychological development. Besides, this is not at all necessary. However, they do permit us to accomplish a task that is urgently required today for theological and pastoral reasons. Namely, today we can once again gain an insight into the original outlines of the message of Jesus as well as his personal lifestyle and destiny, which in the course of the centuries has been obscured and hidden. It should be possible for contemporary humanity to trace the "mental journey" (*itinerarium mentis*) of the first disciples from the baptism to the death of Jesus in order to comprehend why, after his death, he was proclaimed as the living Christ and Son of God. Only from the standpoint of his preaching and lifestyle does the execution of Jesus become comprehensible. It is only from this perspective that the cross and resurrection are not formalized into abstract events of salvation.

No contradiction can be permitted between the Jesus of history and the Christ of faith. We must be able to identify the Christ of faith as the Jesus of history. Naturally historical-critical research into the life of Jesus neither desires nor has the capacity to prove that the man Jesus of Nazareth is in reality the Christ of God. The recognition of Jesus as the Christ always remains a venture of faith and trust or a *metanoia*. However, historical-critical research can aid us in assuring that the Christ in whom we believe is really the man Jesus of Nazareth and not some other person or perhaps no one at all. Our belief in the true Christ can all too easily be distorted into a superstitious attachment to an imaginary Christ or to a mere sign or symbol. A theology that is aware of its responsibilities must take seriously the doubt experienced by so many of our contemporaries concerning the traditional image of Christ. It should defend the Christian faith not only against the assaults of non-belief but also against ecclesiastical short-circuits or distorted descriptions. The projections of belief as well as unbelief must undergo scrutiny from the perspective of the genuine historical reality of Jesus. Therefore, "fides quaerens intellectum historicum"—faith seeking historical understanding—must be combined with "intellectus historicus quaerens fidem"—a historical understanding seeking faith. Thus a faith-interpretation of Jesus, if it is truly to serve the interests of faith, must likewise be a historically plausible interpretation.

Only a theology which seriously considers and, as far as possible, attempts to solve those problems enunciated by history can be seen as functioning at the contemporary level of critical awareness current among those (in the West *and* the East) who have undergone a Western education. Only such scientific theology stands on a par with the scholarly spirit of our time. Thus it is an unavoidably arduous task to employ the historical-critical method in a comprehensive sense in order to find out what we can establish about the Jesus of history with scientific certainty or great probability. The result of this endeavor is not to abrogate the biblical canon or church tradition, for indeed the history of dogma finds its roots at the very beginning of the Christian movement, even in the New Testament.

First Area of Agreement

I am in full agreement with the hermeneutical principles of Edward Schillebeeckx that have been briefly outlined here. In fact, I presented these same principles in yet a different form in *On Being a Christian* and *Existiert Gott?* On the other hand Schillebeeckx might well be in agreement with the hermeneutical conclusions I contemporaneously yet independently worked out in the *Tübinger Theologische Quartalschrift* (1979/Nr. 1) in response to an essay by the exegete Josef Blank, "Exegese als theologische Basiswissenschaft." In that context I outlined some of the elements of the hermeneutical position that has appeared in my work from the programatic hermeneutical discussions with Ernst Käsemann and Hermann Diem (1962), to the initial realization of this program and the turn to the historical Jesus in *The Church* (1967), and continuing up until my latest publications.

Amazingly, Edward Schillebeeckx, originally an exponent of Thomism, has, in the search for sure foundations, traveled along the same path as I. It is a path pointed out by the New Testament itself as one on which alone the authority of Scripture is discovered, its inner unity realized. It is a path that provides a new access to the historical Jesus through the medium of historical-critical methodology. It was this Jesus who was experienced and proclaimed as Lord and Christ by the disciples.

Thus Schillebeeckx is attempting to realize a program similar to the one I formulated, which might serve as a foundation for a future consensus in Catholic theology. *Exegesis that is grounded in the historical-critical method calls for a dogmatics that is likewise historically-critically grounded.* This implies that the results of critical exegesis should not be hindered or ignored by dogmatic theology (neo-scholastic conservatism) nor circumvented, toyed with or domesticated (historical or speculative harmonization). Rather they must be taken up and systematically assimilated (historical-critical responsibility).

According to Vatican II Scripture should be the "soul" and "Principle of Life" of Catholic theology. The same Council also fundamentally affirmed the historical-critical method. Are we mistaken if we see signs among other Catholic theologians that there is a movement in the direction of historical-critical responsibility? Can a serious systematic theology that seeks to deal responsibly with Christian origins ground itself in anything other than the biblical findings attained through historical-critical exegesis, even if this requires a bit more effort on the part of the systematician? If an unhistorical exegesis is definitely out of date in this era, so also is an unhistorical dogmatic theology. If the Bible must undergo critical interpretation, it is all the more imperative that post-biblical dogmas be subject to the same scrutiny. A theology which fails to critically investigate the "data" and remains overtly or covertly authoritarian will in the future, despite protestations to the contrary, lose any viable claim to scientific respectability.

Question I

Edward Schillebeeckx depicts the Catholic as well as Protestant response to his two books about Jesus as "basically positive" (p. 10). He notes a fundamental agreement in all his detailed critical work above by exegetes (including German exegetes) and a fair critique by systematic theologians such as M. Löhrer and P. Schoonenberg. However, there were countless misunderstandings among individual German dogmatic theologians. Some theologians appear to read quite badly. Schillebeeckx often "rubbed his eyes" (v. p. 94) in disbelief when he realized how he was being misunderstood. He rejects interpretations and insinuations such as the label of "liberalism" on the part of W. Kasper, W. Löser and L. Scheffczyk as "unfounded," "false," "incomprehensible," yes even "science fiction." Perhaps this reaction is due to the shock of the Reformation, but why in the land of Luther do Catholic dogmatic theologians feel called upon again in this discussion to stand forth as the defenders of orthodoxy without a genuine understanding of the issues involved? To the "dismay" of those systematic theologians who "don't know what to make of the critical results of modern exegesis" (p. 10) Schillebeeckx states, "one cannot so completely affirm one's own perspective as the only legitimate theological possibility, for in so doing we will lose the capacity for a genuine understanding of other possibilities. There is no need for theologians to contribute further to the ever growing polarization by implying that one theology is more concerned than another in maintaining the purity of the Christian faith. Apparently we find here a more common 'plurality of anxieties' " (p. 114).

One would have to grant to Schillebeeckx that in the midst of the thoroughly justified concern about "orthodoxy," "the other concern, i.e., to transmit the unabbreviated Good News in an understandable fashion" is also justified, and "at certain times can be the more pressing of the two" (p. 10). Naturally that does not mean, according to Schillebeeckx, that we do not find in this case serious and legitimate questions needing to be discussed. It appears to me we need a methodological and substantive clarification if the fundamental consensus we desire is ever to be achieved. Only in this way can we be assured that secondary differences do not conceal or call into question a more primary consensus. This will be clarified briefly by an example which appears in the serious and systematic criticism of Schillebeeckx's larger work, as in his *Interim Report* (pp. 46-57). It touches on the systematic handling of the exegetical problem of Q.[4] To be sure Schillebeeckx has not, as some German critics contend, exhibited a tendentious "predilection" in favor of the source of sayings

---

[4]The same can be said for the concomitant hypothesis of a Palestinian Prophet Christology (v. pp. 77-78).

common to Matthew and Luke (equals Q). However, this hypothesis plays an important role in his historical reconstruction of the primordial level of the Christian *kerygma*. Since this collection of the Lord's sayings make no mention of the death and resurrection of Jesus, Schillebeeckx concludes that the first Christology—under the strong influence of the spirit of Judaism—must not have been an Easter Christology (of the crucified and risen Jesus) but a Parousia Christology (of the departed Jesus who was soon to return).

We really should not immediately raise such a historical question to the level of an issue of faith, as is done by the aforementioned dogmaticians. The solution to historical questions should not be prejudiced on the basis of dogmatic fears, as if what *may* not be, *cannot* be. "What really happened?" This question must be answered in an unprejudiced fashion *qua* historical question. We may assume with historical certainty the existence of a source of sayings that was lost very early. We can also assume with reasonable certainty that there existed at least within a certain context in the period prior to and during the composition of the New Testament a number of distinct Christologies. However, can we, on the basis of the Q hypothesis, proceed to postulate not only the existence of a *compiler* of the Q material but also a Q-community, even one which continued to exist until later? Does this not represent the construction of further, unverified hypotheses on the foundation of another hypothesis? Do not these additional hypotheses become all the more tenuous the higher we pile them? Does not this procedure misconstrue the literary character of the Q-material which essentially presents a collection of sayings of the historical Jesus whose historical credibility is enhanced by the absence of a soteriology of the cross and a Christology centered on the resurrection?

Regardless of how one handles the question of Q, I only mention this example in order to raise the methodological issue of the relationship of exegesis and dogmatics. Is it theologically correct and pastorally helpful (an area of great concern to Schillebeeckx) for systematic theologians to make a case on the basis of hypotheses that are either scarcely verified or represented by only isolated exegetes? We have in mind the kind of overdrawn hypotheses continually being formulated in the research into the historical Jesus and then sooner or later rectified. A systematician ought to avoid getting entangled in the thicket of exegetical hypotheses as if to serve as an arbiter among individual exegetes. He or she is not competent for that. His or her systematic presentation can all too easily divert into extraneous areas and end up as a purely hypothetical affair.

Well, then, how should we react to this myriad of exegetical opinions? Schillebeeckx correctly asserts that we need not as systematicians in every case await the general consensus among exegetes. In many instances such a consensus simply fails to appear. Then, often an individual exegete might prove to be a pathfinder by maintaining a correct insight against a band of colleagues who mutually support one another. Nonetheless, it appears to me that normally— when an issue does not need to be systematically and definitively decided—it is wiser methodologically for a systematic theologian to rely as much as possible on secure exegetical conclusions that are supported by the broad consensus of critical research. For example, the consensus in the research into the life of Jesus is quite extensive. Wherever possible, however, the systematician should leave open those exegetical questions that remain unclarified. I have done something like this in *On Being a Christian* in reference to the debate concerning the title "Son of Man." Schillebeeckx is in accord with this view in the matter of the Q-communities. Such an issue is "to a certain degree" meaningless for a systematic theology. "In terms of content this issue actually has very little significance" (p. 56).

And so what was said about the fundamental hermeneutical consensus is still valid. In fact, the degree of openness, expertise and intensity that Schillebeeckx, the systematic theologian, displays in his two major volumes in handling the biblical findings of critical research is truly amazing. At the same time, it is also amazing that he has provided us with a sensitive translation of ancient concepts into an idiom that is appealing to our age. Thus we have arrived at the second pillar of a possible hermeneutical consensus in Catholic theology.

The Second Source, Pole, and Horizon of Christian Theology Is Our Own Human World of Experience

We can note the following points of agreement:

1. *At issue here are our daily, common, human experiences in all their ambiguity.* It is not a question, as in prior theology, of the elite experiences of intellectual clerics. Nor are we concerned with novel yet nonetheless time-conditioned academic systems and methods. Rather, Schillebeeckx emphasizes that "under consideration here are our daily experiences, the feel for life we find in the world among human beings, our deepest problems of meaning, life, and society" (p. 14). In essence we must explore the common human experience of Christians and non-Christians. We must recognize that the humanities and the social and natural sciences also have important contributions to make in this context.

These experiences today are rarely or never unambiguously religious but rather are essentially ambivalent. In the secular world, in the contemporary crisis of faith, we can perceive a gap between tradition and experience (more precisely between the traditional Christian experience and the individual and collective experiences of today). However, this situation does not require that theology and the Church revert to a private spiritual subjectivity, or take refuge in purely political concerns, or nostalgically long for the Christian society of the past. The religious dimension of human existence, which is not to be equated with specific institutions or dogmas, is still a source of fascination for humanity. Indeed, humanity experiences anew its alienation in the secular, scientific, technological world.

2. *These human experiences stand in need of meaningful religious Christian*

interpretation. These vague non-directed ambiguous experiences that often push humanity to a limit (an ultimate senselessness or a transcendent meaning?) must be referred to a meaningful interpretation. This is possible for humanity only through the medium of a new comprehensive religious experience which integrates all previous experiences. However, by what means can we arrive at such a religious experience? Contemporary secular humanity rarely receives religious experiences directly from on high in the form of a passively endured experience. Instead, in the midst of immediacy and spontaneity, it experiences them more than earlier by means of reflection. As Schillebeeckx correctly mentions, "modern humanity ponders certain experiences and interprets them often in a cautious and groping fashion as religious. The ambiguous experiences that it undergoes are both positive (providing an experience of infinity) as well as negative (providing an experience of finitude). They confront contemporary humanity with a basic decision, i.e., they are a challenge to an honest confrontation with its own experience" (p. 15).

Such a religious confrontation with our experiences does not defacto occur in the abstract, in an isolated fashion. Rather, we find it in a specific culture or religious tradition, whether it be Christian or perhaps Buddhist. However, when does this religious encounter with the ambivalence of human experiences become an experience of Christian faith? "Whenever someone, in the light of what s/he has heard about Christianity, in the midst of this confrontation with human experiences, concludes 'Yes, that's it, that's it.' That which the churches proclaim in their message as an option in life can be experienced by others, and what for them can provisionally only be called a 'project of seeking' (H. Kuitert) will *within* this confrontation with experience (within the project of seeking) ultimately become a completely personal act of Christian faith—a personal faith conviction with a concrete Christian belief content" (pp. 16-17).

3. *Theology has to establish a critical correlation between traditional Christian experience and contemporary experience.* These days people accept the Christian credo less and less on the basis of the mere authority of another. Rather, it is accepted only in and through the confrontation with experience which is interpreted in the light of Christian history of experience as it is transmitted by the Church. According to Schillebeeckx that means "catechesis and preaching must not only illuminate contemporary human experience but must also unfold as responsibly, precisely and suggestively as possible what the Christian view of existence can concretely mean for humanity in our time" (p. 17).

In this process we cannot simply "utilize" an already well-known, purportedly timeless, eternal message. Instead, it calls for a new "translation" of this message in terms of our own world of experience. We have already heard the assertion that the contemporary situation is an inner, constitutive element in our understanding of God's revelation. Indeed, we can only employ the word "God" in a meaningful sense when it is experienced as a liberating response to the genuine problems of life. Our preaching cannot be carried on as a "take it or leave it" proposition. An alien conceptual system does not aid us in proclaiming the Gospel to modern humanity. And certainly we do not seek a type of catechesis that is exclusively experience-oriented without reference to the story of Jesus.

It already became clear as we reflected on the first pole of Christian theology that we cannot simply take over prior interpretations of the salvific significance of Jesus. Neither may we simply relegate the Jesus of history, his message, life-style and destiny to being an arbitrary symbol for our own human experiences. No, a theology that truly wishes to serve the Christian proclamation will not merely strive to find an arbitrary connection, but rather seek a "critical correlation" between past and present, between traditional Christian experience and our contemporary experience. According to Schillebeeckx such a critical correlation demands three things: "1) An analysis of our contemporary world of experience, 2) an investigation of the constant structures of the basic Christian experience spoken of by the New Testament and subsequent Christian tradition and 3) a critical relating of these two 'sources.' This is necessary for these biblical elements must structure our contemporary experience as they structured in a Christian fashion the actual environment of the various biblical authors. Only then can there be continuity in the Christian tradition. This continuity, however, also demands a sensitivity to any change in the horizon of questioning" (p. 63).

Second Area of Agreement

I am also in complete agreement with the foregoing hermeneutical principles of Edward Schillebeeckx. And I am probably not wrong in assuming that Schillebeeckx for his part could agree with the following *ten guiding principles for contemporary theology* that I formulated on the occasion of the publication of *Existiert Gott?*:

1. Theology should not be an esoteric science only for believers but should be intelligible to non-believers as well.

2. Theology should not exalt simple faith nor defend an "ecclesiastical" system but strive for the truth without compromise in intense scholarly fashion.

3. Ideological opponents should not be ignored or hereticized, nor theologically co-opted. Rather their views should be set out in a fair and factual discussion and interpreted *in optimam partem* as tolerantly as possible.

4. We should not only promote but actually practice an interdisciplinary approach. Along with a concentration upon our own field, we must maintain a constant dialogue with related fields.

5. We need neither hostile confrontation nor easy co-existence, but rather a

critical dialogue especially between theology and philosophy, theology and natural science: religion and rationality belong together!

6. Problems of the past should not have priority over the wideranging, multi-faceted dilemmas of contemporary humanity and society.

7. The criterion determining all other criteria of Christian theology can never again be some ecclesiastical or theological tradition or institution, but only the Gospel, the original Christian message itself. Thus, theology must everywhere be oriented toward the biblical findings analyzed by historical-critical analysis.

8. The Gospel should not be proclaimed in biblical archaisms nor in Hellenistic scholastic dogmatisms nor in fashionable philosophic-theological jargon. Rather, it should be expressed in the commonly understood language of contemporary humanity and we should not shy away from any effort in this direction.

9. Credible theory and livable practice, dogmatics and ethics, personal piety and reform of institutions must not be separated but seen in their insepar-able connection.

10. We must avoid a confessionalistic ghetto mentality. Instead we should espouse an ecumenical vision that takes into consideration the world religions as well as contemporary ideologies: as much tolerance as possible toward those things outside the Church, toward the religious in general, and the human in general, and the development of that which is specifically Christian belong together!

If it were possible to achieve agreement in Catholic circles concerning these, or similarly formulated, criteria for doing theology today, then we would not have to concern ourselves with actually establishing a fundamental consensus of content in Catholic theology—and far beyond it. A theology that was pursued according to the foregoing standards would certainly be directed to theologians but not only to theologians. It would be a Christian theology for contemporary humanity.

Question II
The fundamental consensus that we have established will not be altered if we pose a few questions concerning Schillebeeckx's three requirements for a "critical correlation." These questions are offered less in the spirit of criticism than as stimulating suggestions for further inquiry.

1. *Concerning the analysis of our contemporary world of experience* (cf. pp. 67-72): Such an analysis is obviously unavoidable for contemporary theology and it can be pursued in countless ways. However, therein lies the whole diffi-culty, i.e., how can we analytically apprehend this world of experience whose complexity is without precedent and is ever increasing through the effort of the

social and natural sciences? From experience theologians, especially those with political leanings, easily succumb to a twofold temptation. Either they wish to survey and judge this immensely vast and complex world from a quasi-divine perspective, *sub aspectu aeternitatis*, or in an all too earthy manner they simply affiliate themselves with a specific one-sided socio-political analysis with the corresponding pre-programmed conclusions. Is theology at all capable of providing an "analysis of our contemporary world of experience"? Thus Schillebeeckx's analysis briefly outlined in the *Interim Report* (in contrast to *Gerechtigheid en liefdet*) appears to me to come out too general and a bit one-sided. If it is correct that our Western society "stood and still stands under the banner of 'utilitarian individualism'" (p. 68) whose central value is often a purely formal freedom, then it should also be shown concurrently that we are today confronted with entirely different problems than at the time of Hobbes, Locke, Adam Smith and classical liberalism. In today's world it is not only hundreds of millions of people from the banks of the Elbe to the Yellow Sea who suffer under the physical embodiment of the social collective and state socialism and who long for nothing more ardently than civil freedoms. Also in Western Europe and North America, and with increasing industrialization even in the Third World, people from various levels of society are growing anxious in the face of an increasing government, bureaucracy, anonymous powers and regimentation as well as threats to their individual freedom in various areas. Schillebeeckx, as I do, concentrates "on the one hand upon our ineradicable hope for a future that is humanely livable and on the other hand upon an equally tenacious fear which we feel in the face of that future" (p. 68). We must, therefore, include these contrary movements in an analysis of our world of experience.

Briefly stated: our contemporary world of experience must be reflected in theology but not necessarily in the form of a comprehensive economic, political, sociological or philosophic analysis, but rather as a recurrent theme touching upon our contemporary experience and sense of life and current concern. An excellent example of what I have in mind is Schillebeeckx's treatment, in his second volume, of the problem of suffering ("a critical reflection on human suffering") along with the question of redemption and liberation. We can in great measure essentially agree with his conclusions about the relationship between salvation history and secular history, between salvation by God and salvation through human efforts, and between faith and politics.

2. *Concerning the investigation of the constant structures of the fundamental Christian experience in the New Testament and later tradition* (cf. pp. 63-67): Schillebeeckx has determined the following "four formative principles" as "constant structures" in the various New Testament writings: 1) theological and anthropological foundation, 2) Christological mediation, 3) ecclesiastical history and practice, 4) eschatological fulfillment. Expressed in other terms, we can say that in the New Testament we find God and humanity considered in the light of Jesus Christ and experienced in the faith community with a view to the final fulfillment. Naturally we have nothing against constant structures in the

New Testament nor their being systematized theologically. But we can question whether it is necessary to speak of God and humanity, or Jesus Christ and community, and of creation and fulfillment in the context of "four formative principles" and "constant structures" as if these principles and structures were the unifying force of the various New Testament writings and not the very concrete person and history of Jesus. At any rate, I would hesitate, in the face of the numerous attendant questions and problems, to say that "the various New Testament authors did nothing other than reformulate or recompose these four givens of the Christian experience while remaining faithful to their basic history" (p. 64). It appears to me rather that the New Testament authors constantly speak in a new fashion of God and humanity, world and community, in the light of the actual person and history of this Jesus without worrying about any structures and principles. Indeed they do not show concern about these four. If one is so inclined, one can of course find such structures everywhere in the New Testament just as previously Aristotelian scholastics in their milieu discovered the four *causae* (similarly schematic are "the four New Testament credo-models or credo-trends," pp. 82-87).

Let us not overstress this problem that may be just a matter of semantics. We only wish to warn against structuring and systematizing the biblical history and message too rigidly for this can result all too easily in a modern form of Scholasticism. We can only welcome the fact that constant structures have been developed out of the biblical findings which were provided by historical-critical research and can serve as criteria for evaluating the later Church and its theology. Schillebeeckx envisions doing just this in his third volume. Certainly given his expert knowledge of patristic and medieval theology, he will show his adversaries, who constantly speak of tradition, who indeed knows the tradition of the Church. In fact, for those who are truly knowledgeable, it is already clear how much Schillebeeckx's first two volumes were written in the context of the community of the Church and with a full knowledge of its great tradition. Moreover, in contemporary theology we can follow the example of the great patristic and medieval theologians without necessarily repeating the development of traditional doctrines before expounding our own genuine insights.

3. *Concerning the critical relating of both "sources"* (cf. pp. 72-76): No one would gainsay Schillebeeckx's attribution of an "essential, formative power" to the ancient (biblical) sources nor would one question the "productive and critical power" he assigns to "contemporary sources" (cf. p. 67). Actually, both sources are critically important for they serve a reciprocal, hermeneutical function that provokes further understanding. However, what is to be done when biblical and contemporary sources contradict one another or when contemporary "sources" once again present us with a "Führer" or some kind of political "holy movement" or similar modern achievements? Which source should carry the decisive weight in responding to the primary and ultimate questions that confront humanity today? Biblical and contemporary experiences do not always "harmonize" or "click" (cf. pp. 73-74). Very often there is

conflict between them. Must not, then, the "critical correlation" be necessarily transformed into a critical "confrontation"?

In view of the constant possibility of this conflict, it appears to me that Schillebeeckx's criteriology must be sharpened. Schillebeeckx would certainly agree that the definitive norms in dealing with primary and ultimate human questions are the special Christian experiences, or better, the Christian message, the Gospel and Jesus Christ himself. If, along with Schillebeeckx, we distinguish between the time-bound interpretaments and the salvific efficacy itself, we can make it clear that the center of Scripture, the Christian message, the Gospel, is the living Jesus who was experienced as the Christ by the first Christian community and originally proclaimed in the New Testament as he stands for God and humanity. Thus the New Testament, the original witness to this Christ, which today we must interpret historically-critically is and remains for Christians the definitive norm (*norma normans*) for all post-biblical tradition. This tradition can be normative, especially in the binding, universal pronouncements of the Church, but only in a derivative manner, i.e., as a norm that is itself validated by the Gospel (*norma normata*). It should be noted only in passing that in this context the crucial question of Catholic theology concerning infallibility is raised for Schillebeeckx.

But let us end here. It should have become sufficiently clear which path we must follow to arrive at a new fundamental consensus in Catholic, and possibly even ecumenical, theology. That path lies in the middle between ecclesiastical opportunism and unecclesial separatism. It lies in honest scientific research and unshaken faith in our subject matter and in the hope for a just resolution of conflicts.

Translated by Anthony Matteo, LaSalle College, Philadelphia

I BELIEVE IN JESUS OF NAZARETH:
THE CHRIST, THE SON OF GOD, THE LORD

Edward Schillebeeckx

Believing in God is possible only if, by the same act, one believes in humanity. The Christians of the early church in their creed of Christian faith, ancient yet ever new, expressed this experience in the formula which has been matured over the centuries: *"I believe in God*, creator of heaven and earth, and *in Jesus*, the Christ, his only Son, our Lord." This act of faith in the unconditional love of the creator for all that he has given life to on the one hand, and in this man, Jesus of Nazareth, on the other, is so paradoxical that it is possible only by the power of God's Spirit who has filled Jesus as well: *"I believe in the Holy Spirit."*

It is in the framework of this threefold articulation of what has been called from ancient times the Apostles' Creed that I set myself here to elucidate briefly the second article of our creed: the article about faith in Jesus Christ. Of all the names and titles that the New Testament uses to designate Jesus, only three are employed in the Creed: Christ, Only Son of God, Our Lord. It is in these terms that the disciples of Jesus in the past tried to formulate, out of their own experience as Jews, what the Jew Jesus signified for them, not only subjectively but objectively, and precisely as gift of God. What is primary in our Creed is not the formulas as such, despite their undeniable importance. What is basic are these groping attempts of Christians, that is, of believers and their leaders, that look to a witnessing to their concrete experience of salvation in Jesus *as gift of God*, and to expressing it in a way comprehensible to the faithful of the time. Their experience of salvation is primary. Only subsequently does there come progressive reflection on the implications of the rich interior depths of this expression of faith, lived as it is in light of new experiences, new problems, and new inquiries. The original experience out of which this Creed was born is that Jesus of Nazareth, the prophet of the final age, is "the Christ," that is to say, the salvation of God for humanity. Jesus was anointed (*christos*) by the Spirit of God in order to save his people (Is. 61:1, 52:7).

I. Christology As Concentrated Creation

After some generations of Christians, the early church situated this article of faith in the orbit of faith in God, the creator of heaven and earth. The two articles clarify one another mutually just as, in the Old Testament, the two

18

independent traditions of covenant and creation were influenced and enriched, purified, corrected, and reinforced mutually.[1]

Christian faith in creation implies that God loves us without limits or conditions, without merit on our part, unconditionally, infinitely. Creation is a divine act which, on the one hand, puts us unconditionally in our own sphere: finite, non-divine, destined to become truly human; and by which, on the other hand yet simultaneously, God defines himself in a gesture of gratuitous love as *our* God: our salvation and our happiness, the supreme content of the right and good way of being human. God creates a person freely with a view to the salvation and happiness of this human being, this very human being, but by the same no less sovereignly free impulse, he decides to be himself the ultimate meaning, the salvation, and the happiness of his creature. That is the meaning of Christian faith in God the creator. But how? This "how" unfolds in the course of a history that has human beings as its authors, for better or worse. Faith in God the creator is faith in a God who reveals himself. Who God is, that is to say, the way proper to our God of being God, is neither predetermined nor preconditioned but is unveiled for us in the course of our history. Christians also call their God the Lord, knowing in him the master of all history. To dare to create humanity is, on God's part, *a vote of confidence in humanity and its history* without there being posited on humanity's part any condition or guarantee as to what pertains to this vote of confidence. The creation of humanity is a blank check which God alone stands behind. It is a vote of confidence giving to the person who believes in God the creator the power to believe in word and deed that the rule of God, that is to say salvation and human happiness despite all experience to the contrary, is in fact *in the process of being realized*, by reason of the very person of God who calls humanity to realize it.

The struggle of God against all the powers of chaos, against all alienating factors, will be victorious. By their faith in creation Christians confess their belief that the most intimate being of God is, in total freedom, loving toward humanity and all that is free; that it is the salvation, the happiness, and even the enjoyment of the person, for the sake of all. That is why this God is faithful in total freedom, perpetually *a surprise for humanity*: "He is the one who is and who was and who is to come" (Rev. 1:8; 4:8).

Eternal Being, a stranger to any change in status like that of its creatures, is experienced by humanity in virtue of its absolute and eternal freedom as constantly new. Not the least of this newness is that it is always recognizable as the action of the same God. Behold him, new! Since the creative act of God is nothing other than his being eternally and absolutely free himself, it is by this

---

[1]That is why I speak, in this article, of "Christian faith in the creation," without making a distinction between the "Christian" aspects and the "philosophical" aspects of this notion of creation.

very fact relational with respect to his absolute or non-relative being.[2] From the depths of his absolute freedom God decides to be in relation to his creature, humanity in the world. In creating, God participates in the fragility of every creature. For anyone who shares in the Jewish and Christian faith in the living God, humanity is the business of God himself; but that fact does not reduce to the zero point the responsibility of humanity for its own history.

That is why "Christology"—the second article of faith, the salvation that comes to us from God in Jesus—cannot from that point on be understood other than as the emphatic concentration of faith in creation: its ultimate determination or concrete realization deriving from our very history and the historical appearance, in the midst of that history, of the person of Jesus of Nazareth. Faith in creation, then, for the Christian, is directed toward all that is not God, toward all that is creaturely and therefore fragile. Divine Being is manifested as liberating love in Jesus, the Christ.

It seems to us somewhat hard to believe in divine Being deciding in total freedom what he is, exactly what and how he—"it," "he," "she"—*is* (words are inadequate here!). Nonetheless it is indeed what is meant by believing in creation. We can determine freely only in very limited fashion and bound by a great number of conditions who, what, and how we wish to be, in accord with our own design and concept of life. Even in that, we are by and large surprised at our falling short. Divine Being, contrariwise, is always exactly and fully as God would have it be, without more or less and without remainder. God determines freely what he wishes to be for himself insofar as he is God and also for us, not by reason of an arbitrary will but an unconditioned love. For anyone who refuses injustice and alienation and chooses life, this faith in creation is one's basic anchoring point, the place where that person knows he or she is gratuitously but solidly rooted. "God is love. God's love was revealed in our midst in this way: he sent his only son into the world so that we might have life through him" (1 Jn. 4:8-9). The Word who, in the Old Testament, had especially spoken of love has, according to the New Testament, become flesh in Jesus of Nazareth: love made flesh.

That is why Christology is creation underlined, concentrated, and condensed: faith in creation *as God wishes it to be*. It is not a matter of a new plan of God directed toward creation as some religions or sects interpret certain existential experiences, but indeed of the supreme manifestation of being eternally new and at the same time constant and faithful, the being of God that we can perceive to a certain degree only in continued creation: in our history, of which he is Lord. What we confess in the Creed, in which faith in God the creator is essentially tied to faith in the man Jesus—the definitive or eschatological salvation of humanity—is that we declare ourselves ready to accept that fact

---

[2]I consciously use the (somewhat pedantic) word "relational" to avoid the ambiguity of the word "relative." Relative is opposed to absolute, while this is not necessarily the case with the word "relational."

that we are gratuitously and unconditionally loved by a God who takes the side of humanity: the very being human of humanity. Saint Paul expresses this with the greatest force when he writes: "God proves his love for us in this, that while we were still sinners Christ died for us" (Rom. 5:8), or in Johannine terms: "Love, then, consists in this: not that we have loved God, but that he has loved us" (1 Jn. 4:10).

It is only through Christ that we begin to perceive clearly that the divine mystery has depths that all things besides could not make us suspect. God the creator, the faithful one, is the liberating love of humanity, of a sort that fulfills and outruns every human effort, whether it be personal, social, or political.[3]

Evidently one can, one even must, put the question: from what basic data have people who call themselves Christians become convinced that God is in his essence a lover of human beings and not, as it has often been put in the past— even in the ancient settings of the Old Testament revelation—a God who disposes the life and death of humans like a sovereign despot? Christians have learned this from their experience of the life of Jesus: from his message of the rule of God and his way of living in conformity to it, from the concrete circumstances of his death, and finally from the apostolic witness to his resurrection from the dead.

II. The Foundation of Faith in Jesus Christ

a) Doctrine and Practice of the Rule of God

It is striking that the message and the way of life of Jesus, which are at the base of his death and resurrection, are not the object of any mention in the Creed (see below).

The rule of God is the biblical expression, found especially in the New Testament, to designate the divine Being—sovereign love, unconditional and liberating—in the measure in which it is affirmed and revealed in the life of those who do the will of God. It is sufficient to cite one text of the New Testament, among many others, in which the message of Jesus and his lifestyle are reported on. A good example would be the Lucan account of the calling of Peter (Lk. 5:1-11). We are told there of two boats drawn up on the shore and some fishermen who are mending their nets after an unsuccessful night of fishing or, to put it better, a complete waste of time. As if by chance Jesus passed by. He climbed quite casually into one of the empty boats and said to a fisherman, Simon who would be called Peter: "Put out into deep water." Simon looked at this man who was a complete stranger to him and, without particularly knowing why, acquiesced and embarked with Jesus, the others following him. Jesus then began to speak of a mysterious realm which was, however, perfectly concrete:

---

[3]This same pathos for the "humanum," in a scheme of transcendence, seems to me the very heart of the encyclical "Redemptor Hominis" of John Paul II.

"the rule of God," a realm destined for poor fishermen that would be the joy of those who weep, the filling of the hungry. Then suddenly he changed the subject and said: "Put out into deep water and lower your nets for a catch." And, in fact, a few moments later, the nets threatened to break under the weight of the fish. Coming in the wake of what Peter understood by "the rule that is to come," chiefly for the poor, for fishermen whose nets are empty, this catch signified for Peter the coming, the immediate proximity, of God, and he said in anguished tones: "Leave me, Lord. I am a sinful man." To discover God in the course of daily reality seems to make people anxious, as an eagle makes the little birds it is going to devour anxious. But Jesus said, "Do not be afraid"; and the story continues: "With that they brought their boats to land, left everything, and became his followers." The text says: "Do not be afraid. From now on you will be catching humans." But for Peter, then and there, the nub of the story was not in the fact that one day he would become a great apostle but in the reassuring word of Jesus: "Do not be afraid."

What hopes, what fears arising from their deepest emotions do people in fact entertain with respect to God? If they wish to give themselves entirely to God and occupy themselves with only what has to do with him, they expect one besides whom nothing has the right to exist any more, the great rapacious one who swallows up little birds; consequently, he must work for the abolition of himself and the entire creation.

But that all that concerns us is really God's business and vice versa, and that it is that which Jesus means when he speaks to us of the rule, outstrips all that we might be able to achieve of God on our own. Humanity sees God quite other than God sees himself and manifests himself! "Even the sparrow finds a home, and the swallow a nest" (Ps. 84:4). Why should the little bird be the prey of the devourer? When human beings think of God in their human way, that can lead to strange fantasies. Have not humans in the past engaged in human sacrifice to honor God? Are things very different today? What evils, what sufferings are perpetrated in our world in the name of God! But Jesus said: "Do not be afraid." When you hear God drawing near, fear not. God is a God of human beings, a God who, as Leviticus declares, holds human sacrifice in horror (Lv. 18:21-30; 20:1-5). God is a fire, to be sure, but a fire that does not consume the burning bush but leaves it intact. The honor of God consists in human happiness, and humanity finds its happiness in God.

What this happiness and salvation encompass in their fullness—the rule of God—outruns the capacities of our imagination. We only perceive a feeble reflection of this: on the one hand in human expressions of goodness, meaning and love; on the other hand in the mirror image that situations hold up to us in which the human in us experiences itself personally or socially threatened, oppressed and degraded, in a way that would make us rebel. These human experiences acquire their true relief, however, only against the background of the life of Jesus and his beneficent journeyings throughout Palestine. There the vision of what the rule of God can be takes on palpable and expressive form. The

New Testament expresses this truth in one of its oldest reminiscences when it declares that with the coming of Jesus the rule has drawn near (Mt. 12:28; Lk. 11:20; cf. Mt. 3:2; 4:17; 10:7; Mk. 1:15). The rule of God is a new mode of relationship between humanity and God, with a new kind of liberating relationship of people among themselves as its visible and tangible aspect, in the midst of a just and reconciled human community. The wolf and the lamb lie down together; the child plays near the cobra's den (Is. 11:6 and 8). To believe in that, to believe that Jesus is the Christ, essentially signifies confessing and recognizing in an effective way that Jesus has and will forever have a constitutive significance in what concerns the coming of God's rule, and consequently what concerns the healing and the fulfilling of humanity. At stake in the Creed is the proper and the unique relation of Jesus to the rule of God which comes to bring salvation to humanity. "I tell you, whoever acknowledges me before human beings, the son of man will acknowledge before the angels of God [that is to say, on the day of judgment]." Thus does the New Testament express the meaning that Jesus' own existence has for him (Lk. 12:8-9 = Mt. 10:32-33; cf. also Mk. 3:28-29; Mt. 12:32; Lk. 12:10). The person of Jesus has, for believers, a significance for universal history. It is a fundamental Christian conviction that in the coming of Jesus *God makes himself near to us* and it therefore *must*, in one way or another, find a place in the Credo of our faith.

We must indeed remain fully aware that, as in the Yahwist tradition, Jesus does not so much introduce a new doctrine of God as cast a prophetic and particularly penetrating glance on the way in which the notion of God functioned concretely in the society of his time at the expense of the "little ones." Jesus unmasked a conception of divinity that holds humanity in bondage. He fought for a vision of God as liberator of humanity—"Redemptor hominis"— a vision that has to be concretized in the conduct of life of each and of all. That is why the names of God and of Jesus become the bearers in the Gospel of a fruitful and liberating power. All religion that produces, in whatever fashion, dehumanizing fruits is either a false religion or a religion that has lost contact with itself, that no longer understands itself. This criterion of "humanization" proclaimed by Jesus, this passion for humanity's being human, for its healthy state, its identity and its integrity is by no means a reduction of religion, as the enemies of Jesus (then and now) fear. It is, on the contrary, the basic condition of its possibility and human credibility. Moreover, it is the only logical conclusion of the Christian vision of the God who is proclaimed as love.

It is of this God and no other that Jesus is the "great symbol": *the image of the invisible God* (Col. 1:15; cf. 2 Cor. 4:3-4). At the same time Jesus also put himself forward as the model of what the human being must be, the just, true, and good way to be human. What believers knew in one fashion or another, confronted by God himself in the person of Jesus, is expressed in the Creed in these terms: "I believe in Jesus, *the only son of God*." For in Jesus we are not only confronted by God, but indeed *questioned by him*: God confronts us in Jesus with his own divine Being. That is why Jesus is the Word of God, that is to say, not only the interpreter of humanity, someone who shows by word and deed how to realize in a true sense what a human being is, but who in so doing is also the interpreter or the exegete of God, someone who by word and deed makes us see who and how God is. The significance of "God" or even "humanity," Christians learn to spell out beginning with the life of Jesus. Drawing on their own problems, much later and quite different, the fathers of the Council of Chalcedon were animated by the same intent when they wrote: the one and same Jesus Christ is truly man and truly God, the salvation of God in Jesus. The spirit in which we confess the faith in praying the words of the Creed is not a spirit of abstract and nervous orthodoxy but the spirit of the Gospel: "I do believe. Help my lack of trust" (Mk. 9:23).

b) *He Was Crucified, Died, and Was Buried: Under Pontius Pilate*

Death comprises an essential part of everyone's life, and so it was with Jesus. But death takes on a particular meaning when it is premature, *a fortiori* when, as in the case of Jesus, a man is executed. This is not a lynching by a crowd that has been outraged beyond endurance but an execution commanded by those in power, especially when it is an occupying power. It cannot here be a matter of chance, still less of historical misunderstanding, such as is at times said of champions of an enlarged humanity. The message of Jesus about the rule of God was for the religious ruling class of the Jews a prophetic accusation and for the Roman occupiers a mortal, albeit implicit, condemnation. Jesus said to them: "The rulers of the gentiles give them commands and those who exercise authority over them think of themselves as benefactors. It cannot be that way with you" (Lk. 22:25-26). The same point is made even more strongly by Matthew: "Jesus said: 'You know how the rulers of the gentiles lord it over them; their great ones make them feel their power. It cannot be like that with you'" (Mt. 20:25-26). The message of the realm of a God concerned for human beings is in fact capable of mobilizing masses of the people, as is the case today in Latin America. Crucifixion, a form of execution applied by the Romans not only to common law criminals but also to the politically dangerous, is the major historical witness to prove that the message of Jesus actually appeared to be politically perilous. It is always that for those who hold religious and political power, and for anyone who does not seek to realize the genuine good of humanity. The rule of God thwarts all power that can only maintain itself by oppression, impoverishment or, at need, the sacrificing of populations.

"Crucified *under Pontius Pilate*." This last precision was not added without reason. It is, at the heart of the Credo, a dangerously precise historical reference. It is well, therefore, to judge the death of Jesus on the basis of his message and lifestyle and, only afterward, in light of his resurrection. Otherwise, the formula of faith, "he died for our sins," would not have meaning for people of today; it would cease to be credible. It is precisely when one abstracts from the message and conduct that led Jesus to his end that one obscures the message of salvation contained in the death itself. The death of Jesus is the humanly and historically "ineluctable" consequence of the radicalism of both his message and way of life that makes any master-slave relation irreconcilable with the rule of God. The death of Jesus is the expression of the unconditional character of his message and practice—for which he was ready to consider secondary the fatal consequences that resulted for him. The death of Jesus is suffering-by-and-for-others as the crown of an unconditional practice of right-doing and of opposition to evil and suffering. The life and death of Jesus therefore form an indivisible whole. On the other hand, it is not God—"who has a horror of human sacrifice" ··who led Jesus to the cross. It was human beings who eliminated him because they experienced him as a menace to their position. Although God always comes "in power," divine power knows nothing of the use of force, not even in an encounter with those who wished to crucify Jesus. But the abuses of human power *do nothing whatever to restrain God*. The rule of God will come, despite the abuses that humanity makes of its power and in refusing that rule.

The death of Jesus, therefore, can never be interpreted in any other terms than of the gratuitous character or the unconditional love of God, manifested in Jesus even though suppressed in him. Reconciliation can only signify that God, in one stroke, extends his unconditional love and demands to see "the blood" of his son flow first before he will take us into his love. He loved us when we were still sinners! We must therefore recognize in this death an aspect of fiasco (by reason of the abuse of human power). That such a fiasco, in human eyes, constitutes a real aspect of the death of Jesus penetrates still in initial doubts: how can this man of suffering, this humiliated man possibly be the Christ? For his disciples, the increasing perception of the tie between Jesus and Christ is briefly thrown into confusion. It follows that it becomes impossible to bring to light the full identity of Jesus from his message and practice alone. Things *happen* to people, and that contributes to form their identity, precisely by the way in which they integrate these events into the warp and woof of their lives or endure them as absurd. That is why the identity of Jesus, his revelation both of the being of God and of the true way to be human, remains incomplete without the consideration of his death and resurrection. Up until death Jesus maintained his total devotion to the cause of God and to that of humanity, despite the fact that he was liquidated by human beings. The force of the love of God for humanity and of humanity for God can therefore also be revealed in earthly impotence, which becomes perhaps only more disarming and reconciling. What that indicates in one stroke is that the salvation coming from God never saves us from, or outside of, our finitude but that God *is with us* in all that this concrete finitude implies, both in positive experiences and in experiences of frustration, suffering and death. The frontier between God and the creature is ultimately *our frontier*, not God's. That is why the death of Jesus is not the last word on Jesus.

c) *Raised Up from the Dead*

Just as the death of Jesus cannot be viewed apart from his life, so his resurrection cannot be separated from his life and death. We must affirm at the outset that Christian faith in the resurrection is in fact a primary evaluation of his life and his death on the cross, a way of knowing how to recognize the intimate, irrevocable, irreformable significance of the message and the practice of Jesus for the rule of God. The resurrection is voided of its meaning if this aspect is neglected. But this article of faith signifies even more. This "more" is itself also strictly tied to the life and death of Jesus. The resurrection is primarily the coming to light on the great day of something that already existed in his life and his death: his communion of life with God, which even death could not destroy. This unity bears within it the germ of the resurrection: "Life is changed, not taken away." But the resurrection brings with it a corrective besides. It is not only the prolongation of this union beyond death; it is the joyous entry into the realm of God, the elevation of Jesus to Lordship: "I believe in Jesus, *the Lord*." This is to say that, seated at the right hand of the Father, Jesus lives among his own, in his church. That is why the resurrection which was bestowed on the person of Jesus is at the same time a gift of the Spirit to his own. These two aspects cannot be separated; otherwise, the resurrection is situated in a space inaccessible to us and *à propos* of which nothing meaningful can be said. The concept of the resurrection consequently unites two indissoluble ideas: Jesus lives at the Father's side, and as the glorified Christ he manifested himself in his church by the heavenly gift of the Holy Spirit. One cannot therefore understand the resurrection exclusively as a confirmation by God of the message of Jesus and of its permanent value. This is only *one* aspect. Faith in the resurrection is essentially tied to faith in the permanent and constitutive significance of the very person of Jesus for the coming of the rule of God. God does not confirm only goals and ideals. He is a God of people and is therefore identified with the person of Jesus even as Jesus was identified with God: "God is Love."

The Creed puts total stress on the death and resurrection of Jesus and is silent about his message and the conduct of his life. But it must not be forgotten that the Creed is a succinct kind of resume of Christian faith. Now, death and resurrection do in fact sum up the message and conduct of Jesus. Why this is so is evident only when one realizes, from the New Testament, what this message and practice were. Already in their time, the four evangelists reacted against tendencies that wished to bring the Christian creed down to the death and resurrection of Jesus and to underline only this point. Such an enterprise falls under the critique of the message of Jesus proclaiming a God who loves people. Political dictatorships maintained in power by so-called Christians who celebrate the death and resurrection of Jesus every Sunday would be impossible to sustain if the powerful of the world were to realize that this death and resurrection are based on the message and conduct of Jesus: on his practice of the rule of God so long as there reigns a God concerned for people. Otherwise, orthodoxy becomes a mockery of the Gospel and Christianity.

Another aspect has been added to the article of faith concerning death and resurrection—"He descended into hell," an aspect which logically should have been raised before that of the resurrection. I shall speak of it now, however, and in doing so follow the historical genesis of the Creed. It was actually only in the fourth century that between the articles "suffered under Pontius Pilate, was crucified, died and was buried" and "rose again on the third day," the article "descended into hell" was interpolated.

For the Old Testament, to descend to *sheol* (not *gehenna*, which would be hell properly speaking), is a realistic description of what it means to be dead. To descend into *sheol* signifies nothing other than "to really die." In ancient polemics, the supposition that Jesus was not really dead on the cross recurred constantly; his robust health would have triumphed over the agony. Others used to say that, since Jesus was God, his humanity and therefore also his death could only be apparent (docetism); they refused to associate the negative aspects that mark all death with the person of Jesus. With the purpose of reacting against these tendencies, the article "descended into hell" was integrated into the Creed. Jesus in complete solidarity with our human being really partook of death with us and everything about it that is negative: "He was tested in every way that we are . . ." (Heb. 4:15). This certainly implies that Jesus "is no longer here"! Like all the dead he disappeared from our history empirically, and that in order to achieve the good. The time of his visible person among us has definitively passed. This absence can no longer be treated lightly. Christians therefore have no answer for those who say to them: "Your Jesus is dead, just as all mortal humanity will be one day." That is indeed why the death of Jesus was destructive for his faithful disciples at the outset of the unfolding of their own hopes: "We had hoped it was he" (Lk. 24:13-35, the Emmaus narrative).

For a long time, the Old Testament considered death an exclusion not only from the society of the living but even from God and his salvation. In *sheol*, God is a stranger. "Whoever is dead is dead." In the time of Jesus they saw things otherwise. The spirituality of Judaism had arrived at an understanding, as a result of experience, that communion with God cannot be severed by death. The power of God extends even into *sheol*. "Love is stronger than death." To associate the descent into hell with a rejection of Jesus by God, therefore, has no basis in the New Testament. Death, and especially the death of someone who has been rejected from human society by execution, clothes Jesus in a tragic character. The gospel of John nonetheless interprets this painful situation correctly when it makes Jesus say: "An hour is coming—has indeed already come—when you will be scattered and each will go his way, leaving me quite alone. Yet I can never be alone; the Father is with me" (Jn. 16:32). True hell consists of losing all humanity at the same time one loses God. It is precisely this *that had no place* in the case of Jesus and that despite the silence of God. This silence was for Jesus a new revelation of God. That is why from the very depths of an abyss of sorrow he committed his life and death into the hands of the Father.

There is more. At least one text occurs in the New Testament (1 Pet. 3:18-22; cf. 4:6), in which the descent into hell, without becoming a triumphal march (as some Fathers of the church thought it), becomes no less—thanks to the coming of Jesus into the realm of the dead—than a final chance of salvation for all the dead (although the New Testament halts before the mystery and does not say a word on how the dead might have reacted to this last chance at rescue).[4] In any case, what the Creed indicates by the words "descended into hell" is the *universal* saving significance of the death of Jesus: for the living and the dead. Jesus is the hope not only of the living and of future generations but even of those who have disappeared from history: of the dead, people without a future according to the regular order of things, the definitely excluded—even those who have never known Jesus. Viewed in light of resurrection, faith in the descent into hell is the formulation (in terms that are scarcely elaborated) of the conviction that God in Jesus is himself the future of those who no longer have a future. We thus reach the uttermost consequence of the message of Jesus concerning the unconditional love of God as the future of all humanity, "his realm." This aspect of our faith underlines once more the preference of God for the humble, for outsiders. The descent into hell (its mode of presentation abstracted from) is not folklore nor pure myth waiting to be demythicized, but one of the most delicate points of Christian faith: *God wills the salvation of every human being.*

The resurrection is, consequently, not only the basis of the future but also *reconciliation with the past.* Salvation does not concern the future alone but also the ruins of the past. No human ideology can rival Christianity on this point! For God, no human being is lost. (What the modern age calls human rights is a weak but authentic fallout of this Christian vision of humanity.)

We can therefore sum up the meaning of our faith in Jesus as follows: the Christ, the only Son of the Father, our Lord. The question of Christian identity has everything to do with the integrity, the identity, the salvation of humankind. That is why this faith implies: (a) Above all, the confession of faith in the action in God in Jesus Christ. God is revealed as in solidarity with Jesus, prophet of the realm of God, rejected and excluded by humans by reason of his very message: salvation comes from God in Jesus. God not only confirms this message and the practice that corresponds with it but also, definitively, the *very person* of Jesus: He is a God of people, Resurrection. (b) A practice conforms to this faith: a conduct that corresponds to the realm, that is to say: 1) conscious of what the one who believes in Jesus Christ must, as a result, risk in a deed that is at once partisan and disinterested faith, taking the part of the oppressed and the humiliated: of one's neighbor; 2) by knowing well, on the one hand, that

---

[4]See E. Schillebeeckx, *Christus und die Christen: Die Geschichte einer neuen Lebenspraxis* (Freiburg/Br., 1977), pp. 218-223.

whoever acts in this way runs the risk, like Jesus, of her or himself being oppressed and liquidated by "this world": the disciple will fare no better than the master; and 3) on the other hand, convinced in faith that she or he too—always following Jesus—is irrevocably accepted by God: "Since we suffer with him in order to be glorified with him" (Rom. 8:17b). That is New Testament faith which, in spite of all worldly or even ecclesiastical appearances, "overcomes the world" (1 Jn. 5:4).

III. Biblical Counter-Verification

When the son of man comes in his glory, escorted by all the angels of heaven, he will sit upon his royal throne, and all the gentiles will be assembled before him. Then he will separate them into two groups, as a shepherd separates sheep from goats. The sheep he will place on his right hand, the goats on his left. The king will say to those on his right: "Come! You have my Father's blessing! Inherit the realm prepared for you from the creation of the world. For I was hungry and you gave me food. I was thirsty and you gave me drink. I was a stranger and you welcomed me, naked and you clothed me. I was ill and you comforted me, in prison and you came to visit me." Then the just will ask him: "Lord, when did we see you hungry and feed you or see you thirsty and give you to drink? When did we welcome you away from home or clothe you in your nakedness? When did we visit you when you were ill or in prison?" The king will answer them: "I assure you, as long as you did it for one of my least brothers, you did it for me."

Then he will say to those on his left: "Out of my sight, you condemned, into that everlasting fire prepared for the devil and his angels! I was hungry and you gave me no food, I was thirsty and you gave me no drink. I was away from home and you gave me no welcome, naked and you gave me no clothing. I was ill and in prison and you did not come to comfort me." Then they in turn will ask: "Lord, when did we see you hungry or thirsty or away from home or naked or ill or in prison and not attend to you in your needs?" He will answer them: "I assure you as often as you neglected to do it to one of these least ones, you neglected to do it to me." These will go off to eternal punishment and the just to eternal life. (Mt. 25:31-46)

Under the form of a bucolic pastoral narrative we have a vision of the religious future unfolding before our eyes. If one studied this composition of Matthew closely, there is evidence that one could discern there a retrospective view. Matthew does nothing other than tell us how in fact Jesus conducted himself. Here was someone who, from the midst of our history, spoke of the being God of God, that which was expressed in the Jewish way of his time by the words "realm of God"; someone who, moreover, always acted in the spirit of that God, that is to say accomplished the deeds of this realm. He did good toward those who were in need, toward the rejected whom he reestablished in communion. What Jesus said and did is projected by Matthew into the future as a vision of the Judgment, of which Matthew has nothing more to say. But what he can tell us is that in Jesus the being God of God is manifested as a realization of fuller humanity among humans—to give a cup of water to whoever is dying of thirst in the desert, whose lips are cracked with dryness, to provide a garment that can protect by day against a torrid sun and by night against the cold that descends suddenly, for that is the way things go in Palestine.

It is a matter of daily needs, therefore, which the humblest among us suffer in a special way. Matthew's narrative of the Judgment speaks to us therefore of human things, apparently being foreign to the things of God for God is not even mentioned except after the judgment has been rendered: "Come! You have my Father's blessing." The key word here is the human being in need, the human "hardpressed" (whether the prisoner is "good" or "bad," he or she must be visited). It is our attitude toward this human, this little one, the humiliated one, that is the whole point of Judgment. It is therefore that which will serve as the test that will be the criterion according to which the meaning and content of our life will be judged. The first criterion is not therefore knowing whether, in praying to God in the liturgy as sovereign in the universe, we have praised and adored him, whether we have paid in person for the church and its institutions. No, the question at Judgment is short and sweet: *have we—whether personally or through structures—seen to the hardpressed?*

It is not a matter here of human in the abstract, of someone belonging to the genus "homo," but rather of our attitude to little people, the underdog, the needy, as much in the material domain as the spiritual, whether near to us or far, provided a person be in need, in a state of want, and aspires to a little of the space we cling to in life and judge perhaps quite indispensible for us. Every concrete individual.

Thus, at first glance, Matthew's gospel has nothing specifically Christian about it. The narrative accentuates this, for the group of those we call Christians nowhere appears there. The judgment is passed on "all the gentiles," without any distinction being made between the holy and the heathen (Mt. 25:32). All will be judged on the gift of a cup of water coming not from a vast reservoir—which the desert of those times did not know—but from the little that remains in the bottom of the dipper. The situation in such case is more immediately critical. Such are the kinds of situations Matthew has in mind in the scene he envisions. The ultimate, the definitive is present seminally in the midst of our daily life.

In looking into the matter a little closer, however, this is only the exterior side of Matthew's narrative; it is still not yet the specifically Christian that Matthew contemplates. His vision of the judgment has nothing atheistic about it, despite all that has been said in our time about a Christian "a-theism." Matthew has by no means forgotten what he wrote several pages before: "What recompense do you deserve? *Do not the heathen do as much?*" (Mt. 5:46). Moreover, one can find in this same period, not only in (pre-Christian) Jewish literature but also in Egypt and among neighboring peoples the same images of a cup of water, clothing, and the prisoner used to indicate how it is fitting to act the role of brother or sister to all. Therefore we have here a very old and human wisdom of the ancient Middle East which did not exist independently even then. But anyone who reads only that in Matthew's narrative misses the essential point, precisely what he wished to tell us on the basis of the reminiscences of the Christian community of his time: the identification of the judge who will judge in the final instance concerning the lowly who is in need. "*Whatever you have done for one of these least you have done to me*" (Mt. 25:40). "To me"—that is to say, the son of man, of whom the narrative speaks from the beginning.

It is, therefore, in a very particular way that Matthew interprets the Christian sense of merciful love toward those who are in need, and that in twofold fashion. First, there are the needy themselves who will judge us according to the measure of evil that has been done to them. That is doubtless why the condemnation is so severe toward those who are on the evil side: "Depart from me, you condemned." Are they not justly held at such distance of the curse of the wretched that they cannot understand their reaction to the present situation? But the identification is reciprocal. These little ones—these lowly—are in the presence of the son of man in his quality of judge, and for Matthew this is indeed Jesus himself, the Christ, who identifies himself to the little ones, to all these "sons and daughters of men." To take the part of the oppressed is to follow God himself, God who has shown his profoundest compassion for humanity in Jesus. "He loved us when we were still godless." The care of God for humanity becomes the criterion, the measure—without measure, however—of our care of the oppressed and of those in need. This unlimited sensitivity to human needs develops fully only as a result of a personal experience of the divine toward all humanity: you can be yourself, you can be there, an expression of the very being of God, justification by grace alone, as the theologians say, learned words to say simply that God is loving toward humanity. It is precisely this divine excess, this absence of limits that is evident to us human beings; it transcends what we understand by solidarity among people or human intersubjectivity. But it becomes evident to anyone who experiences the divine mercy on other terms: to the religious person it is also the touchstone of our liturgical prayer which is celebrated in Jesus our Lord.

"I myself will look after and tend my sheep" (Ez. 34:11; cf. 34:12-17). God is more human than any human being. This surpasses anything that anyone can comprehend. But the grandiose vision of the Judgment that Matthew unfolds before our eyes allows us to see something of the incomprehensible love of God for humanity. This also helps us to understand the harshness of the divine judgment toward anyone, of any sort whatever, who tramples a neighbor underfoot or wounds the neighbor's innermost being, be it by a twist of the head. It is only then that we grasp something of the exquisite sensitivity of God, at the precise point that God has dearest to heart: humanity, and especially humanity in need. According to many apocryphal writings the angels themselves have stumbled over this preference of God for humanity.

Finally, is not Jesus whom we call the sole-begotten and only beloved son human even as you and I, with the immense difference that he is more and better? To love human beings—the point at which we understand Matthew—is a *religious* event *par excellence*. It goes without saying that we cannot separate the narrative of Judgment and the totality of the Old and New Testaments, but all this cannot in turn wipe out the proper tenor of this short passage. Moreover, this preference for those in need cannot make us forget the others. We must understand what it says in Ezekiel: "I myself will pasture my sheep; I myself will give them rest," joined to what precedes: "In good pastures will I pasture them. . . . in rich pastures shall they be pastured on the mountains of Israel" (15:14). The good shepherd does not leave the healthy sheep to one side. Where it says that in Scripture, it is only a manner of speaking to underline the interest accorded the lost sheep. Christianity is therefore a "complexio oppositorum," that is to say, a very complex affair, almost a contradictory one, and yet quite simple. But it surely demands some creative imagination, so that the preference for the lowly who is in need does not tolerate any inhumanity toward the ninety-nine who are well fed—who represent today only a third of the world's population.

I think—I say this not without a certain hesitation—that *perhaps* on the day of Judgment all humanity will be found at the right hand of the son of man: "Come all you who are human, my beloved, the blessed of my Father, because in spite of all your inhumanity you one day gave a cup of water *when I was in need*. Come!" Has he not gone on before us? And is not his name the "Good Shepherd"?

Translated (from the French) by Gerard Sloyan, Temple University

PARTICULAR QUESTIONS WITHIN GENERAL CONSENSUS

David Tracy

Hans Küng has provided a masterly analysis of both the collapse of the neo-Scholastic paradigm in Catholic theology in the recent past as well as the emergence of the need for some new consensus on criteria and method for the present. Only the latter will assure the existence of a critical community of theologians in our pluralistic present. As John Courtney Murray observed in an earlier period, every community needs enough consensus to assure that even the disagreements are both focussed and critically discussable.

In my judgment, Hans Küng has once again put the community of "Catholic and ecumenical" theologians in his debt by articulating a general set of methodological criteria on which agreement is possible and by means of which disagreements can become both focussed and critically, rather than polemically, discussable again. I will set forth my own responses to his article, therefore, by concentrating on two central issues: first, the general consensus possible for "Catholic and ecumenical" theology on the basis of the general criteria set forth by Küng and Schillebeeckx; second, my own "further questions" in relationship to Küng's position within the context of that first central methodological consensus.

Since the issues involved in both areas are central for any theology and the space available is limited, I will articulate my own position as clearly and briefly as possible. I will not, therefore, discuss the several other important issues relevant to both Küng's paper and the wider issues: for example, his typically forthright analysis of the pre-Vatican II situation; his brief (for myself, much too brief) comments on political and liberation theologies as well as the transcendental theology of Rahner and others; his disagreements with Schillebeeckx's use of the Q materials, and Schillebeeckx's analysis of the contemporary situation. All these issues are important but not the central thesis of Küng's paper.

I. The Consensus Possible: Critical Correlation of Two Sources

Both Schillebeeckx and Küng establish broad and important areas of the real methodological consensus available to contemporary theologians. To recall that consensus: for Schillebeeckx the contemporary theologian "must seek a critical correlation" between past and present, between traditional Christian experience and our contemporary experience. This analysis will demand three things: (1) an analysis of our contemporary world of experience, (2) an investigation of the basic Christian experience spoken of by the New Testament and subsequent Christian tradition, and (3) a critical relating of these two sources. With these general critieria, I am in full agreement for the reasons advanced

33

by both Schillebeeckx and Küng. In my own model for fundamental theology (in *Blessed Rage for Order*) I advanced a model which, unless I misread them, is in substantial methodological agreement with both Schillebeeckx and Küng. My own formulation is that the task of contemporary Christian theology demands the critical correlation of the meaning and truth of the interpreted Christian fact (including therefore the texts, symbols, witnesses, and tradition of the past and present) and the meaning and truth of the interpreted contemporary situation. For myself, these *general* methodological criteria can (and should) be further specified to show the particular form they take in the three major forms of theology: fundamental, systematic, and practical. The clearest criteriological way to achieve this consensus would seem to be to explicate criteria of "relative adequacy" for each particular kind of theology within the horizon of the general model for theology itself noted above. For example, fundamental theology will formulate criteria of relative adequacy as criteria of meaning, meaningfulness, and truth to *common* human experience for that critical correlation. Systematic and practical theologies will explicate criteria of relative adequacy as criteria of disclosure and transformation with a major emphasis on disclosure for systematics and on transformation for practical.

This is obviously not the place to explicate my own formulations of those criteria. In fact, I have tried to articulate those general criteria for fundamental theology in *Blessed Rage for Order* and for systematic theology in the forthcoming *The Analogical Imagination*. I hope next to turn my attention to the attempt to render explicit the *praxis* criteria of personal, social, cultural, historical, and religious transformation for practical theology. What is of interest in Küng's call for consensus to me, therefore, is this singular fact: however much individual theologians may disagree with my own and other attempts at formulating criteria of relative adequacy for the three principal sub-disciplines in theology (fundamental, systematic, and practical theologies), the kind of basic consensus on a general model for contemporary theology articulated by Schillebeeckx and Küng could still stand.

That general consensus is on the need for any theology as critical correlation (actually, the phrase Schillebeeckx used in his earlier formulations, "mutually critical correlations," seems a clearer formulation) between the two "sources" (Schillebeeckx) or "poles" (Küng): the "source" of the basic Christian experience spoken of by the New Testament and subsequent Christian tradition and the "source" of an analysis of our contemporary world of experience. This general consensus on method and criteria is *the* major point of both Schillebeeckx and Küng and, for myself, the major hope for the kind of general consensus now badly needed and, thanks to Schillebeeckx and Küng, once again available for public and consensual use.

In sum, the major point of the positions of Küng and Schillebeeckx is also the major contribution of Küng's excellent article. If the general methodological consensus he articulates can receive the community-wide support it deserves, the present chaos can move into a responsible pluralism of theologies based on real and fundamental methodological consensus. The heart of a responsible pluralism in any community of inquiry is to achieve enough basic consensus (especially on methodology and criteria) to allow critical discussion of both agreements and disagreements within the relevant community of inquiry. In my judgment, the general kind of methodological consensus formulated by Küng and Schillebeeckx is precisely the one now needing acceptance by the wider community of Christian theologians ("Catholic and ecumenical"). Thus can theologians fight communally against the rising forces of neo-authoritarianism as well as disallow a collapse of criteria and consensus in the face of a mindless, chaotic pluralism of pure subjectivities. To test whether this general consensus can also serve to aid the formulation of further questions and possible disagreements *within* that general consensus, I shall now turn to some further questions of my own on Hans Küng's further specifications of this general consensus model for theological method.

II. Further Questions

1. "Concerning the Critical Relating of Both Sources"

Hans Küng, the reader will recall, provides a powerful but not, for me, persuasive case for shifting Schillebeeckx's language of "critical correlation" into Küng's familiar language of "confrontation." Since I prefer to stay with the language of "mutually critical correlation," my warrants for this important but not decisive choice seem necessary here. I do not doubt Küng's major point here: viz., that "biblical and contemporary sources are not always in agreement. Very often there is conflict between them." This observation is entirely true. Indeed, as Küng's brilliant use of a model of "confrontation" in both *On Being a Christian* and *Existiert Gott?* demonstrate, confrontation of the contemporary world by the Christian message or confrontation of the tradition and church by the Gospel and by better contemporary self-understanding (e.g., from the natural and human sciences) *often* do account for the particular form that "critical correlation" needs to take on particular issues.

And yet to *assume* that "confrontation" rather than "critical correlation" should prove the more relatively adequate general language for a consensus model is, I believe, unwarranted. The reasons are partly semantic, partly substantive. First, the semantics: logically, "critical correlation" can allow for those necessary moments of confrontation which, as Küng correctly reminds us, are "very often" needed. Yet the reverse, logically, is not the case. A pure confrontation model as a general model cannot account for those identities between the meaning and truth of the two sources, nor even adequately account for the radical continuities between the two. Semantically, "critical correlation" is a preferable term precisely because it allows for the full spectrum of logical possibilities from identity through continuity and similarity to paradoxical and dialectical relationships to radical (confrontational) non-identity.

The substantive issue buried in this seemingly "merely" semantic difference is also worth noting. As H. Richard Niebuhr showed in his little classic *Christ and Culture*, the spectrum of responsible Christian theological ways of correlating "Christ" and "Culture" (his formulation of the two "sources") ranges from positions of "Christ against Culture" (Tertullian and Tolstoy) to "Christ in Identity with Culture" (Harnack and Ritschl), with two further models "Christ above Culture" (Aquinas) and "Christ in Paradox with Culture" (Luther) filling mediating logical positions. Moreover, the model of "Christ the Transformer of Culture" which Niebuhr himself implicitly (in *Christ and Culture*) and explicitly elsewhere employed as a more relatively adequate substantive model deserves further reflection for contemporary ecumenical discussions of possible substantive consensus.

Substantively, a model of "transformation," like the logical model of "critical correlation," can account for the strengths of the alternative positions without assuming the necessity of either identity or confrontation. I think Hans Küng could agree with this point since his own theology, although it often employs a confrontation model, also employs other modalities in the fuller spectrum provided by the logical model of "critical correlation" and by the substantive model of transformation (not confrontation) implicitly employed in both *On Being a Christian* and *Existiert Gott?*. For those logical and substantive reasons, therefore, I prefer the Schillebeeckx model of "mutually critical correlations" (assuming this model leaves open the possibilities of confrontation whenever needed) to the Küng "necessary" transformation of that model into "critical confrontation."

2. The Theological Role of Historical-Critical Research on the Jesus of History

So central is this issue to the positions of both Hans Küng and Edward Schillebeeckx in their recent Christologies, as well as in their reflections on general theological method, that the issue should occasion far more reflection than I can accord it here. In fact, my further questions to the position presented in this paper on historical criticism are indeed "further questions" which may or may not occasion a real disagreement on theological method. For purposes of clarity, I will first state which positions of Küng's do seem to warrant agreement.

First, if the critical correlation method is accepted, it does follow that theologians should attempt some correlation of the results of historico-critical research into the message and person of Jesus (on Küng's model of the "broad consensus of exegetes") correlated with personal Christian faith in Jesus of Nazareth as the Christ.

Second, this particular theological model of correlation should play a central role in any theology which attempts fidelity to the Christian Gospel and contemporary scholarship.

This much seems to me sound on general methodological grounds. Still I must raise some further questions which may signal some real differences, even disagreements, especially with Küng's formulation, "The source, standard and criterion of Christian faith is the living Jesus of history." Perhaps the clearest way to state my own position methodologically is as follows. The results of historico-critical exegesis of the New Testament and particularly on the Jesus of history should play a corrective rather than constitutive role for developing a Christian theology and specifically a Christology. I hold to this position for three reasons.

First, on methodological grounds, historico-critical exegesis is a major but not sole method of analysis for these texts. A hermeneutical method with a more literary-critical than historico-critical bent has, in my judgment, also proved itself for theological usage. Minimally hermeneutical-literary critical methods provide another and distinct route to the Christian mode of being-in-the-world disclosed in front of (not behind) these New Testament christological texts. As the work, for example, on the parables of Jesus by Perrin, Via, Funk, Crossan, and, in Germany, Jüngel shows, as the more general work on hermeneutical grounds, as such related work on narrative as those of Childs, Frei, and others seems to show in a different way, historico-critical method is a necessary but not sufficient method for an analysis of the world of religious meaning disclosed by these texts. Greater sensitivity to these literary-critical and hermeneutical concerns promises at least as secure and, in general, a more relatively adequate methodological approach to the New Testament, including questions of the person and message of Jesus.

The hermeneutical approach is more relatively adequate insofar as it does take account of the historical-critical work (Perrin, Crossan, *et al.* do speak of the "parables *of Jesus*"—i.e., of the parables as reconstructed by historico-critical exegetes like Dodd and Jeremias into the parables of the historical Jesus). This new (and, in the United States, at least, increasingly influential) approach geared toward hermeneutical theory and literary criticism merits the attention of theologians as a further and necessary step for recovering the religious worlds of meaning *in front of* the christological and. the Jesuanic texts in the New Testament.

I realize that I have not here provided the full warrants necessary for my claim of greater relative adequacy for this hermeneutical approach (I have tried to provide those warrants in published work elsewhere). With the command that both Küng and Schillebeeckx demonstrate in their published work on general hermeneutical theory, I find it surprising that the "literary-critical turn" (e.g., on genre not as taxonomic for historico-critical purposes, but as productive of meaning) seems to find little mention in this article. For myself, only this further step (along with the kinds of ideology-critique based on *praxis* provided by political and liberation theologians) would provide a sufficient methodological base for contemporary theologians.

In sum, the further developments among some exegetes and hermeneutical theorists along with the praxis-oriented various methods of ideology-critique demand at least as much methodological attention from contemporary theologians as do the earlier and more familiar historico-critical methods of most exegetes. To ignore these further methodological resources is to ignore the further possibilities provided by "contemporary scholarship." I repeat that this first methodological concern is merely a further question for Küng and Schillebeeckx and may not prove a disagreement. However, the silence of the present article upon these issues leads me to ask where they stand on these presently burning issues among both exegetes and hermeneutes and, therefore, among those contemporary theologians who relate to both those communities of scholarly inquiry.

My second question—and it remains a question—is a more central theological one: namely, that all methods (historico-critical, literary, and ideology-critique) contain corrective but not constitutive truth for Christian theology. The constitutive truth for Christian faith is to be found elsewhere: in the personal response of faith in the faith-community as that faith is mediated by the community and the tradition. Both Küng and Schillebeeckx, if I read them correctly, agree with this point (e.g., Küng: "The recognition of Jesus as the Christ always remains a venture of faith and trust in a *metanoia*"). The community of faith and the tradition are, moreover, the major mediators of that personal faith response. Yet, as Küng and Schillebeeckx correctly insist, the results of historico-critical method should play a corrective role upon all possible "distortions" which may also be mediated by the tradition. This strikes me as exactly right—and exposes the danger of simple (as with traditionalists) or complex-speculative (as with Kasper) appeals to "tradition." In these latter positions, "tradition" is employed as a kind of *deus ex machina* to spare us the real and burning difficulties posed by historical consciousness, hermeneutical consciousness, and ideology-critique as these methods expose the possible distortions also present in the tradition.

Yet the further question does recur. Granted that faith is a "personal venture," granted the corrective roles of historico-critical methods (and, to recall my first question, of methods of hermeneutical literary criticism and ideology-critique), still do we not need to say more about the constitutive mediating roles of tradition and community? Recall, for example, a classic debate in modern theology on this issue: the Loisy-Harnack debate and the reflections of Ernst Troeltsch upon that debate. In my own language, which I believe to be faithful to Troeltsch's major point, the following central point can be made: the "Catholic" position (Loisy), by insisting upon the constitutive role of "tradition," is more relatively adequate theologically and historically than Harnack's attempt to judge the tradition through the *constitutive* (not merely corrective) role of historical criticism of the Gospel and the tradition. This remains the case, I repeat, as long as "tradition" as mediating of personal faith in Jesus Christ is also open to the real critique of historico-critical method (as Troeltsch clearly insisted). Otherwise, the logic of the alternative position lands us in a dilemma:

an attempt not merely to correct the tradition but in effect to replace it with historico-critical reconstruction of the message and person of Jesus.

To be clear: by all means, let these historico-critical (or literary-critical or ideology-critique) reconstructions provide checks, critiques, exposures of the distortions in the tradition. Clearly the recent Christologies of both Küng and Schillebeeckx have done exactly that. But let us be as clear as theologically possible that finally the mediating realities of tradition and community and the "personal venture" of faith in Jesus Christ are the major constitutive realities for Christian systematic theology. Without clarity on that issue we risk entering the unsteady path of expecting too much from "old" and "new" quests for the historical Jesus. Indeed we can turn those welcome paths into labyrinths by asking them to provide what, in principle, they cannot: constitutive rather than corrective truth. If anyone still doubts that those "quests" can become either liberating or corrective but can also become new forms of entrapment, Van Harvey's magisterial work *The Historian and the Believer* exists to demonstrate some of the traps that some of our theological predecessors wandered into by expecting too much from "old" and "new" quests for the historical Jesus.

I do not assume that either Hans Küng or Edward Schillebeeckx *necessarily* disagrees with my further questions on the constitutive role of personal faith mediated through community and tradition and the corrective role of historico-critical, literary-critical, and ideology-critique methods. Rather, I raise these further questions—in the context of the fundamental methodological consensus which Küng's article provides—in the hope of asking for further reflections on (1) the use of other methods than the historico-critical and (2) the proposal of the constitutive role of faith mediated through tradition and community as distinct from the corrective role of the historically reconstructed message and person of Jesus. Because the fundamental methodological consensus which Küng articulates is, in my judgment, both ground-breaking and sound, my "further questions" may signal the presence of some critical questions and possible disagreements necessarily present in any critical community of inquiry really grounded in a fundamental methodological consensus.

ECUMENISM AND THEOLOGICAL METHOD

Avery Dulles

Surveying recent developments in theology, one can see great and growing possibilities of a broad consensus regarding method. Theology, as I understand it, is a disciplined reflection on religious faith. As late as a few decades ago, Catholics frequently spoke as though faith did not exist beyond the confines of their own church, but today they generally recognize that divine and salvific faith exists among members of other Christian communities, among adherents of non-Christian religions, and even among people who are not formally religious. The Second Vatican Council, in several important texts, encouraged this new tendency.[1] Since the Council Catholics such as Raimundo Panikkar have argued that faith is a "constitutive dimension of man,"[2] while Protestants such as Wilfred Cantwell Smith contend that faith is "generically human" and is "constitutive of man as human."[3]

If theology is understood as faith seeking understanding, the presence of faith among nonbiblical and unevangelized peoples appears to ground the possibility that they too can do theology. It suggests, further, the possibility that all who wish to converse seriously about questions of ultimate meaning in the light of an existential engagement may engage in a joint theological enterprise. A generic commonality in theology does not necessarily presuppose a common creed, common Scriptures, or common ecclesiastical authorities. Rather, the articulation of creeds, the canonization of Scriptures, and the recognition of magisterial authorities result, in part, from the use of theological reason.

Notwithstanding the tension among rival faiths, which shows no sign of abating, the coming decades, I suspect, will witness the maturation of a broadly ecumenical theology in which adherents of different religions and ideologies can fruitfully collaborate. Such a theology would be a shared reflection, from different perspectives, on the experience of involvement in the all-embracing, transcendent mystery—an experience which Christians interpret as a responsive involvement with the God most fully revealed in Jesus Christ. All who find themselves caught up in the quest for transcendence could profitably meditate together on what is implied in phenomena such as prayer and worship, self-sacrifice for ideals, altruistic love, obedience to conscience, and hope in the face of inevitable death. Thus far Christian theologians have generally addressed these

---

[1] *Ad gentes* 7. Compare *Dei Verbum* 3, *Lumen gentium* 16, *Gaudium et spes* 22, and *Nostra aetate* 2. In this article I shall cite the council documents by their Latin titles and adhere to the translations in W. M. Abbott, ed., *The Documents of Vatican II* (New York: America Press, 1966).

[2] R. Panikkar, "Faith—A Constitutive Dimension of Man," *Journal of Ecumenical Studies* 8 (1971): 223-253.

[3] W. C. Smith, *Faith and Belief* (Princeton: Princeton University Press, 1979), p. 129.

questions within the relatively narrow confines of their own tradition. If we are looking for a truly foundational theology, we shall have to widen our horizons so as to approach universal human questions within horizons that are equally universal.

The method of shared reflection on the basic human orientation to the transcendent still remains to be worked out in practice. Initially we may assert with Wolfhart Pannenberg that such a reflection should not be a mere psychology, sociology, or phenomenology of religion, but rather a theology in the sense of being preoccupied with the truth about God and God's self-communication.[4] Pannenberg would seem to be on solid ground in maintaining also that such a theology of religion should not methodologically presuppose that any given tradition has the definitive truth. In my opinion such a theology should be dialogic in method. All participants, no matter how committed they may be to the authenticity of their own traditions, must be prepared to receive as well as to give, acknowledging that insights coming from other traditions may confirm, nuance, perfect, and even correct certain doctrinal tenets which they themselves have brought to the dialogue. While I do not deny the possibility of a purely dogmatic theology of the religions, elaborated within the perspectives of a single tradition, I would not regard this as an adequate substitute for the dialogic theology I am here envisaging.

Interreligious dialogic theology could of course be carried out on a more modest scale, and with the expectation of more concrete results, by adherents of different faiths linked to each other by close historic ties. Jews and Christians, for example, could very profitably engage in a joint theological reflection on the ways in which they find access to the living God through the religious heritage of ancient Israel. Christians taking part in such a joint reflection, while finding no need to disguise their distinctive convictions, need not take Christ as the thematic center and starting point of this particular theological enterprise.

Within this wider ecumenism, extending to all religions and to all quasi-religious ideologies, one may situate the more narrowly ecumenical theology practiced among Christians. Such a theology builds on the common conviction, shared by all Christians, that the revelatory and redemptive center of human and cosmic history is to be found in Jesus Christ, as attested by apostolic tradition and by the canonical Scriptures. At a point logically prior to their separation into different confessional bodies, Christians are one in their fundamental faith. In view of their shared responsibility to bear credible and effective witness to God's saving work in Jesus, Christians can profitably meditate together on the contemporary situation of Christianity and on the sources of their common faith.

In an ecumenical approach to the fundamental Christian mystery, one might have several different objectives; for example, to arrive at an agreed picture of

---

[4]W. Pannenberg, *Theology and the Philosophy of Science* (Philadelphia: Westminster Press, 1976), pp. 319, 365.

how the biblical authors represent Christ, and on the existential power of the Christ-figure they depict. Not satisfied with this objective, Hans Küng[5] and Edward Schillebeeckx[6] maintain that the Christian cannot be content with finding a message, a picture, a fiction, or a literary symbol, but only with finding Jesus himself, whom the church acknowledges as its living Lord. From the standpoint of normative Christology, I would share this concern. According to the main Christian tradition, we are not redeemed primarily by a message or by a picture, but by the living person of Jesus, in whom God is present and active. Christians who share this conviction can profitably collaborate in seeking to find clues in the New Testament regarding the person of Jesus and the message which he has for us.

For an ecumenical theology of Christian origins to live up to its full promise, it should, in my opinion, be dialogical. That is to say, the participants from different traditions should bring to the common endeavor their own particular insights and emphases, while seeking also to draw profit from the insights and emphases of the others, insofar as these too are pertinent to the task at hand. This does not mean, of course, that the participants should absolutize the past positions of their own church, especially positions not dogmatically defined. On the contrary, it implies that all should be ready to enrich and modify their own prior positions when such adjustments seem indicated by the common scrutiny of the shared sources. Any participant may, of course, urge that the partial or inadequate formulas of other traditions should be amended on the basis of a better reading of the sources. A dialogic theology, which reflects on how the original message has been received in the lives of diverse congregations, seems to me more honest and fruitful than theology which would purport to make a new beginning from the biblical foundations. As Schillebeeckx explains, a study such as his own volume on Jesus "has not been nor possibly could be carried out by a process of skipping over what twenty centuries of Christian history have mediated to us of the churches' credal profession and actual conduct."[7]

A contemporary theological approach to Jesus as the norm and center of Christian faith would have to attend closely to the New Testament, recognized by all Christians as the fundamental and indispensable source. In so doing it would rely heavily on the exegetical techniques now common among Scripture scholars and currently approved in official Roman Catholic directives, including Vatican II's Dogmatic Constitution on Divine Revelation.[8] There can be no question in our day of going back to the uncritical style of exegesis characteristic

---

[5]H. Küng, *On Being a Christian* (Garden City: Doubleday, 1976), p. 418.

[6]E. Schillebeeckx, *Die Auferstehung Jesu als Grund der Erlösung: Zwischenbericht über die Prolegomena zu einer Christologie*, Quaestiones Disputatae 78 (Freiburg: Herder, 1979), p. 37.

[7]E. Schillebeeckx, *Jesus–An Experiment in Christology* (New York: Seabury, 1979), p. 35.

[8]*Dei Verbum* 12.

of Catholic dogmatics in the first half of the present century. In this sense one may endorse what Küng, in the focal essay to which I am here responding, calls the "historical-critical method."

Yet there are serious ambiguities in the terms "historical" and "critical." As Schillebeeckx observes, quoting Ernst Troeltsch, "A whole world view lies behind the historico-critical method."[9] The method has been used by positivistic thinkers to impose evidential rules unacceptable to believing Christians. Although a positivistic historiography, with its methodological postulates, can be serviceable, up to a certain point, in Christian apologetics, it cannot suffice for a properly theological inquiry. I would therefore agree with Schillebeeckx when he calls for a "post-critical" study of the New Testament[10] and for a specifically "theological exegesis."[11] Drawing on the Christian conviction that the living community continues to experience Jesus Christ in faith, Schillebeeckx maintains that later witnesses can correct and supplement the inadequacy of certain early formulations.[12] In view of the presuppositions of faith about the continuing presence of the Holy Spirit in the church, one may wish to qualify Küng's principle that the criterion of all theology must be "the original Christian message itself . . . analyzed by historical critical analysis" (the seventh of Küng's principles proposed on the occasion of the publication of his *Existiert Gott?*, as quoted in the focal essay above).

A common, dialogic approach to the basic Christian witness found in the New Testament is so rich in promise that one may wonder whether there is still need, in addition, for a distinct dogmatic theology conducted within the confines of a single church or tradition. In the past we have had a great variety of dogmatic theologies, Catholic, Protestant, and Orthodox. Should these theologies now allow themselves to be superseded by an ecumenical theology based on the New Testament, so that all dogmas can now be validated by their conformity to the Bible as *norma normans*?

Küng's focal essay forcefully describes the limitations of the "Denzinger" theology of the period between the two Vatican Councils. Drawing on the prior work of Schillebeeckx, he puts his finger on the fundamental flaw in that style of theology: its undialectical identification of revelation with the content of dogmatic statements. A sound theology of revelation demands a more critical approach to all authoritative statements, whether biblical or dogmatic, and thus allows for hermeneutical processes designed to recapture the profound intention

---

[9]Schillebeeckx, *Jesus*, p. 38.

[10]Ibid., p. 77.

[11]Ibid., p. 39.

[12]Ibid., p. 54. On purely historical grounds Peter Chirico criticizes Küng's exclusive reliance on the "original message." "According to the critical method practiced by historians in most fields today, initial interpretations tend to be narrow and limited, whereas later interpretations tend to reflect a more comprehensive perspective" ("Hans Küng's Christology: An Evaluation of Its Presuppositions," *Theological Studies* 40 [1979]: 256-272, quotation from p. 266).

of outdated formulations. Theology can serve the church by assisting in reformu-
lating the tradition, with full faithfulness to its genuine meaning, in order that
Christians may speak effectively to contemporary questions in the idiom of their
own day.

Without seeking to revive the authoritarian ghetto-theology that Küng
deplores, one may contend for the legitimacy of a dogmatic theology done
within a specific ecclesial tradition. Christians who are seriously committed to
a particular church or communion cannot be content with a confessionally
neutral theological method. They will wish to approach any given question with
the help of all the aids that may be useful for settling the points at issue. To ask
theologians to disregard the tradition of their own church out of respect for the
canons of ecumenicity would be to deprive them of what they may properly
esteem as a precious instrument in their search for truth. One is reminded in this
connection of John Henry Newman's complaints against William Paley's
apologetical method: "Why am I to begin with taking up a position not my own,
and unclothing my mind of that large outfit of existing thoughts, principles,
likings, desires, and hopes which make me what I am?"[13]

It could be objected, of course, that to adhere to a confessional tradition is
arbitrary and subjective. This objection, however, ignores the role of authority
in the quest for knowledge.[14] To use church tradition as a *locus theologicus* is no
more authoritarian and unscientific than to accept Jesus or the canonical
Scriptures as normative. Whatever may be the case with Christians of other
affiliations, the Catholic is committed by the very fact of church membership to
accept the teaching authority of the ecclesiastical magisterium, not out of
"ecclesiastical opportunism," nor out of subservience to the "ecclesiastical
system" (Küng's phrases), but precisely for the sake of better attaining the truth
of revelation. To depart without solid reasons from the approved doctrinal
norms of the ecclesial body to which one belongs, far from being scholarly and
scientific, would be subjective, arbitrary, and even self-contradictory.

The Second Vatican Council, in its Decree on Ecumenism, took note of the
methodological difference between Roman Catholics and other Christians in
their use of Scripture. In the words of the Decree,

> But when Christians separated from us affirm the divine authority of
> the sacred Books, they think differently from us—different ones in
> different ways—about the relationship between the Scriptures and
> the Church. In the Church, according to Catholic belief, an authentic
> teaching office plays a special role in the explanation and proclama-
> tion of the written word of God.[15]

---

[13]J. H. Newman, *Essay in Aid of a Grammar of Assent*, chap. 10, part II, no. 3 (Garden
City: Doubleday Image Books, 1955), p. 330.

[14]Cf. A. Dulles, "Authority and Criticism in Systematic Theology," *Theology Digest* 26
(1978): 387-399.

[15]*Unitatis redintegratio* 21.

Does it follow from this that Catholics are bound to follow a purely "regressive" method—to use the term coined by Ambroise Gardeil?[16] Must they work back from the recent teaching of the hierarchical magisterium as an absolute norm, and use the sources of Scripture and tradition simply to confirm what the magisterium has already declared? Even Pius XII, in commending the regressive method, called attention to the need for continual renewal through fresh study of the sacred sources.[17] In the light of the teaching of Vatican II we may confidently acknowledge the critical and creative role of exegetes and theologians. They may frankly call attention to what they see as deficiencies in past doctrinal formulations[18] and strive to mature the judgment of the church on questions currently under discussion.[19] In all this endeavor, Catholic theologians will seek to work in close relationship with the teaching authorities of their own church, respecting the authority and charisms of those called to pastoral office.[20]

In the present age it is no longer possible to draw a sharp line of demarcation between a dogmatic theology which would be narrowly confessional and an ecumenical theology which would be confessionally neutral. Even when addressing readers of their own communion, theologians will strive to take cognizance of what Christians in other traditions are saying, and even when writing for an ecumenical audience, they will strive to speak faithfully from out of their own tradition. Thus the distinction between ecumenical and dogmatic theology is more a matter of proportion and emphasis than one of specific difference. The theologian is bound to be critical, but criticism is a two-edged sword. It impels one both to probe the validity of the formulations current in one's own church and to test the adequacy of contrary formulations proposed by other groups. In criticizing either side, the theologian will strive to use no other standard than the truth of the gospel itself.

Among the means by which the gospel becomes manifest, Scripture is to be acknowledged as having a certain primacy. Officially acknowledged by Vatican II as the "soul of sacred theology,"[21] Scripture is the original and canonically approved record of the decisive events and interpretations on which the church is founded. As an inspired record, Scripture may be called the "word of God." With Catholic theologians of recent decades, one may admit a measure of truth in the classical Protestant position that the Bible alone is the definitive norm, *norma normans*. This formula does not deny, but rather implies, the normative character of church tradition, but it also suggests that tradition has only derivative and subordinate authority.

---

[16]Gardeil himself was concerned to show that the method he proposed was scientific, critical, and open to progress. See his first, programmatic article, "La réforme de la théologie catholique, Idée d'une méthode régressive," *Revue Thomiste* II (1903): 5-19.
[17]*AAS* 42 (1950): 568-569; DS 3886.
[18]Cf. *Unitatis redintegratio* 6, *Lumen gentium* 37, *Gaudium et spes* 62.
[19]Cf. *Dei Verbum* 12.
[20]Cf. *Dei Verbum* 8, *Lumen gentium* 12, 25.
[21]*Dei Verbum* 24; cf. *Optatam totius* 16.

To speak of the Bible as *norma normans*, in my opinion, is unsatisfactory. For one thing, the term seems to suggest that Scripture and tradition are two separable quantities, the second of which must be measured by the first. This dualism between Scripture and tradition was rejected both by the Faith and Order Commission at Montreal in 1963 and by Vatican II's Dogmatic Constitution on Revelation. According to a Commission Report received at Montreal, the exclusive sufficiency of Scripture is indefensible in the face of "the historical actuality of *Scriptura numquam sola*! Scripture is nowhere by itself alone."[22] Vatican II insisted that Scripture and tradition, "flowing from the same divine wellspring, in a certain way merge into a unity and tend toward the same end."[23] Going further, the Council maintained that tradition, Scripture, and the teaching authority of the church "are so linked and joined together that one cannot stand without the others."[24] For the Bible to be used with theological responsibility as a means of purifying tradition, it must itself be read in the light of tradition. The ultimate norm, if this term is to be used at all, is neither Scripture nor tradition, still less the magisterium, but all three of them in their convergent unity, insofar as they succeed in bearing witness to Christ himself, who is Lord of both Scripture and church.

The idea that the Bible alone is *norma normans* contains yet a further difficulty. It raises the question: who is the judge as to whether a given statement of the magisterium is or is not in accord with the Scripture? At one point Küng's focal essay seems to demand that all "post-biblical dogmas" be scrutinized in the light of "the biblical findings attained through historical-critical exegesis." This procedure would seem to subject dogmatic theology and the ecclesiastical teaching office to a magisterium of exegetes. Schillebeeckx, as I understand him, would accept no such proposal. While he accords an "indispensable place" to exegesis, he approvingly quotes Yves Congar as rejecting any magisterium of exegetes.[25]

In order to offset the extravagant claims sometimes made for critical exegesis, I see it as important to insist that, in addition to an exegetical theology that is primarily concerned with the biblical sources, there is need for a historical and dogmatic theology that seeks to serve the understanding of faith by a study of tradition in its various stages of development, with due regard for church pronouncements. Such dogmatic theology, as I have already indicated, must not isolate itself from other branches of theology, but remain in lively dialogue with them.

We are perhaps now in a position to make summary response to Küng's

---

[22]"The Renewal of the Christian Tradition: The Report of the North American Section," in L. Vischer, ed., *Report of the Theological Commission on Tradition and Traditions*, Faith and Order Paper 40 (Geneva: World Council of Churches, 1963), p. 21.
[23]*Dei Verbum* 10.
[24]Ibid.
[25]Schillebeeckx, *Jesus*, p. 40, quoting Y. Congar, *Vraie et fausse Réforme dans l'Eglise* (Paris: Cerf, 1950), pp. 498-499.

proposal for a unitary theological method having two poles: first, "God's revelational address in the history of Israel and the history of Jesus" and, second, "our own human empirical world."

As regards the first pole, I have already expressed my reservations. In limiting the first pole to the biblical history, Küng (in contrast to Schillebeeckx, who does not so limit it) appears to minimize the cognitive import of twenty centuries of Christian tradition. He seems to exaggerate the capacities of a theologically neutral historical-critical method to grasp the reality of Jesus and to underestimate the possibilities of authentic doctrinal development.

The second pole of theology, as proposed by Schillebeeckx and Küng, quite properly emphasizes the inescapable role of contemporary experience in the life of faith. The positive role of the inquiring subject in the theological process has been recognized by practically all working theologians since Tillich set forth his "method of correlation." In view of the possible tensions between the tradition of faith and one's personal experience, it is good to speak of "critical correlation" (Schillebeeckx) and perhaps on occasion of "critical confrontation" (Küng).

With regard to Küng's personal formulation of the "second pole," I have some questions which I shall here indicate very briefly. In speaking of "our own empirical world" (unserer heutigen Erfahrungswelt) I wonder to what extent he acknowledges that Christian experience can be shaped by the ecclesial situation of the subject. More generally, does Küng's formula sufficiently allow for the many diverse ways in which men and women of our day experience the world? In castigating an "esoteric theology for believers" and insisting that theology speak "the language of contemporary humanity" does he neglect the value of using technical terminology in the discussion of technical questions? Does he identify theology too closely with proclamation?

Finally, there is the question whether it is necessary or even desirable to have a general consensus regarding theological method. I am not sure whether Küng intends to propose the method he attributes to Schillebeeckx and himself as a universal norm for all theology. In the neo-Scholastic era the Catholic Church experienced the domination of a single method, and the situation was not a healthy one. By emphasizing that revelation is a divine mystery, the Second Vatican Council seemed to authorize a diversity of theologies, each approaching the mystery from a particular point of view.

Among all legitimate theologies there would be certain common features, for all would be concerned with a contemporary understanding of the saving action of God, which, according to Christian belief, was decisively given in Jesus Christ. This generic similarity does not in my mind eliminate the pluralism. Theology takes different forms according to the starting points, backgrounds, antecedent convictions, conceptual structures, concerns, and objectives of different groups of practitioners. This was already true in New Testament times, for, as Schillebeeckx notes, the Synoptic Gospels, the Pauline epistles, and the Johannine writings—to mention only three major streams—differ considerably in style and approach.[26] History furnishes many other examples of theological methodology, such as the homiletic theology of the Church Fathers, the contemplative theology of the monastic tradition, and the Scholastic theology of the medieval universities. In our own day the various demands of widely differing audiences would seem to call for a corresponding variety of theologies. The kerygmatic, patristic, and transcendental currents, as well as political and liberation theology—to mention only the methods that Küng judges insufficient—have seemed to answer to real needs. While the different methods ought not to lead to contradictory results, I see no reason why they should be swept aside to make room for a single method such as Küng's historical-critical approach to New Testament materials.

The kind of theology exemplified by the Jesus-books of Küng and Schillebeeckx (which actually differ rather markedly from each other) has genuine value and meets a real need of our day. Still, it represents only one theological option, as Schillebeeckx himself seems to recognize:

> I know that a scientific-cum-critical approach (my scientifically disciplined standpoint in this book as a believer) is only one of many possibilities. This relativizes the whole book. Yet even this albeit relative standpoint has its own right of existence and, in the end, an inalienable pastoral value of its own.[27]

In place of any proposal for a new consensus founded on a single method I would therefore argue for a pluralism of theologies, unified only in the sense that each theology attempts to articulate the meaning of God's action as experienced in human history. Some theology can be done in interfaith dialogue, without requiring express adherence to Christ or the church. Some can be done in a Christian ecumenical context, without specific appeal to the doctrinal standards of any particular church. Some, finally, is to be done within a given church or tradition, with deliberate adherence to the doctrinal norms implied in such an ecclesial commitment.

---

[26]Schillebeeckx, *Auferstehung*, p. 23.
[27]Schillebeeckx, *Jesus*, p. 40.

JESUS OF NAZARETH: TODAY'S WAY TO GOD

Gerard Sloyan

The differences between Professors Schillebeeckx and Küng on the needed new consensus in Catholic (and ecumenical) theology, as the latter perceives them, are relatively few. Küng's refinements of Schillebeeckx, while important, are a matter for Schillebeeckx to respond to. They will not be the subject of this essay.

What I prefer to do is comment on the areas where the two European theologians are agreed and ask whether their perceptions are correct. They hold in common the Catholic tradition of Christian faith. Hence, neither is a biblicist who thinks that the truth of faith is arrived at by individuals apart from the consensus of a worldwide community that has had a corporate life of twenty centuries. The Bible, especially the New Testament, is normative for all post-biblical tradition: a recognizable Catholic position. Equally Catholic is the conviction that the Church can make binding pronouncements but that these cannot come "out of the blue." They must be on matters that are demonstrably part of the apostolic preaching to which the twenty-seven canonical books testify. The teaching contained therein is highly diverse and on certain essential points contradictory.

Both theologians have a primarily pastoral concern in the practice of their discipline. While yielding nothing as to the rigor that should attend it, they are convinced that theology is a good of the whole Church. It is not an exercise in harmless mental gymnastics which the *ecclesia docens et discens* endures, seeing in it the way the academically minded reflect on the revealed message. Theology for both these thinkers is a service provided by believers to other believers, whatever the latter's role or function in the community. The reason for its need is clear. Changing cultural and linguistic patterns, which is a way of describing the varying perceptions people have of the meaning of life on the globe, require that God's activity in Jesus Christ on human behalf through the Spirit's power be constantly reinterpreted afresh. Otherwise the venture of faith will be impossible.

Continuing to identify what Schillebeeckx and Küng hold in common about theology's task, we find them agreed that the sources of that discipline are chiefly two: God's revelatory address in the history of Israel and the history of Jesus, and the human empirical world, both that in which we live at present and the worlds inhabited by the Christians who have lived before us. The hermeneutical problems attending an interpretation of the latter in terms of the former are immense but the Church cannot shirk them. Indeed, in every age it has taken them on as the condition of professing a religion rooted in history.

Up to this point, the positions taken by Schillebeeckx and Küng are familiar. The two introduce a new element in their joint conviction that post-

49

Enlightenment historical criticality has placed a new burden on the Church, hence on theology. It is this: that human modes of knowing both past and present are not the same as those that went before. While the New Testament, the patristic, the medieval, and the renaissance periods were convinced of the importance of human history and its general availability to later ages, they did not challenge it in a critical way. They accepted as a "given" the historical character of the biblical accounts and of the various struggles to express biblical truth in the language of the time (be it Hellenist Jewish, Graeco-Roman, Byzantine, Italian, or Frankish). The problem of history of the last three hundred years, the two theologians maintain, is different. Neither the Church nor theology can turn back the clock after the change. Without attending to a theoretical Asian or African way of doing contemporary theology, both authors hold for the ineluctability of the challenge posed by the historical-critical problem that arose in the West and now prevails everywhere.

Finally, they maintain a position that has met with the clear resistance of those who do Catholic theology in another mold, one that can rightly be claimed as traditional. The two so exclusively hold for the biblical revelation as normative that they do not allow the conciliar teaching of subsequent ages ("Church teaching") to be similarly normative. The position in possession in Catholicity would seem to be that the creeds, the councils, and certain teachers of the past (e.g., the Cappadocians, Augustine, Aquinas) not only convey New Testament teaching faithfully but comprise the dependable norm of biblical faith. Schillebeeckx and Küng, to the contrary, find expressions of that faith like those of Chalcedon, Trent, and Vatican I to be so time-conditioned that they are *normae normatae*, not *normae normantes* as they are widely taken to be by Catholic theologians.

The extent of this difference of perception cannot be overstressed. Schillebeeckx and Küng are not so much thought to deviate from the Catholic tradition over particular doctrines, as their recent "trials by media" might lead us to believe; they seem to their theological opponents to differ from other Catholics on how the faith is to be known. Küng, however, in his approving summary of Schillebeeckx, affirms that the familiar way not only will not serve the present and the future but was not authentically Catholic in its presuppositions. That way is the way of development (the two might say "accretion") in which whatever was once thought to be a binding statement of apostolic faith remains such forever. Those statements were rather, Schillebeeckx and Küng would hold, a perfectly satisfactory means in their time of not describing the divine-human relationship erroneously. (Exhausting the mystery is simply not in question.) As to a "theology of the high-water mark" in which the latest conciliar statement is the unimprovable best, it does not characterize a Church that will always be protecting its faith by declaring in the language of the time those formulas that do not adequately reflect that faith.

The clear difference of outlook is not that two contemporary Catholic theologians are declaring their Church non-traditional. They are proposing a theory on how the tradition operates which goes counter to the conventional wisdom. In it, the whole Church that is always the repository of right faith protects this faith from error by reexamining the revelation of the apostolic age in light of the life lived by its members in successive ages. It does so with a lively sense of previous examinations. These it does not hesitate to call on when they prove useful. But when this is not so or when the contrary may be the case, while it need not actively repudiate them, it must proceed to the challenge of the new situation. The earthly Jesus who is none other than the Christ of the apostolic Church's faith is always the norm in such exploration. The results of former explorations may prove helpful—it is even to be expected—but they are not sacrosanct.

The position of Schillebeeckx and Küng on Jesus as normative is helpful in its clarity. It is attended by certain risks. For one, it does not bother to explore "the tradition" operating at its best, contenting itself with a summary of the ills of an unhistorical dogmatic theology. But a dogmatic theology carried on in the historical-critical spirit demanded has already come to birth and is operative in much current theological education. Secondly, insufficient attention is paid to the vigorous position directly opposite to the one assumed by the authors to be axiomatic. For the lifestyle and teachings of Jesus have simply not been the bedrock of the theological enterprise; rather, a quite different view of Jesus has. His life has been to the fore in popular preaching, but in theology it has had a shadowy existence as his "humanity"—a necessary condition for human salvation; but his human selfhood has not been the essence of God's deed accomplished in him. Whether the latter was taken to be the Johannine enfleshment of God's eternal Word or the Pauline one of the power of the cross (cross and resurrection, Catholics would say more freely than others), the impact of the living Jesus of history on theology has not been nearly as great as the two theologians require. In their demand, therefore, they are being radical in the strictest sense. A third risk is that of supposing that the whole Church is in one and the same condition at the present time, hence needs the same theology. While the critical-historical challenge to religious faith is everywhere in the air, many believers transcend it by professing a faith that is inadequate to it in theory but quite adequate in practice. This condition may be stigmatized as a "ghetto existence"; it may at the same time be recognized as a conscious means of resisting the erosions of a culturally conditioned life. God alone is unchanging, dependable, firm. People choose the transient signs of the divine reality that they will—often the least satisfactory signs from a purist point of view, but signs adequate to their needs (an infallible, inerrant word of Scripture innocent of any hermeneutical problem, for example).

In citing the risks Schillebeeckx and Küng have taken, I have not engaged in a critique of their position. Let me tentatively do so now, expressing my respect for each of them in wrestling with the contemporary problem of Catholic belief. I turn to Schillebeeckx first because, as an exegete, I am closer to his project than to Küng the historical theologian. My critique of Schillebeeckx is entirely favorable in the area I am best able to judge. He has analyzed and synthesized the scholarship on the Jesus of the gospels in a way that should be a model for future systematic theologians. In doing so he has not yielded to the delusion that the Church must track down the historical Jesus before it can believe in him. He has shown, however, the roots of the various Christologies found in the New Testament. The assumption that there was not only a Q collection but a Q community is not such a minority position as Professor Küng suggests. Neither is it an Achilles heel in Schillebeeckx's prolegomenon to a theology. For he simply wants it to be known that there may have been a time in Christian life (i.e., between A.D. 40 and 70) when Jesus was venerated as the eschatological bringer of salvation through his teaching and not through his death and resurrection. If St. Paul viewed him as the savior through the cross and resurrection only, and the four evangelists through this and his life and teaching as well, the evidence should be brought forward—including importantly the pre-Coptic original of Thomas—that Jesus was seen by some early Christians as having saved us by the heavenly wisdom he spoke in his summons to faith (cf. Mt. 7:28; Jn. 7:46).

Schillebeeckx at no point assumes that the faith of the Church is based on the sources of the gospels rather than the gospels themselves. He does not invite anyone to hold a Catholic faith that replicates the hypothetical one of A.D. 65 or a theology that is pre-Nicaean. He does invite the whole Church to construct a theology, looking to the present and future, that is based on Jesus the revealer of God through his lifestyle and teaching as one of its two fundaments. It is in this venture that the (putative) exclusive significance of Jesus' teaching to some early Christians is important. The theological venture proposed can go on without it, as any exegete who denies Q but holds Schillebeeckx's general theological position will testify.

The attempt to build a theology on such a base is a new one, as has been indicated above. Hence, no one should be surprised at the resistance Schillebeeckx and Küng are meeting with. The christological, trinitarian, and pneumatological structures that were completed by the fifth century scarcely needed to hear Jesus of Nazareth speak in his own person. They did require the utterances put on his lips by John the theologian. St. Paul for his part constructed a Christology via soteriology. It needed no data from Jesus' life except that, born under the Law, he died in perfect obedience to God on a cross. The synoptic authors met a need of their times that Schillebeeckx and Küng think is the chief need of our times. They presented not a God who acted in time through an eternal Word nor one who did a deed of utter gratuity in our behalf making us one with God through Christ, but a human being, a Jew filled with God, who taught how humans ought to live before God, but first lived that way himself. The proposal that is novel is that the Church build a new theology on Jesus under this aspect. Essential to the matter is the unbroken Catholic tradition that he and the Christ of glory are one; moreover, that he is sufficiently available in the four portraits of the gospels to be an object of reasonable faith. A theology that is exclusively Pauline or Johannine or based on the two in combination can declare the history of Jesus expendable. Kähler and Bultmann did just that, but without falling into the gnostic trap by retaining the historicity of the cross. The importance of Matthew and Luke—with Mark erroneously taken to be Matthew's Petrine abbreviator—was never minimized in the Catholic tradition. The dialectic between the synoptics and John and Paul, it is true, was never taken seriously. Still, commitment to the synoptics as faithful interpreters of the meaning of Jesus is a Catholic tradition that not only survives critical scrutiny but welcomes it. In following the critical path of the past two centuries Schillebeeckx and Küng are very much in this tradition: not the historical skepticism that attended the search but the search's capacity to identify what is historical about Jesus.

The Schillebeeckx assumption, in which Küng joins him, is twofold: that these times are open to a Jesus of deed and word (who, for believers, is always the Christ) as they are not open to any other New Testament reading of his significance, and that the critical-historical scrutiny of all religious data—biblical, creedal, conciliar, etc.—is in possession in Catholic theology or is shortly to be so. Both poles of the axis require serious exploration but, on the basis of what has already been done, the assumption is likely to prove true.

The best elements of humanity in both hemispheres resonate to a person who lives in holiness and speaks wisdom. Whether a culture views the ultimate. predominantly as transcendent or immanent, it can recognize a sign of the ultimacy it knows in a mystic and a sage like Jesus. He convinces some by his lifestyle, others by his words and deeds. The claim of a reconciling act of God through a particular human nature used as "conjoined instrument" leaves many religious people puzzled, including many Christians. They do not think of God from God's side, as it were, but from their own. They recognize deity in their midst only with great difficulty, if at all. Authentic signs of ineffable deity are another matter. The God who speaks in Christ through the Spirit may be heard in the Jesus who speaks, and above all who does what he says.

The second part of the assumption about the modern critical spirit is more open to question. Much Catholic theology today can be categorized as familiar with critical method and willing to use it, so long as it does not impinge on dogmas thought to be incapable of reformulation. Interest in history as the condition of theology wanes as soon as it shows all created things—Bible, creeds, councils, magisterium—to be relative to the one absolute, God. The theological tendency to multiply quasi-absolutes is still vigorous in Catholicity. The papal/ episcopal magisterium is widely viewed as resistant to the corrosions invited by taking critical history seriously. While this outlook is widespread, the spirit of contemporary Catholic theology is in fact running in the other direction. There are many expositors of the pronouncements of Vatican II at ease with the contradictory spirit these represent, when it comes to a critical view of the Christian past. But such expositors tend to be systematic or dogmatic theologians long familiar with placing historical realities in the appropriate places in a doctrinal schema. The historians, the biblers, the individual and social moralists are not as impervious to history as this. They tend to fit their discipline into history rather than use the aspects of it that suit them. Professor Schillebeeckx predicts that the last named spirit will not prevail in Catholic theology. He is confident that the fabulous invalid of unhistorical theology is on its deathbed.

A distinction is in order. As to the spirit of orthodoxy innocent of history, the observation is correct as regards Catholic *theology*. There is no upcoming generation of Catholic theologians of any state in life likely to continue the tradition of non-critical-historical theology. Increasing numbers will come abreast of the exegete's task because no other respectable option is open to them. The same is not true of apology, many of whose practitioners will be theologians in appearance. An equally numerous generation of apologists is to be seen on the horizon. Both groups will claim the preservation of Catholic faith as a pastoral necessity of their discipline. One would be rash to predict which will prevail in the short run, say, of fifty or one hundred years. But one can safely say with the two European thinkers that the critical-historical spirit will prevail in any Catholic theology of the foreseeable future. This seems true outside the West as well. It will also be accompanied in West and East by an increasing attention to the *symbol*, the poetry, the liturgy of religious faith, an aspect of the theologian's art that neither Schillebeeckx nor Küng seems sufficiently aware of. Attention to both history and symbol will make possible the hermeneutical task of the future. It will not be so if theology is thought to be a matter of God's self-revelation in *history* only.

The second origin or source of the Catholic theology that needs to be constructed is identified by Professor Küng as "our human empirical experience." Here he places us squarely on a moving staircase, the more so as he contrasts it with "traditional Christian experience." The human capacity for living in two worlds, a religious and an empirical one, seems boundless. Witness the Muslim situation, perhaps the firmest widescale religious adherence in the world. Witness, too, the easy coexistence that many achieve in both the technological West and a Christianity of biblical authoritarianism. Their flight from ambiguity to certainty regardless of the cost is precisely what Professors Küng and Schillebeeckx say cannot happen. These two project a natural home for people who experience the ambiguity of life within a Church that knows the ambiguity of faith. But is not the opposite more the case? Are not large numbers, terrified by life in a Church "without answers" (their term), stampeding toward the certitudes of literal biblicism, a Christ who heals all ills, and spiritual authority that absolves from responsible inquiry? The answer is so clearly yes that a Catholic theology that goes in the other direction is prophetic indeed. Yet this is precisely what is being called for. It will provide us with a struggle that is counter to the spirit of the age—no new thing for Catholicity. It includes the struggle for a Church and *magisterium* that are authoritative rather than authoritarian. And yet the terms of the struggle can be discouraging, since some theologians most committed to the claims of God upon believers are most readily dismissed as disloyal to God through human representatives of the divine. The problem is an old one. It will not go away or get any easier of solution with time.

Part of the problem is that "traditional Christian experience" includes patterns of thought and language that, despite being centuries old and scarcely comprehensible in the terms of their initial framing, are *also* part of "our human empirical experience." Hence it is false to set them against one another as mutually exclusive. The age-old pain of humanity is alienation: from oneself, from the community, from God. Yet if revealed truth and reconciliation have been held out and accepted in a language characteristic of no other human experience, it remains valid language from the fact that God has been perceived and reconciliation accepted. This seems to be the chief weakness of the supposition of Küng and Schillebeeckx that human empirical experience has no capacity to include traditional Christian experience. The two are mutually inclusive in many cases. It seems unwise to separate them so neatly.

As to the construction of a theology in every age that is forged from human experience: it has never been done otherwise. Hence, we should expect it in our time. The human experience of the landless proletariat of Egypt and Ethiopia and East Syria required a God who walked as a man, transcending the grinding limitation of humanity. The human experience of Antioch, from which orbit all three synoptic gospels may have come, required a human Jesus whose deity did not threaten his humanity, leaving it independent and free. The human experience of Rome, adept at compromise without losing sight of the rights attending rival claims, required a settlement like Leo's *Tome* that became Chalcedon. The human experience of a tired Europe, drained by the plague and unending serfdom to princes, required a God who did much on behalf of a humanity that did little, least of all by its athleticism and commerce of spirit. The theologians have always been the ones to perceive the needs of the times and give them answer in the framing of the message once delivered to the saints. They pay a price for this, like the prophets. A religious community will always kill the visionaries and erect their tombs.

The article Professor Küng has provided us with is a distinct service, in his clear rendition of the Schillebeeckx position in two volumes and an interim response. Can the same be said of his ten guiding principles? The answer is yes and no. As guides to doing theology in a spirit of Catholic fidelity and fresh inquiry, who can be against them? Yet in their Cartesian clarity and spirit of mild accusation, who can be for them? When Küng asks for fairness, tolerance, and the absence of hostility, he only describes Christian behavior. When he distinguishes between "some ecclesiastical traditions" and the gospel, he is evidently opposing the rigidification of human tradition as Jesus did. But he has left no room for those Church traditions of which it can be said they are legitimate developments of the gospel message. His intent is clear and Catholic, for the Church does not in principle promulgate human teachings with gospel force. Will his strong appeal against what the Church has done unconsciously in every age—namely, identify the culturally time-bound in theology with the gospel—be heard? It almost cannot be heard when it is delivered in these words.

Yet the exhortation of these two teachers will prevail in theology because, before God, there is no higher court of appeal than the life and teachings of Jesus and the realities of human experience. The change will come slowly, dialectically, painfully. Its beginnings are already present in that there are no substantial numbers of creative theologians in formation except those who think critically and are wedded to Jesus and his teaching. It will meet with resistance because anything done faithfully in his name meets resistance. It will proceed more slowly than it needs to because the world is not nearly as rational as the Küng essay, nor as anguished over human suffering as Schillebeeckx. And the world, as even John the theologian perceived, has always had a comfortable place in the Church.

HISTORY, SOCIOLOGY AND DIALOGUE:
ELEMENTS IN CONTEMPORARY THEOLOGICAL METHOD

Leonard Swidler

At least two types of change or growth can be seen taking place in the formation of religious doctrinal positions.

A) One begins either at the very start of a religious idea, or at some early stage which authentically and quite directly expresses the nuclear event and/or insight. Then the growth of the original idea moves in the direction of expansion and extrapolation that is other than, foreign to, and even in opposition to the nuclear event and/or insight. An obvious example might be the legend-building expansion of the image of child Jesus in its spare outline in Luke's gospel to the wonder-working, self-impressed child Jesus of some of the apocryphal gospels. A negative example of this sort of development within the canonical gospels which continued this "expanding" move is the image of "the Jews" in Mark, where it is rather mixed, to a highly negative one in John; this anti-Jewish trajectory continued in ever-expanding fashion with the early Fathers and much of subsequent Christian tradition almost to the present.

B) A second type of change occurs by way of "evolution," that is, an explicitation of what was implicit in the initial event and/or insight, or at least a development of it in a way that is in keeping with the nuclear event/idea, i.e., by responding to new circumstances and demands within the inspiration of the initial principles. For example, Jesus' almost exclusive preaching of the Good News to his fellow Jews was understood by some early Christians to imply that we Gentiles ought to have the Good News preached by Jesus' followers—thus explicitating what they perceived to be implicit in Jesus' preaching. In the kindred matter of not requiring all of us Gentiles to take on the full responsibility of the Torah, those Christians (with Paul again in the lead) moved the doctrinal development "beyond" or "away from" the position taught by Jesus by responding to the new circumstances within the inspiration of what they perceived to be the initial principles embodied and expressed by Jesus.

In studying the growth of the doctrine about the significance of Jesus, i.e., Christology, one has to decide whether that growth in all or some instances is type A or B, or both, or neither—the only four possibilities.

The act of decision is unavoidable. The initial event cannot simply be "repeated." It must somehow be assimilated by the now living person(s), otherwise it does not become a "doctrine," a teaching. It simply remains a past fact which has no effect on anyone's life. Hence, it is not possible simply to point to or repeat the initial event or fact and claim that that is the teaching or doctrine. A living person or persons must somehow perceive the initial event and state, at first internally, that such and such is its significance. It is that internal understanding, and perhaps eventual outward statement, that transmits and determines the direction and form of the power of the initial event to the lives of living persons. A number of persons might perceive the same event with some reacting with total indifference and others reacting positively or negatively in a great variety of ways. It is that "reaction to," understanding of, statement to oneself and perhaps eventually others about the significance of the initial event that is the power-transmitting and shaping instrument. It is usually called doctrine or teaching.

Hence, when speaking of the doctrine of Christology it is not sufficient to attempt to point to or "repeat" the Jesus-event. In fact, as seen, it is impossible to do so. Living persons must somehow perceive or apprehend the Jesus-event and respond to it with something more than indifference in order to produce a doctrine (Christology) which will have an effect on their lives. Thus, there clearly are two poles involved in any doctrine, the initial event and the living person, and the relationship between the two. It is, then, no invention on the part of Küng or Schillebeeckx to speak of the two poles or sources of Christian doctrine and their relationship—it is in the very nature of things. The source of the differences between Küng, Schillebeeckx and like-minded Christian thinkers and, say, pre-Vatican II Catholic thinkers (and many still live after 1965) is in the assessment of what precisely the two poles and their relationship are. For Christians this dispute comes to a critical head in the doctrine of Christology.

In Christianity many persons have somehow perceived the Jesus-event and have reacted to it vigorously. It produced a deep effect on their lives. But not all actual "reactions to" or doctrines of Christology have been or are accepted by all committed Christians. No concerned Christian can affirm both the world-fleeing Christologies of some gnostic Christians and the world-affirming Christologies of the synoptic gospels. Somewhere these Christians have a measuring stick by which to judge a "correct" (coming from "rectus" in Latin, meaning "straight"—in Greek it is "ortho," "straight," and hence, "ortho-doxy," "straight teaching") Christology. For some, it is contemporary church authority (*Magisterium*). For others it is some past church authority (*Traditio*), either in whole or part (e.g., the first seven ecumenical councils). For still others it is the Scriptures (*sola Scriptura*), although most Protestants now recognize that Scripture itself is really the earliest set of traditions.

Küng, Schillebeeckx and like-minded Christian thinkers are putting forth a christological method that attempts to go behind tradition (whether *Magisterium*, *Traditio* or *Scriptura*) and locate the initial event fundamentally not in any foreshortened "reaction to" or doctrine about the Jesus-event, but in the living Jesus of history. The living Christian(s) today, and tomorrow, must as best as possible apprehend and "react to" this living Jesus of history, that is, the Jesus of Nazareth who lived in Israel two thousand years ago. It is no longer sufficient in a world that is historically conscious for a Christian to "react to" earlier "reactions to," doctrines about, the Jesus-event. An historically conscious person wants to base her/his judgments and actions as much as possible on the primary facts; the Catholic experience with Galileo, the American experience of

Watergate, and other similar experiences drive contemporary Christians in this direction.

In a way the sixteenth-century Reformation attempted such a move by trying to go behind the *Magisterium* and *Traditio* to where it thought the initial event lay, the *Scriptura*, and in some ways that instinct was right. However, it had two shortcomings. One, it tended to act as if human communities could exist without developing *Traditio*, which is an impossibility. Two, it did not (indeed, at that time, could not) know that the New Testament, including the gospels, was already a series of *Traditiones*, doctrines, "reactions to," the Jesus-event. This perception of the *Scriptura* arose only with the development of the historical-critical method, and particularly form and redaction criticism in this century.

With the help of the historical-critical method we are now able to perceive the major outlines of the Jesus of Nazareth of two thousand years ago who had such a massive impact on his followers. This perception of course will continue to be refined, but the essential elements are already reasonably sure. It is that living Jesus of history, the one who lived then and there in Israel two thousand years ago (whatever else he might be or do), who must be the touchstone for all "reactions to," doctrines about, him, including the various ones in the New Testament itself. It cannot be objected that the image of the historical Jesus produced by the help of the historical-critical method is simply a contemporary "image" and can make no more claim to allegiance by Christians than any other "image" of Jesus, as, for example, that of Paul, who never knew Jesus, or a gnostic Christian, or the Council of Chalcedon (451 A.D.). For there is nothing in a living person's mind that is not an "image." But there is a fundamental difference between the image formed of a person from the words and actions of the person him/herself and the image of what someone else thinks of that person.

Due modesty in the claims made by the historical-critical method, of course, must be maintained. In the case of Jesus, the faith-statement nature of the gospels severely limits the degree to which one can hope to obtain primary data on the historical Jesus. Further, there is the "pull" that the whole history of the understanding of statements (Gadamer *et al.*) about Jesus doubtless exerts on the contemporary Christian thinker which may skew the image of the historical Jesus. On the other hand, that history of understandings (*Traditio*) can also be extremely enlightening. It would at the same time be foolish to pass up such insights and also disastrous to attempt to skip over that history—because it is impossible! It is already in some form, often badly distorted, in our heads, for we are the product of all that has gone before us. What makes us specifically human, however, is not simply action, but conscious, knowing and freely-willed action. Hence, the more we learn our history (including here the history of the understandings of Jesus), the more precisely we are able to make distinctions, decisions and knowing free affirmations about it. Still further, each person stands in a particular historical context (von Ranke *et al.*) and a particular place in the world so that all perceptions are fundamentally influenced by that fact (Mannheim *et al.*), including perceptions of historical-critical images. Again, an awareness of this limitation will allow the human being to avoid naive absolute certitude on the one hand and total scepticism on the other. And yet further, we are now becoming aware that human language is both a liberating and a limiting instrument (Wittgenstein *et al.*). A growing awareness of its limiting as well as its liberating powers will enable humans to proceed with modesty though also security, always being open to new evidence, insights, perspectives, and, hence, change. But of course all this proper modesty is appropriate not only for the image of the historical Jesus that is derived from the "primary data," but *a fortiori* also for all images of the "reactions to" him.

At one point in the first half of the twentieth century some Christian New Testament scholars (Bultmann *et al.*) gave up the search for the historical Jesus and focussed on the early "reaction to" him, the proclamation (*Kerygma*) about him, so that merely the "that" Jesus had existed was all that was seen as important about the historical Jesus. "What" Jesus' life consisted of was not important. The proclamation about Jesus was perceived as God's instrument (*Scriptura*) to challenge contemporary humans to respond to God's message of the meaning of life. This approach would seem to fall into the category of neither A nor B in reference to Christology, that is, if Christology is conceived of as having something substantive to do with Jesus. In any case, it has tended to fade from dominance as New Testament scholars again gained confidence, though chastened, in the project of the search for the historical Jesus. Furthermore, this disjuncture between the historical Jesus and the proclamation about him, the "Christ of faith," was felt by the vast majority of Christians to be fundamentally off the mark. Most Christians over the centuries have from the beginning—gnosticizing minorities aside—always understood the historical Jesus, what he said and did, to be centrally important. It has for the most part been argued that a particular teaching about Jesus was right, orthodox, because it ultimately really fit with the historical Jesus who lived two thousand years ago. True, some teachings may well have been directly based only on some later *Traditio*, but then the claim was at least implicit that such a procedure was a sure way to link up with the real, historical Jesus. There would be few Christians, if any, who would be willing to affirm the statements about Jesus in the Council of Nicea (325 A.D.) or Constantinople (381 A.D.) *even if* they could not be said of the historical Jesus of Nazareth.

The difficulty that Küng and Schillebeeckx point to in this situation is that the "reactions to," the statements about, Jesus, whether past (*Traditio*) or present (*Magisterium*), tend too often to be the yardstick for understanding the historical Jesus, when it should be the other way around. That this is not just a dispute about some abstract theory, consider the following contrast: Contemporary Catholic scholars[1] perceive the historical Jesus to have continued to affirm

---

[1]Gerard Sloyan, *Is Christ the End of the Law?* (Philadelphia: Westminster Press, 1978); Franz Mussner, *Traktat über die Juden* (Munich: Kösel Verlag, 1979).

and carry out the Torah, Law, through the whole of his life and to teach his followers to do the same; he set up no opposition whatsoever between Law and grace, nor did he in any way reject his people the Jews—in fact, he felt himself to be sent to the Jews (cf. Mk. 7:24-30). Contrast that image of the historical Jesus emerging from careful historical-critical analysis with the "reactions to" Jesus developed by Paul in the letters to the Galatians and Romans and subsequent Christian thinkers who set up varying oppositions between the Law and grace in Jesus leading to the "replacement" of the Jewish people by the Christian Church as the People of God, which in turn provided the setting for the horrors of Antisemitism which has reached its abyss only in our lifetime.[2] Thus it is apparent that our Christian *Traditio* about the Jewish people must be "corrected" by the image of the historical Jesus the Jew emerging from historical-critical research if for no other reason than *reductio ad horrorem*.

But this very example highlights clearly the limitation of the historical-critical method. It was precisely Protestant German New Testament scholarship that developed the historical-critical analysis of the Scriptures, and yet it was from Germany that the greatest cataclysm of Antisemitism came. It would seem that the historical-critical method by itself cannot solve the crucial problems of Christology and doctrine in general. It is here that contemporary experience must play a balancing role, and not solely in the manner alluded to in Küng's essay. It now appears clear that the Protestant distortion of the image of the Jews, Jesus' attitude toward the Law, and even Paul's attitude toward the Law and the Jewish people was twisted in its negative direction by the Protestant desire to carry on the sixteenth-century polemic of faith-works, etc. against the Catholics. There were no work-righteous Catholics in the New Testament to contrast with faith-righteous Protestants, and so the Jews stood in for the Catholics and the "Christians" for the Protestants.[3] The contemporary sensitivity to our cultural, including religious, limitedness in all of our perceptions of reality is leading to a proper humility and openness to and even desire for dialogue with persons of other cultures and religions and theologies. The former Catholic-Protestant, Christian-Jew, etc. hostilities are shrinking, and consequently the distortions in historical-critical scholarship due to them are also shrinking.

Thus today in doing Christian theology there are at least three new elements which must be formative: 1) The historical-critical method which gradually is providing us with an ever clearer image of the living Jesus (the Jew) of history to which our "reactions to," our doctrines, our Christology ought to conform—no disjuncture between the Jesus of history and the Christ of faith. 2) An awareness of the limitedness of our knowledge: historically limited (historicism), culturally and socially and individually limited (sociology of knowledge), and linguistically limited (linguistic analysis)—no doctrinal statement is ever complete, is not in need of "correction." 3) Because of the limitedness of our knowledge we need

---

[2]Cf. Edward Flannery, *The Anguish of the Jews* (New York: Macmillan, 1965); Lucy S. Dawidowicz, *The War against the Jews: 1933-1945* (New York: Bantam Books, 1976).

[3]Cf. E. P. Sanders, *Paul and Palestinian Judaism* (Philadelphia: Fortress Press, 1977).

to be "in dialogue" with others constantly to compensate as best we can for our limitations—no "going it alone" by any individual or group has any credibility today. Moreover, the partners with whom we Christians need to dialogue are not just our contemporaries in other cultures, religions, theologies, etc., but also our "source," the living Jesus of history, reached through the *Scriptura*; all the other Christians who have ever lived, *Traditio*, for their lessons of both what to believe and do and what not to believe and do are invaluable; the contemporary *Magisterium*, for that is the believing community within which we must live out our Christian lives, from whom we receive nourishment and whom we in turn nourish—but this *Magisterium* is not just a small group of hierarchs; rather it includes the whole community in various ways as it believes, prays, and lives, and hence teaches.

IS A NEW CHRISTIAN CONSENSUS POSSIBLE?

Rosemary Radford Ruether

Hans Küng believes that the Second Vatican Council, while conducted primarily on pastoral lines, had revolutionary theological implications. It opened the way for Catholic theology to absorb the questions of critical biblical scholarship and of modern secular society that had been resisted by a closed ecclesiastical establishment since the Reformation. But, because the pastoral questions were not integrated into explicit theological and exegetical reflection, but papered over with a traditional neo-scholastic theology, a new consensus has failed to emerge. Rather, what has happened is a disintegration of all consensus, a sharp party conflict between traditional scholastical theology, with its doctrinal view of biblical foundations, and those theologians who have absorbed the historical-critical method.

This "liberal" wing of Catholic theology itself has ramified into a number of distinct movements. Specifically, those theologians who are primarily interested in translating biblical faith to the contemporary secular scientific consciousness are in a significantly different place from those who see the modern world as a crisis of Western hegemony over the oppressed peoples of the earth. Küng seems to be more comfortable with the first emphasis and is nervous about the second, that of liberation theologians, who wish to find in theology a reflection upon a concrete human struggle against injustices.

Küng, in his book on *Jesus* sees Jesus (and himself) as the great "middle-of-the-roaders," "neither Left nor Right." But he seems to imagine that this position transcends and judges all politics, instead of itself corresponding to a political option, namely, that of the liberal, bourgeois establishment. The liberation theologians, however, would not recognize themselves in the caricature of persons who "in an all too earthy manner . . . simply affiliate themselves with a specific one-sided socio-political analysis with the corresponding pre-programmed conclusions." Miranda, Gutierrez and Segunda, as much as Küng, are interested in establishing the critical correlation between "return to the source in the Gospel of Jesus" and "reflection on contemporary historical experience." But both their picture of Jesus and their contemporary experience is different from Küng's, and so they come up with a significantly different kind of correlation.

As Küng has noted elsewhere, the problem of the implementation of Vatican II in a new consensus is not simply a matter of the gap between pastoral applications and the reigning model of theological method. More fundamentally it is a problem of ecclesiastical power structures. The Vatican council enunciated a new collegial model of the Church on the theoretical plane. In practice, it was not able to translate this into a new collegial polity in the Church. Consequently, we have the contradiction of a hierarchical church leadership who are in charge of implementing a document advocating collegial processes. Not surprisingly this leadership has not only combatted the possibility of any democratization of the Church, but also sought to subvert the authority of the new theology.

The old scholastic theology, with its formal doctrinal view of Christ as the founder of the ecclesiastical hierarchy, is necessary to validate this type of polity. As long as that centralized power structure is intact, there is little likelihood of moving forward to a new Catholic consensus. On the contrary, what we can expect is constant rear-guard actions from those in control of the Vatican offices against the conciliar theology. In fact, since Küng wrote this article, Edward Schillebeeckx (whom Küng sees as his theological counterpart in the making of the new consensus) is under new attack by the Holy Office. The Curial establishment appears to have begun a whole new drive to displace theologians such as Küng and Schillebeeckx from makers of a new center to the margins of a Church life still very much dominated by the old center. They would like to define the conciliar thinkers as heretics, while claiming the authority of the Council itself.

This leads me to the critical problem with Küng's treatment of the theological crisis in Catholicism today. He approaches the making of a new theological consensus here as though it were primarily a matter of a better education, an updating of people's consciousness to include historical-critical method and modern social issues. Those with this improved education can create a new consensus (based in the networks of theological academia, rather than in the ecclesiastical hierarchy and the Curia) where, in a "gentlemanly" fashion, they can all agree on the general rules of the game, if not in all matters of detail.

I believe there is something like this new consensus within a particular network of theological scholars and biblical exegetes. This group shares a common historical-critical method, as well as a common social base in Western affluent universities. This group of people already has, for some decades, established a working consensus on method that allows them to share common presuppositions, while debating endlessly about details of exegesis and interpretation. But can this academic consensus really claim to be the overarching center which can place Curial neo-scholastic theology on their right and the liberation theologians on their left as two extremes?

The guardians of the ecclesiastical hierarchy cannot concede a legitimate place to the new theology, certainly not as the new consensus, but, in fact, not even as a legitimate option for Catholic theology. The old neo-scholastic theology and formalistic exegesis of Scripture is necessary to legitimize the kind of Church structure that they dominate. Such theology and exegesis operates as the ideology of this ecclesiastical ruling class. Without it, they would lose the fundamental sanction of their existence. They know this very well. Consequently they intend to give no quarter in their struggle to delegitimize the new theology and exegesis.

As is evident from the sloppy scholarship in the recent Declaration of the Vatican against the ordination of women, the group of official theological defenders of the *status quo* are not very interested in whether their methodology is scientifically respectable or not. They do not subject themselves to the academic standards of the university. The contempt of university scholars for their scientific method falls wide of the mark with them. They are interested in defending a certain traditional ecclesiastical system. If a particular theologian or biblical scholar doesn't agree with the conclusions that are desired, he can simply be dropped from the commission. The free search for truth is not a value for them. Truth is already incarnate in the traditional Church institution. To defend it by any means necessary is to defend truth. Their methods are apologetic, not scientific. Facts that do not fit these ideological needs do not count.

Once we realize how totally different the values of the defenders of Curial theology are from the values which Küng would prescribe as the basis of the new consensus, I think we can put aside any hope for such a new consensus as long as this polity is still in power. There is simply no agreement on a common scientific methodology between the two camps. The lack of consensus in the Catholic Church on basic theological and exegetical matters has nothing to do with academic disagreement and cannot be resolved on this basis. Fundamentally, it is a schism between two magisteria, the magisterium of the professors and the magisterium of the pope and the hierarchy. It is a power struggle, not an intellectual debate. The inability to understand the new thinking has more to do with sin than with ignorance or education. Any biblical, historical or sociological findings that threaten this system of dominance (that reaches all the way from control over Curial commissions to control over the sexuality of lay women in the family) cannot be taken into account.

On the personal level, no one knows this better than Küng himself. Yet he seems to think that, on the theological level, he can discount this reality of power struggle and speak of a new consensus only in terms of the academy. But this is not the source of the schism. The schism cannot be resolved by consensus between Küng and Schillebeeckx. The use of theology as ideology in defense of the traditional power structure is itself the fact that needs to be reflected upon theologically. By taking this fact itself into our theological consciousness, we begin to understand the apostacy of the hierarchy from the Gospel. But understanding this does not create a new consensus.

A new consensus could only come about if this traditional power could be deposed and the Church restructured on conciliar, democratic lines accountable to the people. Then the theological consensus of the academy could serve as a guide for the pastoral teaching of the Church. This is really what Küng is calling for: that the academy replace the hierarchy as the teaching magisterium of the Church. This cannot be accomplished by the academy itself. It entails the equivalent of the French Revolution in the Church, the deposing of a monarchical for a democratic constitution of the Church. No one has seriously discussed how this is to be done. But one thing is sure. It will not be legislated by the present power holders. It demands a revolution from below of a type that is difficult to imagine, much less to organize.

In the immediate future we cannot hope for a new consensus that will overcome this theological split between the academy and the hierarchy. Rather, the best we can hope for is the defense of pluralism. Pluralism will not be conceded as a theological principle by the Curial theology. The Curia demands not only a consensus, but a consensus that is fundamentally subservient to the defense of the traditional power structure. Pluralism can be defended only by making sure that this hierarchical power structure is not strong enough to repress successfully the independent institutional bases of conciliar and liberation theology.

There are a number of institutional bases of the new theologies. These are Catholic academic institutions, Catholic faculties of theology at colleges and universities, seminaries (primarily order rather than diocesan seminaries), renewed religious orders, lay-run base communities, independent study and action centers and movements concerned with social justice, and the independent Catholic media. The reason why there is any significant intellectual pluralism in the Catholic Church today is primarily because the hierarchy has lost control of a number of important institutions, especially educational institutions and Catholic media. In addition, new kinds of Catholic movements have developed, outside of direct ecclesiastical control. These are the social bases of liberal and liberationist theology.

We can expect to see in the coming years, under the new pontificate of Pope John Paul II, a concerted effort by the Vatican and national hierarchies to recapture control over these Catholic groups, especially educational institutions and religious orders, and to marginalize and delegitimize the catholicity of those autonomous lay movements, action centers and media which they cannot control. Already we have seen a number of evidences of this. The Jesuits have been issued a directive by Arrupe not to engage in any popular protest on controversial issues opposed by the Vatican. Seminaries have been told that they must take a new loyalty oath to the traditional Catholic teaching authority.

Study and action centers, that have been the source of critical protest, will be attacked by disciplining members of religious orders who belong to them. Already Bill Callahan, S.J., of the Quixote Center in Washington, DC, one of the major sources of organization around issues of sex discrimination, has been told that he must leave off all work on the ordination of women and end his connection with the Priests for Equality. He can los_ his Jesuit standing if he does not comply. By removing priest members of such groups, the hierarchy seeks to impugn the center's right to call itself Catholic. We can expect major moves by the Vatican and the bishops to regain control of renewed women's religious orders, especially in the United States, which are seen as the source of the agitation over women's rights in the Church.

The defense of theological pluralism in the Catholic Church (which is to say, the survival of conciliar and liberation theologies as options for Catholics in the future) fundamentally hinges on the successful defense of these independent bases of Catholic thought and life. Catholics must learn to fight in new and more political ways to defend the freedom they have achieved. When the faculty of

The Catholic University is threatened by the bishops with withdrawal of funds if they don't conform to a certain doctrinal line, one must do more than appeal to Church authority. One must demonstrate the large amount of funding of this university that comes from American governmental sources. One must threaten the possible loss of this American funding if investigation turns up serious violations of academic freedom.

When priests with tenure on religion faculties are threatened with dismissal when they marry, one should take the case to the American Association of University Professors as a violation of tenure contract. In short, one must use the liberal institutions of the secular society against the illiberal practices of the monarchial Church to limit the latter's power. Above all, one must cease to internalize the authority of unjust power. What the Pope says is not necessarily right because he says it. If, as I contend, the lack of consensus in theology is rooted in power struggle, then the liberal wing of this dissension must defend the autonomy and Catholicity of its institutional power bases, if it hopes to survive as an option for the future.

So far I have spoken of the conflict in Catholic theology in terms of the academy and the hierarchy. But there is a second equally important split between the theology of the academy and the theology of the social justice movement, between what I would call liberal establishment theology and liberationist theology. Küng, in his article, speaks as though a general consensus about who Jesus was can be recovered through historical-critical method. We also can know what contemporary experience is about through consulting the contemporary experience of persons like Küng himself. Then the two can be put together to create a new theology.

But, in fact, there are very different contemporary experiences which depend on one's class situation and consciousness. People who view contemporary experience primarily in terms of the conflicts of secularity, scientific methodology, and the problems of boredom and meaninglessness in an affluent society think out of a very different social base than those whose contemporary experience is primarily that of life-and-death struggle of the poor of the world for survival. Küng fundamentally belongs to the first camp.

Academic theology belongs to the intelligentsia of this liberal, bourgeois establishment. The Jesus that they recover from the Scriptures, despite the best historical-critical method, turns out to be a Jesus that answers the questions of this liberal bourgeoisie, not a Jesus who answers the questions of the poor. The theology of the academy expresses a perspective that privatizes religious commitment. Its claims of universality and transcendence of politics masks its partisanship of this social establishment.

Academic theology tends to seek to delegitimize liberation theology which unmasks this bias. It does this by accusing liberation theology of one-sided and socially limited partisanship. Liberation theology rejects this ideology of neutrality in favor of a clarified moral commitment to the side of the poor in the conflicts of our time. This is not a question of an option of partisanship or non-partisanship. It is a question of what kind of option maintains an unjust *status quo* and what option helps revolutionize society in the direction of greater justice for all. In the reality of unjust power relations, claims of non-partisanship serve the ruling classes, while the option for the poor is ultimately the option for a new whole.

Academic neutrality functions as an element in the ideology of the academic, bourgeois establishment, just as neo-scholasticism is a part of the ideology of the ecclesiastical hierarchy. The academy will fight liberation theology by attacking its academic respectability and denying university credentials to its spokespersons. Although liberation theology will probably maintain some marginal bases in the academy, it cannot expect unqualified support from it. Its primary contexts are the peace and justice movements and the base communities.

For the foreseeable future we cannot expect a new consensus in the Catholic Church. This itself perhaps represents an artificial and static ideal. Rather we must seek to defend the survival of both of these critical options, conciliar and liberation theologies. We can do this only by limiting the power and authority of the Vatican and the hierarchy. This means not just theological but ecclesiastical pluralism in the Church—in effect, an internal schism. This pluralism does not exist as a tolerated right of free thought, but rather as a standoff in the struggle against an institution which does not concede the right of any other view to exist outside of its own authority. The Vatican and hierarchies must be prevented from repressing the freedom of the academy and the academy must be prevented from repressing or co-opting liberation theology. When both these critical options have the minimal freedom to continue to develop, then perhaps some new institutional realities will begin to emerge that can be the beginning of new dialogue.

THE EXPERIENTIAL "WORD OF GOD"

Bernard Cooke

I understand that the purpose of these responses to Hans Küng's essay is to further discussion about appropriate theological method, more specifically to test the possibility of a consensus on this matter among Catholic theologians and beyond that on an ecumenical basis. Such a purpose demands that the responses be straightforward, even blunt, and that they be as precise as possible, especially in their criticism. Lest this obscure one's appreciation for the contribution made by both Küng and Schillebeeckx, let me at the very beginning acknowledge the major contribution these two have made to present-day theological reflection.

Yet, I cannot avoid the impression that our base essay is ambiguous in its thrust and slightly behind the times, two criticisms I would hope to expand. First, while I agree that theologians' attitudes toward their task and the purpose they have in mind have an inevitable impact on their mode of operation, I think one must separate the questions that have to do with attitude and those that have to do with technical procedure. Küng fails to do this as far as I can see.

The essay is meant to explore the existence of a consensus between Küng himself and Schillebeeckx, a consensus whose breadth is being tested by these present responses. But consensus on what? On the utilization of experience as a source of reflection? I think considerable agreement could be reached on this, but (as I plan to expand later) this is nothing new. Perhaps the chief indication Küng gives of something beyond this comes in the list of guiding principles (drawn from his *Existiert Gott?*) for contemporary theology. Most of these principles are attitudinal in nature—we should be honest, non-polemical yet carefully critical, fair to other opinions; we should avoid mystifying language, stay in context of everyday life as we reflect, deal with today's world, and keep theory and practice together. Certainly, we would hope for a consensus on such points, not only in theology but in any worthwhile human discourse. Certainly, none of us practice all these virtues perfectly—who of us does not occasionally use less than clear language to hide the fact that our thought is unclear? But my own impression is that there is a widespread attempt among theologians today to function in this open fashion.

Even with respect to these attitudes, we need more clarification than Küng's principles provide. For example, as we move beyond mere tolerance of other opinions into an authentically pluralistic approach to human understanding, and specifically to theological understanding, vague goodwill can betray us. We should respect others' intelligence and sincerity, to the point where we listen to them in the hope of learning; but our respect should be grounded in a clear grasp of the *bases for our differences*—whether these be philosophical, social, analytic, cultural, or more strictly on the level of faith and belief. The extent and nature of our agreement or disagreement is, obviously, conditioned by our awareness of which of these various bases are in question.

When one comes to the more technical guidelines mentioned by Küng, there seems to be again less precision than one might desire. In some instances there is a broad generalization: we "must practice an interdisciplinary approach"—that would find broad acceptance; the question is what such goals mean in the specifics of concrete scholarly work. In other instances the desired precision touches on very central issues; let us take as example an issue that has frequently figured in theologians' reaction to Küng and that is prominent in the present essay: the relation of "original Gospel" to the Church's emergent historical understanding.

I must confess that I am still not quite certain just how Küng is using the notion of "Gospel." In some instances it seems to refer to the New Testament teaching as a whole; in other cases it apparently points to the central message of the New Testament writings; and at other times it seems to refer to the Christ-event itself which underlies the earliest Christian formulations. What really is it that is normative as Gospel of our own present faith and criterion for any judgments we pass on the past twenty centuries of Christian history?

Küng says, of course, in so many words that it is the historical Jesus of Nazareth which is the criterion; but is this Jesus exactly as he was or as he is understood by the authors of the Gospels and Paul? And even when he lays emphasis on the life of Jesus as *norma normans*, it is not clear whether his stress on what precedes Jesus' death is meant to exclude any really new insight coming with Jesus' resurrection. (As Peter Chirico's recent article [*Theological Studies* 40 (1979): 256-272] indicates, this question is already raised by Küng's *Christ sein*.) This leads to another question, which seems to find no treatment in Küng's explanation, though it would seem to be central to any discussion of this matter: given that whatever ontological status one wishes to assign to Jesus' "risen state," it clearly transcends the sequence of temporal history, why is not the final stage of the Christ-event as much a present reality to Christians today as it was to the earliest Christians whose experience is reflected in the New Testament pages? And if this be true, then why grant to the New Testament texts the supreme normative role that Küng gives them? Would it not be just as logical to give an equal role to the eucharistic celebrations whose very essence is to be a unique form of *anamnesis*?

I am not quite clear what many of Küng's statements mean. The words are clear enough when he says that "only the Gospel, the original Christian message itself" can be the "definitive criterion" of Christian theology. But what is this "original Christian message"? I know that Küng is perfectly aware of the multiple theologies one finds in the New Testament literature, aware also of the development that takes place during the first generation or two (perhaps even during Jesus' own ministry), aware therefore that the New Testament texts can not serve as their own interpreter. So, I am puzzled by the extent to which in Küng's thought the New Testament literature has a kind of a-historical ultimacy.

It is perfectly possible that what Küng is pointing to, in quite general fashion, is the pre-eminence of the primitive Christian experience (as we find this expressed in the New Testament writings) over against later historical developments. If so, I would find it difficult to follow him very far. While there is clear evidence that many of earliest Christianity's key insights were gradually obscured or almost forgotten, there is also considerable evidence of growth and learning and maturity over the centuries—growth that was influenced in no little way by the continuing influence of the New Testament Scriptures themselves. As a matter of fact, if one is to speak of a normative role of the Scriptures, then he or she will have to speak in terms of the actual normative role these Scriptures have played in the historical unfolding of Christian faith and life, a role that was itself an historically developing one.

One of the critical methodological challenges facing us today is utilization of history in our theological reflection, not just historical "data" distilled from the multitude of detailed historical researches but the very modality of consciousness that has come in recent centuries from increasing awareness of the historical nature of our human existence. Beyond the questions of how far we can reconstruct events of the past "as they really happened," lies the deeper heuristic issue of how vicarious experience functions to give us insight. Ultimately the reason for studying history (or any of its cultural expressions, such as literature) is to transcend the narrow limits of our own direct experience and enrich our consciousness by sharing in the experiences of others. This, of course, is specially relevant in the matter of religious awareness where present-day believers claim a community in faith and belief with previous generations. Given the importance of this matter, I think that any attempt to work toward a consensus in method must investigate the role being assigned to historical understanding.

In short, then, I find it hard to judge whether or not the consensus that Küng advocates is shared by many or should be so shared—the reason for the difficulty in judging being the indefiniteness of the consensus to which he refers. But perhaps the central issue to which he is pointing and with regard to which he senses a new agreement in method is the utilization of experience as a starting point for theological reasoning. If this is a correct reading of his essay—and I think it can be supported—it brings me to my second area of comment: the non-novelty of Küng's approach.

It probably sounds a bit too harsh to say that many an American (North or South America) theologian would read through Küng's description of using experience as one of the two poles of theological reflection with a certain sense of *deja vu*. For a number of well-known reasons, the tendency of thinking on this side of the Atlantic has been to avoid abstractness and to deal with concrete realities—it has been described as "pragmatic," with the term being used somewhat pejoratively. Be that as it may, more than a generation of American theologians take it for granted that genuine theology must work from human experience (religious in a very wide sense), not to gain some sort of "relevance" but simply to be theology. Moreover, the experience of *all* humans has gradually come to be respected as a source of religious insight, so much so that in some circles there is an excessive egalitarianism that makes little discrimination between the experiences of the sensitive and the experiences of the dulled.

Latin America's widely-heralded "theology of liberation" is probably the best known instance of this use of human experience as a starting-point for theology. While biblical thought and imagery is certainly a basic resource of these liberation theologians, as are classical theological reflection and modern patterns of social and behavioral analysis, it is the painful experience of participating in their people's struggle to free themselves from economic and social oppression which provides the foremost "word of God" upon which they reflect. And, as their Christian adaptation of the Marxist notion of *praxis* makes evident, authentic theological reflection must remain inseparable from involvement in social liberation, for it is an intrinsic element in that liberation.

Nor is this mode of reflection limited to Latin America. The incredible rapidity with which North American "feminist theology" has developed into a sizable corpus of solid and creative thought testifies to the widespread acceptance of a theological method rooted in experience. When feminist theologians began to insist that the Church's theological enterprise was badly truncated because it had not drawn from the experience of half of humanity, they were obviously able to appeal to the assumption that theology was meant to work out of such experience. The distinctiveness of women's experience, whatever that may turn out to be as our cultural stereotyping dissolves, promises to be a source of major enrichment for theology in the future.

Without belaboring the point, it seems to me that for quite some time now, our theological question has not been *whether* experience is a basic source of theology, but *how* we can accurately and critically use it as such. This has raised questions about the way in which social and behavioral sciences can clarify the reality of these experiences, questions about the way in which literary criticism can clarify the interaction of experience with the production and reading of literary works, questions about the manner in which historical studies can provide a sharper genetic understanding of our present human situation—clarifications that give theological reflection a starting-point that corresponds more accurately with reality. At present, much of this process of questioning focuses on the interaction between theology and the somewhat amorphous enterprise of "religious studies."

Some consensus would be extremely helpful in this area. We need to find some way of arriving at agreement, at least in general lines, about the relative validity of various methodologies, which means we must have some commonly accepted description of the various methodologies so that we can intelligently relate them to one another. There is growing conviction that the prevailing divisions of material and method are no longer productive; we are struggling to find shared views about objectives and procedures in research that will permit us to work corporately and therefore more productively.

At present there seems to be (on the North American scene) a tendency to "cluster" in response to these needs and possibilities—the arrangements of task force groups of scholars in different but related fields to study questions of mutual concern have become a regular feature of the annual conventions of professional societies (such as the American Academy of Religion, the Society for Biblical Literature, or the Catholic Theological Society). And this is extended into numerous conferences conducted at university centers. Just recently, for instance, we held a seminar at our own university which gathered together scholars from a variety of disciplinary backgrounds (social science, history, literary criticism, philosophy, religious studies) and representing a wide range of religious positions (Muslim, Buddhist, Hindu, Jewish, as well as Christian), in order to examine together the interaction of religious sacred writings and historical experience. Moreover, definite movements can be discerned, movements that already have had an identifiable impact on theological method—one thinks, for example, of the development of "structuralism" within New Testament studies, or of the application of "process thought" to religious reflection.

All of this recent North American (and somewhat analogously Latin American) activity seems to confirm the approach to theological reflection that Küng advocates in his essay. What I find exciting is not only the extent of convergence, but the possibilities of new insights that could come with extended interaction between European and American theologians.

So far, most of this essay has been a critical appraisal of Küng's proposals; and it would be both unproductive and ungracious not to go further and make some positive suggestions which he in turn can evaluate and so advance the discussion. Let me, then, sketch very quickly an alternative model for the theological enterprise—using "alternative" rather loosely, because it will quickly become apparent that it is basically open to the kind of thrust that Küng describes in his own method. Instead of viewing the theological task as one of bringing two poles, "the Gospel" and human experience, into creative contact with one another, I see a person's experience (and by extension a community's experience) as the basic and, to some extent, all-encompassing "word of God." For each of us, it is the sequence of experienced happenings that tells us ultimately who and what we are, what the world around us is all about, what transcendent influence works with and upon us, and what response we are called to give as we help shape the future.

Obviously, the happenings that make up a given person's experience are being constantly interpreted—necessarily so, because in many instances the meaning of the happenings is obscure or ambiguous. And the very factors that enter into the interpretation—explanations given by family or friends, education and reading and discussion, "hearing the Gospel," religious doctrines and catechesis, exposure to the arts and literature, and other expressions of human culture—are all integral elements in the experience itself. Perhaps most basically, any given experience is interpreted in the light of other experiences, either one's own recalled past experiences or the experiences of others in which one has shared vicariously. These experiences of others, which for them were an immediate "word of God," function also for me as "revelation" in proportion as together we form one truly sharing community of belief. Each person is, then, sacramental in some very fundamental sense; each true believer is a "theological source" more ultimate than any doctrinal or theological formulation—though, clearly, the generalizations that take place in doctrine and theology have an indispensable role in creating a unity of understanding and making interchange of personal belief possible.

In order that the experiential "word of God" be genuinely fruitful for each of us, it must be read with accuracy. This is where theological input occurs, hopefully. No brief summation of theology's task is satisfactory, partly because the very boundaries of theological reflection are expanding as new modern disciplines of knowledge become part of theological method. Let me suggest just three or four contributions theology can and should make.

1. Theology should help one discover and identify the religious components in the implicit and explicit structures of interpretation that influence any given experience. That there are such presuppositional structures is certain, that they both limit and enrich our perception of "reality" is well known; and the recognition of religious presuppositions in this "hermeneutic of experience" is required if we wish to ascertain what in our experience is revealing word of God. Not only should theology provide the categorial clarifications enabling us to identify these religious presuppositions, it should also, by situating such understandings relative to established credal and theological traditions, indicate the extent of historical relativity in our presuppositional structure.

2. Theology should describe as accurately and critically as possible (as a basis for comparative evaluation) those principles for interpreting one's own experience which are provided by previous expressions of faith—including the Scriptures. A distinctive element in this task is the critical examination, in historical perspective, of the various *logoi* or structuring categories that people used to give rational theological structure to their religious understandings.

3. Theology should help suggest the (providentially directed) pattern of ongoing religio-human development into which our own experience fits. This would include a practical extrapolation of our present historical dynamics, a hypothetical projection of what the future could (and according to the Gospel imperative should) become, so that this could influence practical moral decisions.

4. Christian theology must as its basic function guide each believer as he or she responds personally to the perennial question: "Who do you say that I am?" Perhaps it is in drawing us back insistently to this question about Jesus of Nazareth that Hans Küng has most profoundly affected our theological endeavor. For this we are all in his debt.

METHODOLOGICAL CONSENSUS?
A PROTESTANT PERSPECTIVE

Arthur B. Crabtree

In his doctoral dissertation Hans Küng demonstrated, to the surprise of Barth and many others, that Barth's teaching on justification was Catholic as well as Protestant. In this brief essay I shall attempt to show, though not to the surprise of Küng, that Küng's theological method is Protestant as well as Catholic. I shall do this firstly by a short survey of the development of Protestant theology and secondly by a study of several twentieth-century Protestant theologians—Barth, Brunner, Bultmann, Tillich, Kaufman, and Pannenberg.

The Protestant Reformation was in one respect the child of Renaissance humanism. In common with the humanism of Petrarch, Boccaccio, Manetti, Reuchlin, Lefèvre d'Etaples, and Erasmus, it advocated a movement *ad fontes*, a return, that is, to early Christian sources—in particular to Scripture and the Church Fathers. In stressing *sola scriptura* Luther and Calvin meant that Scripture should be regarded as the sole norm, not the sole source, of doctrine. They were concerned however not only with the norm of doctrine but also with the problems of their age in church and society, and it was on the basis of this dipolar interest that they produced the Catechisms and Confessions of Faith which formed the foundation of the Protestant Orthodoxy of the seventeenth century.

When this Orthodoxy became divorced from life and morality it was again a combination of a return to sources (the Bible and Luther) and contemporary concerns which produced Spener's *Pia Desideria* (1675), Pietism on the European continent, the Wesleyan evangelical revival in England, and the Great Awakening in the United States. When the Enlightenment swept across Europe, Protestants responded with the Deism of Herbert of Cherbury, Toland, Tindal, and Chubb, though it must be confessed that Deism owed more to the Enlightenment than it did to early Christianity.

When Romanticism succeeded the Enlightenment, the Moravian Pietist, Schleiermacher, developed his Romantic Pietism, stressing the importance of both early Christianity and Romanticism, and insisting that sound Christianity must ever maintain constancy and change.

When the Romanticism of Schelling and Schlegel became the romantic idealism of Fichte and Hegel, Protestant theologians (and also Catholic theologians such as the Tübingen Catholic school of Drey, Möhler, Hirscher, Staudenmaier) began to unite biblical theology with Hegelianism: Neander and Marheinecke in Berlin (where Hegel himself was teaching); Baur, Zeller, and Schwegler in the Tübingen Protestant school; and Biedermann in Zürich. In Britain the brothers Caird followed the same path, John in Glasgow and Edward in Oxford, where the latter influenced William Temple.

Following the death of Hegel in 1831 there was a resurgence of Kantianism manifest in the Neokantianism of the Marburg (Cohen, Natorp, Cassirer) and Heidelberg (Rickert and Windelband) schools, stressing phenomenological ontology, the distinction between natural and cultural science, and the supreme importance of ethics (Kant) and values (Lotze). Recognizing the importance of Neokantianism, Albrecht Ritschl formed a new dipolar synthesis of early Christianity and Neokantianism, and his influence continued in the Ritschlian school of Harnack, Herrmann, and Troeltsch. Its impact was felt in the Christian Socialism of Kutter, Ragaz, Brunner, Barth, and Tillich, and in the Social Gospel of Rauschenbusch.

The First World War shattered the hopeful expectations of Protestant liberalism and evoked a new beginning. This new beginning was made by Thurneysen, Barth, Brunner, Bultmann, and Gogarten in the movement variously known as theology of crisis, dialectical theology, and neo-orthodoxy. It was a new synthesis of biblical theology with the existentialism of Kierkegaard and Heidegger, accompanied with ideas derived from Otto and Dostoevsky. Its *foci* remained however the Bible and the spirit of the age.

After Hitler's accession to power in 1933 dialectical theology diverged into the schools of Barth, Brunner, Gogarten, and Bultmann (plus the Post-Bultmannians such as Käsemann, Bornkamm, Fuchs, and Braun).

In the nineteen-sixties and -seventies new impulses came from the horizons of the modern world: the process philosophy of Bergson and Teilhard in France, of Whitehead in England and the United States, and of Nicolai Hartmann in Germany; the Marxist philosophy of Bloch; and the liberation movement among Africans, Asians, Afroamericans, Amerindians, and Latin Americans. These are producing new syntheses of biblical religion with the modern world in both Protestant and Catholic theology.

Having surveyed very broadly the history of Protestant dipolar syntheses, let us now study in particular the methodology of Barth, Bultmann, Tillich, Kaufman, and Pannenberg.

Until World War One Barth was a liberal Protestant, very close to one of his teachers, Harnack. During the war however, as pastor in Safenwil, Switzerland, he found his liberal synthesis inadequate for his own needs and the needs of his parishioners. Along with his friend Thurneysen he sought a new theology. He found it in the synthesis of Scripture with the existentialism of Kierkegaard and Heidegger together with Otto's teaching in *Das Heilige* of 1917 that God as the *mysterium tremendum* is wholly other, and Dostoevsky's perception of the fathomless depth of human sin. This new synthesis produced his *Römerbrief* of 1919 and the more influential second edition of the *Römerbrief* in 1922. It created his *Christliche Dogmatik* of 1927, of which he wrote only the first volume, and his *Kirchliche Dogmatik* from 1932 onwards. As he wrote his *Church Dogmatics*, which abounds in both biblical exegesis and reactions to modern life, he increasingly stressed the power of divine grace, as Berkhouwer has indicated, and turned toward the analogy of being, which he initially denied, as von Balthasar has shown. But his thought, changing though it was, was constantly moving between the poles of the Bible and modern life.

Brunner clearly states his dipolar method in the Prolegomena section of the first volume of his *Dogmatics*. In his chapter entitled "Scripture as the norm of doctrine" he writes: "Scripture has normative authority . . . because it is the primary witness to the revelation of God in Jesus Christ."[1] And in his chapter entitled "the contemporeity of doctrine" he writes: "Just as the Bible of the missionizing church must be translated into the most diverse languages . . . so must the gospel ever and again be translated into the 'language of the age'–a task which the church must take far more seriously than it has recently done."[2]

Bultmann began as a biblical scholar, and remained New Testament Professor throughout his long teaching career in Marburg. As New Testament Professor his primary concern was to understand the New Testament in its setting in the ancient world and the early church, and this concern is manifest in works such as *The History of the Synoptic Tradition, Jesus and the Word, Earliest Christianity*, and *Theology of the New Testament*. But Bultmann was also a preacher and as both New Testament scholar and preacher was vividly aware of the enormous gap between the world of the New Testament and the world of today. How does one interpret the New Testament, with its three-storey view of the world (heaven and God up there, earth down here, and hell beneath the earth), its angels and demons, its apocalyptic expectancy of the near advent of a new age, its concept of Christ as coming down from heaven and ascending to heaven like a gnostic redeemer God–how does one interpret this New Testament to modern people who believe in a universe of galaxies beyond galaxies; a universe in which there is no "up" or "down," but in which all motion, like all time and space, or rather space-time, is relative; a universe in which we know that sickness is due not to demons who must be exorcised but to viruses and bacteria and multitudinous poisons and bad health habits such as smoking and overeating and lack of exercise?

It was this question with which he dealt in an address first delivered to pastors of the Confessing Church in Frankfurt on April 21, 1941, and later published that same year under the title, *New Testament and Mythology*. The first thing to recognize, he says, is that the New Testament concept of the world (*Weltbild*), the apocalyptic imagery, and the concept of a divine redeemer who descends to earth as a man, ascends to heaven, and will return to complete his work, is all mythological speech, and consequently *erledigt* (finished, impossible to accept) for modern people. What are we then to do with the New Testament, with the biblical pole of our theological method, with the norm of theology according to prevalent Protestant tradition? Demythologize it, says Bultmann, by which he makes clear he means not removing the myth but reinterpreting it anthropologically, or rather, existentially–"Myth should be interpreted not

---

[1]Emil Brunner, *Dogmatik*, I, p. 53.
[2]Ibid., I, pp. 79-80.

cosmologically but anthropologically, or better, *existential interpretiert*."[3] It should be noted that Bultmann says "existenti*al* interpretiert," not "existen-ti*ell* interpretiert." What he means is that it should be interpreted in terms of Heidegger's concepts of *Angst* and *Sorge* (dread and care) and the unavoidability of decision to be authentic (*eigentlich*) or inauthentic (*uneigentlich*). For such is our sinful life—a life from which we can be rescued, not, says Bultmann, as Heidegger imagined, by obeying the voice of our own conscience, but only by Christ.

Now whatever one may think (and there are diverse opinions, as the essays collected in Hans Werner Bartsch's volumes, *Kerygma and Myth* illustrate), one thing is clear: Bultmann moves incessantly between the poles of the New Testament and the modern world and tries to relate them to one another.

Tillich in his *Systematic Theology*, like Brunner in his *Dogmatics*, tells us precisely what his theological method is. He begins his *Systematic Theology* with a section on "Message and Situation," which opens with the words: "Theology, as a function of the Christian Church, must serve the needs of the church. A theological system is supposed to satisfy two basic needs: the statement of the truth of the Christian message and the interpretation of this truth for every new generation. Theology moves back and forth between these two poles, the eternal truth of its foundation and the temporal situation in which the eternal truth must be received."[4] It is therefore necessary, he continues, "to seek a theological method in which message and situation are related in such a way that neither of them is obliterated. . . . The following system is an attempt to use the 'method of correlation' as a way of uniting message and situation. It tries to correlate the questions implied in the situation with the answers implied in the message."[5] He selects five basic questions—the question of reason, the question of being, the question of existence (in the modern sense of Schelling, Kierkegaard, and Heidegger), the question of life, and the question of history. His system of theology accordingly comprises five parts: reason and revelation, being and God, existence and Christ, life and the Spirit, history and the Kingdom. Thus his whole theology moves, in his own words, "back and forth between these two poles, the eternal truth of its foundation and the temporal situation in which the eternal truth must be received."[6]

Gordon Kaufman writes his *Systematic Theology* from what he calls a "historicist perspective," taking account both of the *Heilsgeschichte* in which the supreme redemptive and revelatory event of Jesus Christ is located and general world history.[7] "Since theology," he writes, "is the attempt of the

---

[3]Rudolf Bultmann, *Neues Testament und Mythologie*, in Bartsch, *Kerygma und Mythos*, I, p. 22.

[4]Paul Tillich, *Systematic Theology*, I, p. 3.

[5]Ibid., I, p. 8.

[6]Ibid., I, p. 3.

[7]Gordon D. Kaufman, *Systematic Theology*, p. xii.

Christian community to understand its rootage in revelatory history, it must be founded upon the study, analysis, and interpretation of the biblical documents. . . . All subsequent Christian writings are historically, and thus theologically, derivative from those collected here. . . . The Bible's authority derives from the revelatory events of which it contains the primary reports."[8] Nevertheless, "We are twentieth century men, who know modern physics and psychoanalysis, communist tyranny and Hiroshima, Freud and Marx, Einstein and Hitler; and we must seek to grasp God's historical act in Jesus Christ in terms *we* can understand, accept and believe."[9] Consequently, "theology has a two-pronged task. On the one hand, it must see *all human existence* in the light of God's act. This will involve careful study of contemporary views of the self, society, and the world; understanding of the problems of individual and society; insight into the significant movements in contemporary culture and into other religions and cultures. . . . On the other hand, it is necessary *to appropriate God's act(s)* from our situation."[10]

Pannenberg displays a similar historical interest. "History," he writes, "is the most comprehensive horizon of Christian theology. All theological questions and answers have meaning only within the framework of history."[11] And this historical interest has two poles: "Systematic theology always occurs in the tension between two tendencies. On the one hand it is concerned with the faithfulness of theology itself (and beyond itself to the Christian Church) to its origin, to the revelation of God in Jesus Christ, as this is attested in Scriptures. On the other hand, however, the task of theology goes beyond this special theme and includes all truth whatsoever."[12]

Examples such as these leave no doubt that the dipolar method of moving incessantly between Christian origins and the modern world is characteristically Protestant, and we can rejoice that it is now common to Catholics and Protestants. It has indeed ever been the method of Christian theology whenever theologians have had a sense of history and relevance. It was the method of patristic theology, both Eastern and Western, where the Fathers related Christianity to Stoicism, Platonism and Neoplatonism of the ancient Hellenistic world. It was the method of Alexander of Hales, Albert the Great, and St. Thomas Aquinas as they related Christianity to the resurgent Aristotelianism of their day. It was the method of the nineteenth-century theologians of the Catholic Tübingen School as they related Christianity to Schelling's romanticism and Hegel's idealism. And it remains the method of the resurgent Catholic Tübingen School of Adam, Geiselmann, and Küng.

Three concluding observations:

1. The principal methodological contrast today is not between Catholics

---

[8]Ibid., pp. 62-63.
[9]Ibid., p. 72.
[10]Ibid., p. 75.
[11]Wolfhart Pannenberg, *Grundfragen Systematischer Theologie*, p. 22.
[12]Ibid., p. 11.

and Protestants but between those, whether Catholics or Protestants, who think historically and dynamically and those who think unhistorically and statically.

2. The gap between early Christianity and the modern world is bridged by the living Christian tradition, as Pannenberg has suggested.

3. The future of humankind is now so menacing and the threats to human survival so grave that we must seek insights into cosmic connectivity such as those found in Taoism (as Jung Young Lee does in his *Cosmic Religion* [Harper, 1973]) and join with all people of goodwill in transforming our present civilization of selfishness, exploitation, and hatred into the civilization of love envisioned by Pope Paul VI.

THE BIBLE AS REALISTIC NARRATIVE

George Lindbeck

At the heart of Küng's proposed theological method is what in this country has come to be known as "the New Quest for the Historical Jesus." That, to be sure, is not the name he gives. He speaks rather of "a path that provides a new access to the historical Jesus through the medium of historical-critical" study. "Today we can once again gain insight into the original message of Jesus, as well as his personal lifestyle and destiny, which in the course of the centuries has been obscured and hidden." We can thus distinguish without separating the Jesus of history from the faith responses of the early Christians as embodied in their various images of the Christ of faith. A "fundamental hermeneutical consensus" —or, as I would prefer to say, "convergence"—is now finally available. The existence of this convergence is, it would appear, the initial and basic premise of Küng's methodological proposal.

A second premise is that, "The source, standard and criterion of Christian faith is the living Jesus of history." The theologically most important function of Scripture for Küng is to supply the data for the historical reconstruction of who and what Jesus was in his life upon earth. Now that such a reconstruction is possible, it must be normative for theology in general. The New Testament historically-critically interpreted is the *norma normans*. "Exegesis that is grounded in the historical-critical method calls for a dogmatics that is likewise historically-critically grounded."

The third premise is that the "critical correlation" of the Jesus of history and early Christian experience with contemporary experience can lead to convergence in all areas of theology. Those who agree on these three premises will employ similar standards in critically evaluating, interpreting, and appropriating traditional faith responses and correlating these with contemporary experience. They will not automatically or entirely agree (just as Küng is in some ways very different from Schillebeeckx), but their conclusions will be mutually complementary and corrective. The dangerous pluralism of contemporary theology, in which the practitioners of different methods are often not able even meaningfully to disagree, can thus be overcome. A consensus will develop, not in the sense of uniformity, but in the sense of cooperative and cumulative work.

Küng's motives in proposing this program are at one and the same time reformatory, ecumenical, and Catholic. For him, as his other writings make clear, the appeal to Scripture provides leverage for the reform of the church; but this appeal now need no longer be divisive, as it was in the sixteenth century, because we have the scholarly means for reaching consensus on the interpretation of Scripture. Thus he views his proposal as both reformatory and ecumenical. It is also, he holds, thoroughly Roman Catholic because it was, in effect, endorsed by Vatican II when the latter "fundamentally affirmed" the historical-

81

critical method and also asserted that Scripture should be the "soul" and "principle of life" of Catholic theology. In short, thanks to modern historical studies, the Bible can at last function as the *norma normans* to generate an *ecclesia semper reformanda* which, unlike fissiparous Protestantism, remains united and attached to its apostolic origins.

This is an appealing vision, not least to a Lutheran Protestant such as myself. There can be no quarrel with Küng's goal, but at most with the adequacy of some of his methodological means. This should be remembered as I now sketch certain difficulties and suggest modifications.

In reference to what I have called the first premise, it is true that the contemporary historical-critical convergence is of great theological importance. This importance, however, is chiefly negative, and perhaps does not bear the positive weight Küng wishes to place on it. The negative function of historical scholarship is to make impossible many of the traditional arguments for post-biblical developments and positions. To mention a familiar and in a sense minor example, neither Catholics nor Protestants can now cite Mt. 16:18 as a proof-text for either their papal or their anti-papal views as they have done in the past. Yet this negative conclusion does not, of course, settle the issue, because it is always possible to discover new arguments. Catholics, for example, may no longer hold that the historical Jesus founded the papacy, but they can maintain instead that this institution is a God-willed and irreversible providential development. Küng criticizes the use of the notion of "irreversibility" in this context as an instance of the non-historical "speculative harmonization" (of which Karl Rahner is a prime practitioner) of traditional doctrine with contemporary knowledge and experience ("Historisch-kritische Exegese als Provokation für die Dogmatik," *Tübinger Theologische Quartalschrift* [1979], pp. 24-36). On the other hand, however, he regards speculative harmonization as preferable to the flatly anti-historical proof-texting methods of traditional scholasticism. As anyone who has been involved in ecumenical discussions can testify, the old positions become much more flexible when they are argued in new ways which respect the veto power of historical-critical research.

The question, however, is whether historical-critical research has more than this negative function and can instead serve as the basis for positive theological construction. Hans Küng, as we have noted, believes that it can. The consensus on the historical Jesus and the original Christian experience is now sufficiently solid to constitute a criterion for all theological work. My impression, however, is that this judgment is possible, if at all, only when one confines attention to continental, and especially German, biblical studies. David Flusser of Jerusalem and Krister Stendahl of Harvard, for example, would hold that the scholars on whom Küng relies (e.g., in *On Being a Christian*) greatly underestimate the degree to which Jesus and St. Paul were and remained faithful Jews. This is not simply a minor difference, but involves major shifts in the picture of both the historical Jesus and the early Christian message. Although it can be argued in reply that historical-critical studies will eventually resolve such oppositions, the fact remains that Küng's methodological proposal insofar as it depends on a positive scholarly consensus seems premature.

The second premise also raises problems, One must, to be sure, applaud the desire for a common theological standard which leads Küng and Schillebeeckx to insist on the Jesus of history as the decisive norm. Yet it needs to be pointed out that most theologians, Protestant as well as Catholic, think that what is theologically most significant is some version or other of the Christ of faith. They do not read the Bible primarily as a source of data for reconstructing historically what actually happened. For them, rather, the theologically important content of Scripture is, for example, its symbolizations of religious experience (Tillich, Ricoeur and, in part, Rahner and Tracy), or its disclosures of authentic existence (Bultmann), or the concepts it employs (as in the "biblical theology" which until recently dominated in World Council of Churches circles), or biblical stories and symbols of deliverance from political and psycho-social oppression (liberation theology). Traditional Catholic and Protestant scholasticisms, whether orthodox or heretical, read Scripture in still another way, viz., as a source of doctrinal propositions; but there is some evidence that even this approach can be pursued in such a way as to avoid actually contradicting the results of historical research. All these various kinds of contents, it should be pointed out, are actually to be found in the Bible, and no approach need confine itself to a single kind of content. Nevertheless, it makes a great difference which is made primary. The "Christs of faith" which result from the varying starting points often seem utterly diverse and sometimes even contradictory, and they certainly differ from the theologically normative Jesus of history which a Küng or a Schillebeeckx sketches.

If one asks why theologians look for such different things in the Bible (and in Jesus), the answer is that they differ in their analyses of what human beings need, i.e., in their anthropologies and/or in their analyses of the requirements of the contemporary situation and experiences. They adopt some extra-biblical hermeneutical or interpretive framework (e.g., phenomenological, existentialist, transcendental Thomist, Marxist, evolutionary—as in the case of Teilhard de Chardin—or simply traditional) within which to read the Bible. The frameworks at least partly determine the kinds of questions which are asked and therefore also influence the answers received—the pictures of Jesus which emerge. One can sympathize with why theologians proceed in this way. They want to make the Gospel relevant to human experience especially in its currently salient aspects; or, in the case of traditionalists, they want to keep the church fixed in some one of the patterns supplied by the past. Nevertheless, the result of this multiplicity of apologetic, correlational, and traditionalist approaches is a pluralism which threatens to become chaos. There seems little sign of an emerging consensus around the "living Jesus of history" for which Küng hopes.

These observations, needless to say, are not against him, but in his favor. Even if the scholarly consensus on the historical Jesus is not as firm as he thinks, it seems to supply the one common point of reference for Christian theology—

Catholic and non-Catholic—taken as a whole. Furthermore, there is some merit in his contention that biblical scholarship has now advanced to the point where, unlike the nineteenth-century liberal quest, it strongly resists projections of current ideas and values on the historical Jesus. The good historians of our day emphasize the strangeness and alienness of Jesus. The Jesus of history discovered by historical-critical work, so it can be argued, is the closest thing we have to a criterion which stands over against us, judging and correcting us, rather than himself being ruled or normed by some contemporary or traditional worldview or set of values.

The importance of this norming function for Küng becomes apparent once again in his treatment of the third premise, the "critical correlation" of the sources with contemporary experience. He insists on the criteriological priority to contemporary experience of "special Christian experiences, i.e., the Christian message, the Gospel, and Jesus Christ himself." This leads him to express some discomfort with Schillebeeckx's tendency to over-elaborate and systematize an "analysis of our contemporary world of experience" in the terminology I used earlier, to develop an extra-biblical hermeneutical framework. Fortunately, this is counter-balanced in Schillebeeckx's recent work by his emphasis on the historical study of "the living Jesus of history."

In all this, Küng's instincts are sound. He is quite right in seeking to find a criterion in the sources of Christian faith which has enough independence of later hermeneutical frameworks to enable theology to escape from the unmanageable pluralism of both traditional contemporary apologetic, correlational, and speculative approaches. My one and only question is whether there might not be a better way to meet the challenge.

It seems to me worth asking whether Scripture does not perhaps supply its own interpretive framework. Everyone recognizes that correct interpretation requires the ascertaining of the literary genre of the work to be interpreted. What then is the literary genre of the Bible as a whole in its canonical unity? What holds together the diverse materials it contains: poetic, prophetic, legal, liturgical, sapiential, mythical, legendary, and historical? These are all embraced, it would seem, in an over-arching story which has the specific literary features of realistic narrative as exemplified in diverse ways, for example, by certain kinds of parables, novels, and historical accounts. It is as if the Bible were "a vast, loosely-structured, non-fictional novel" (to use a phrase applied to Karl Barth's view of Scripture in David Kelsey's *The Uses of Scripture in Recent Theology* [Philadelphia: Fortress, 1975], p. 48).

Furthermore, we can specify the primary purpose of the canonical narrative (which is also the pre-canonical purpose of many of its most important component stories from the pentateuch to the gospels). It is to "render a character . . . offer an identity description of an agent," viz., God (ibid.). Its primary purpose is not to tell the reader what actually happened in the sense of either profane or salvation history, and even less to provide doctrinal propositions, theological concepts, or symbolic expressions or re-presentations of religious experience or authentic *Existenz*—although it may do all these things as well. Given this canonical intent, it is not surprising that the Bible is often "history-like" rather than "likely history." As is illustrated by a parable such as that of the prodigal son, the ability of realistic narrative to depict who and what God is like in relation to creation is not in every case logically dependent on facticity.

Among the many consequences of adopting such a canonical interpretive framework, I shall mention only two. First, it gives more theological weight to the Old Testament than appears to be possible in an approach such as Küng's. The fundamental identity description of God is provided by the stories of Israel, Exodus, and Creation. This identity description is then completed or fulfilled by the stories of Jesus' life, death, and resurrection, but the latter stories must be read in the context of what went before. In contrast to this, the historical-critical focus on what actually happened tends to neglect, for example, the Exodus because so little can be reliably known about this in comparison to Jesus. Second, when looked at canonically rather than historically-critically, the purpose of the gospels is not at all to provide information for its own sake about the earthly Jesus, but rather to tell about the risen, ascended, and now-present Christ whose identity as the divine-human agent is irreplaceably enacted in the stories of Jesus of Nazareth.

There is nothing novel about this canonical approach with its emphasis on a realistic narrative framework for the interpretation of Scripture. If Hans Frei is right in his *The Eclipse of Biblical Narrative* (New Haven: Yale University Press, 1974), it was, apart from allegorizing, the most common pre-critical way of reading the Bible until after the Reformation, when doctrinal, pietistic, and, last of all, historical-critical methods displaced it. Frei further suggests (as does also Kelsey) that Barth revives this exegetical tradition in a partly post-critical form; and that the revival can be carried further and be made more rigorous by the use of ordinary language philosophical analysis, on the one hand, and of techniques of literary analysis developed by such critics as Erich Auerbach and René Wellek, on the other. I myself have elsewhere argued for the feasibility of such an approach in terms of contemporary philosophy of science ("Theologische Methode und Wissenschaftstheorie," *Theologische Revue* 74 [1978]: 266-279).

It must be admitted in conclusion, however, that there is no certainty that the alternative I have just outlined can supply a basis for convergence in theological method better than the one favored by Küng and Schillebeeckx. Methods are proved only by performance, and up until now there are no major theological performances to the credit of a post-Barthian realistic narrative approach. Thus what I have presented is more a theoretical than a practical option. Küng and Schillebeeckx cannot be faulted for not adopting it. Rather they should be praised for their strenuous reminders that the common study of Scripture must be at the heart of Christian theological method and convergence, and that the historical-critical enterprise is absolutely indispensible in keeping theologians and the church honest.

CATHOLIC-ECUMENICAL THEOLOGICAL CONSENSUS?
—A REFORMED PERSPECTIVE

David Willis

Professor Küng's essay is of particular importance for the way it delineates a new theological consensus emerging among Roman Catholic theologians and for the suggestions it contains for moving ahead to a more fully ecumenical consensus. It reflects and builds upon a widely shared theological orientation, and the acceptance or rejection of the *main lines* of Küng's position appear to have far-reaching consequences for the immediate future of serious ecumenical dialogue. I want to show that his proposal is for the most part quite consistent with the main features of Reformed theology as found in representative Reformed theologians and as found in the multi-lateral confessional dialogues in which the World Alliance of Reformed Churches has participated. Then I want to show that Küng's way of moving toward a fuller ecumenical consensus and the consensus-building process of those dialogues are mutually enriching and correcting.

According to Reformed theology, the one, holy, catholic and apostolic Church is *semper reformans et reformanda* according to the Word which God effectively addresses to us by the power of the Holy Spirit. The Reformed tradition is Christocentric in its understanding of God and the human condition and in its understanding of the freedom of Christian men and women to know, praise and serve God in their worldly vocations. Reformed theology has always taken with utmost seriousness the dogmas of the first four ecumenical councils as necessary standards subordinate to Scripture and has repeatedly felt compelled to transmit and reinterpret these dogmas in subsequent confessions of the apostolic faith. Sound doctrine, indeed all wholeness, is but a response to the Triune God who graciously accommodated itself in the fulfillment of the covenanting purposes in Christ, and who continues to accommodate to our condition through the human ministry of the communion of saints. This view of God's accommodation to the people of God in successive cultures is an important emphasis in Calvin's ecclesiology.

> To make us aware . . . that an inestimable treasure is given us in earthen vessels [2 Cor. 4:7], God himself appears in our midst, and as Author of this order, would have men recognize him as present in his institution. Accordingly, after he forebade his people to devote themselves to auguries, divinations, magic arts, necromancy, and other superstitions [Deut. 18:10-11; Lev. 19:31], he added that he would give what ought to suffice for all: that they should never be destitute of prophets [Deut. 18:15]. But as he did not entrust the ancient folk to angels but raised up teachers from the earth to perform the angelic office, so also today it is his will to teach us

through human means. . . . For although God's power is not bound to outward means, he has nonetheless bound us to this ordinary means of teaching.[1]

H. Richard Niebuhr and John Calvin stand on opposite sides of the watershed of the critical-historical scholarship of the nineteenth and twentieth centuries. This view of revelation as God's accommodation, however, serves Niebuhr's affirmation of the cultural contexts in which God encounters us.[2] For Niebuhr, cultural relativity is not set over against revelation but is the material used by God to bear God's message. The community of faith is not finally determined by those changing cultural contexts, for Christ transforms culture and keeps alive the community of memory and interpretation in which confessional theology occurs.

For all their differences, both Niebuhr and Karl Barth teach that in Christ God takes on the human condition to make it serve God's own revelatory purposes, and both combat a docetic ecclesiology that would have salvation minus the humanity of the Church. There is a definite development in Barth's thought from his early emphasis on the total otherness of God to his "correction of a correction" in his giving more nuanced weight to the humanity of God.[3] This development is not through a radical departure from the original momentum of Barth's theology. The humanity of God is that assumed by the Eternal Word, and it is finally only in the incarnate Word that we fully see the co-humanity for which men and women are created as God's covenant partners. This priority of God over creation is also seen, for example, in Barth's treatment of sanctification. It is really a human subject which is awakened to conversion, but this conversion occurs only after the manner of the divine presence and action in Christ.

> . . . There can be no question of co-ordination between two comparable elements, but only of the absolute primacy of the divine over the creaturely. The creaturely is made serviceable to the divine and does actually serve it. It is used by God as His organ or instrument. Its creatureliness is not impaired, but is given by God a special function or character. Being qualified and claimed by God for co-operation, it co-operates in such a way that the whole is still an action that is specifically divine.[4]

---

[1]John Calvin, *Institutes of the Christian Religion*, ed. J. T. McNeill, trans. F. L. Battles (Philadelphia: Westminster, 1960), 4,1,5; pp. 1017-1018.

[2]H. Richard Niebuhr, *The Meaning of Revelation* (New York: Macmillian, 1962). Cf. also chapter six of his *Christ and Culture* (New York: Harpers, 1951).

[3]Karl Barth, *The Humanity of God*, trans. J. N. Thomas and T. Wieser (Atlanta: John Knox Press, 1978), 13th pr., pp. 37ff.

[4]Karl Barth, *Church Dogmatics*, IV,2, trans. G. W. Bromiley (T. & T. Clark, 1958), p. 557.

The sovereignty and inclusiveness of God's reconciling act in Jesus Christ is taken so seriously that Barth argues, in II,2 of the *Church Dogmatics*, that all men and women are elected in Christ; this is an accomplished fact, but the realization of it must be lived out in all the ambiguities of individual and corporate life. This same triumph of grace also applies, for Barth, to the way God's fidelity keeps the Church faithful in doctrine. God's fidelity in tradition, God's handing over and down, of the Word, Jesus Christ, is ultimately sovereign over the betrayal, the false tradition, of that Word which is also apparent in the Church.

This sovereignty and priority of God's grace in Christ is the primary motivation for Reformed participation in the consensus-building process involved in contemporary ecumenical dialogues. That motivation can and must also be seen as a struggle to be obedient to Christ's will that his disciples be united and that their scandalous divisions not serve as impediments to the credibility of the Gospel. But the ecumenical imperative is really a variation on the indicative of Christian freedom, otherwise the quest for greater visible unity would become another form of works-righteousness and living under the compulsion of the law. Freed by the already accomplished fact of God's reconciling work in Christ, those whom he has joined to himself are freed to become more visibly united to one another and to bear a common witness to him in the world. That is the importance of the starting point as expressed in the report of the dialogues between the World Alliance of Reformed Churches and the Vatican's Secretariat for Promoting Christian Unity: "The starting point of these discussions was the recognition that, in Jesus Christ, God has made joint cause with sinful humanity and aims at the renewal of the world. Therefore all those who are connected with the name of Jesus Christ have the joint task of bearing witness to this Gospel."[5] Carrying out this task is really the discipline of faithful response to the presently active Head of the Church who, by the Word and Spirit, will ultimately triumph in uniting all followers in a more visible unity of confession, witness and praise.

For a dozen years now, the world confessional bodies have been engaged in a series of dialogues. The results of those dialogues are in the process of being collated and evaluated in the forum, jointly sponsored by these world confessional bodies and the Faith and Order Commission of the World Council of Churches, on bi-lateral conversations. At its second meeting, this forum summed up, among other things, the results of these conversations on the question of consensus. "Consensus in the full sense may be defined as that articulation of faith which is necessary to enable the establishment of visible unity."[6] It, consensus, is more than convergence on particular doctrines and less than a

---

[5]*The Presence of Christ in Church and World* (Geneva: World Alliance of Reformed Churches, and Vatican: Secretariate for Promoting Christian Unity, 1977), p. 7.

[6]"Report from the Second Forum on Bilateral Conversations," *Bi-annual Bulletin of the Centro pro Unione*, Rome, Fall, 1979, p. 4.

confession of faith; it will come about in stages, and at each stage of the consensus-building process, a basic trust in the *intentio fidei* of the dialogue partners is a prerequisite. Where this basic trust exists, "it will be possible to accept the separated tradition of another church without the imposition of the particular formulations of faith of one's own. An example of this would be the Common Declaration between Pope Paul VI and Pope Shenouda III, in which there was a joint profession of faith on the mystery of the incarnate Word without the use of either the terms 'person' or 'nature.'"[7]

> Consensus is not to be identified with complete unanimity and uniformity of theological understanding. Such is not found within the existing unity of particular churches and should not be expected from dialogue between churches. Yet there is a tendency to require a greater doctrinal precision of another church than exists within one's own church. . . . There is a legitimate necessity for unity in fundamental faith; there is also an equally necessary freedom in the diversity of its spiritual, liturgical and theological expression.[8]

The decisive stage in the consensus process is acceptance by the churches concerned, but

> throughout the dialogue continuing interaction with the churches is essential. This will stimulate the consensus process, both among those directly involved and in the churches themselves. Interaction will be a protection against the introduction of mere transient theological novelty, for the churches will scrutinize the emerging consensus for its continuity with the apostolic tradition. Reciprocally, the insights of the dialogues will purify and deepen the churches' own understanding of the tradition.[9]

Reformed theologians, not just privately but as representative of the World Alliance of Reformed Churches, have had a part both in the years of confessional dialogues and in the present forums on the bi-lateral conversations. On consensus, as on any other of the topics taken up, what emerges is obviously not just a Reformed—any more than it would be just a Roman Catholic, Lutheran, Anglican, Eastern Orthodox or Methodist, etc.—view. That is precisely part of the point of these dialogues, that through them a fuller understanding of a particular doctrine or practice will emerge than that which already existed in a completed form in any of the traditions, and yet one which will be consistent with, and will be an often corrected amplification of, a tradition's understanding of the matter upon entering into the dialogue. After all, the aim of these dialogues is not just church unification or (to use a more pejorative term) church merger. The visible unity of the churches will come only as a part of a much

---

[7]Ibid., p. 5.
[8]Ibid.
[9]Ibid.

larger reality, and this applies to the meaning of consensus as well: "The attempt to formulate consensus aims at enabling the churches to confess together the apostolic faith. This necessarily involves the continuous restatement of the apostolic faith in ways appropriate to changing historical and cultural situations, which themselves impose upon the Church such an obligation."[10]

Küng's lead essay touches directly on the phenomenon to which the bi-lateral forum's report also refers, namely, "Consensus is not to be identified with complete unanimity and conformity of theological understanding. Such is not found within the existing unity of particular churches and should not be expected from dialogue between churches." The focus of the report, however, is on that kind of consensus which can help *establish* greater visible unity among the churches in dialogue; whereas Küng's focus, in *this* essay,[11] is on that kind of consensus which can help *maintain*, as it were, the already established unity which exists in his own church. The crisis, as he sees it, is that the "artificial yet nonetheless actual consensus" of "Vatican Denzinger theology" has been undermined and that a new consensus has not been provided either by "defensive positivist Vatican theology," or by the new patristic theology, or by speculative mediating theology. He argues that the new consensus which is needed entails "a theology of Christian origins and center enunciated within the horizon of the contemporary world." He finds that he and Schillebeeckx are in essential agreement on the basic outlines of this effort, and he is convinced that this bi-polar theology is important for the quest for a fuller ecumenical consensus. The main agreement which Küng sees between himself and Schillibeeckx, the one of which the other agreements are subdivisions, is hermeneutical. Contemporary scientific theology must work with a hermeneutic of two sources or two poles. The two "sources" for Schillebeeckx are "the traditional experience of the great Judeo-Christian movement . . . and the contemporary human experiences of Christians and non-Christians." The two "poles" for Küng are "God's revelational address in the history of Israel and the history of Jesus" and "our own human empirical world."

I am not going to evaluate here the accuracy of Küng's piling his and Schillebeeckx's theologies in the same basket with certain things dangling out over the edges; nor surely am I interested in seeing anyone drive a wedge between their two methods. But I am interested in noting that from a Reformed perspective, discernible both in representative Reformed theologians and in the consensus-building process of confessional dialogues in which the Reformed are participating, Küng's description of the two poles is more helpful than Schillebeeckx's description of the two sources. His first pole is more specific than Schillebeeckx's first source, and, above all, he makes clearer than does Schille-

---

[10]Ibid., p. 6.

[11]For a recent example of his work on the larger issue, see his editing with Jürgen Moltmann of the issue of *Concilium* entitled *An Ecumenical Confession of Faith?* (New York: Seabury, 1979).

beeckx the relative importance of the second pole or source in relation to the first pole or source. When Küng designates the first pole as "standard" and the second as "horizon," he rightly underlines the fact for Christian theology these do not have *equal* weight. The horizon of human experience is *never separable* from God's revelational address (whether in the history of Israel and of Jesus, or in contemporary experience); but the horizon of human experience is never *equal* to or with the revelational address (whether in the history of Israel and of Jesus, or in contemporary experience). In both contexts, the saving priority and initiative remain God's. This inseparable-but-unequal polarity of the subject matter of theology is apparent in both main sections of Küng's essay.

In the first section he agrees with Schillebeeckx that

> For the Christian faith, Jesus is the definitive revelation of God in the history of Israel because he was so experienced by his first disciples (subjectively) and he was such for them (objectively). . . . Certainly the faith of Jesus' disciples does not constitute God's revelation, salvation and grace. However, without their experience of faith they could proclaim nothing about Jesus as God's revelation, salvation and grace. . . . Thus we have the image of revelation coming "from above," from God but continually experienced, interpreted, verified and then made the object of theological reflection "from below" by humanity.

What Küng calls "the living Jesus of history," who is "the source, standard and criterion of Christian faith" is not available to us apart from the interpretive community which proclaimed Jesus the Christ. By studying the structure and content of primitive Christian belief, critical-historical scholarship is an indispensable discipline, for both Küng and Schillebeeckx, in clarifying for us the identity of Jesus.

In the main section, Küng points out that both theologians take "our daily, common human experiences in all their ambiguity" as a given fact with which contemporary scientific theology must work. In establishing a critical correlation between traditional Christian experience and contemporary experience, theology employs the word " 'God' in a meaningful sense when it is experienced as a liberating response to the genuine problems of life." Vast numbers of modern men and women do not experience or interpret these problems in religious categories at all; many are unconscious of the religious dimension implied in the non-religious search for meaning and for workable solutions to these problems, and many are adherents of non-Christian religions. All these are part of the horizon of the modern world with which theology must work. For Küng, however, "our contemporary world of experience must be reflected in theology but not necessarily in the form of a comprehensive economic, political, sociological or philosophic analysis, but rather as a recurrent theme touching upon our contemporary experience and sense of life and current concern."

To the extent that Küng holds together and interrelates God's standard revelatory address and the horizon of human experience as inseparable but unequal poles or sources for contemporary theology, his procedure and that of the inter-confessional dialogues are reciprocally enriching and correcting. I think it is fair to say that the historical-critical scholarship done by individual participants in the intensive dialogues over the years is not always sufficiently apparent in the final reports on these dialogues. The reports are, moreover, usually couched in terms which are meant for discussion by the respective ecclesiastical authorities who must act on them if the consensus-building process is to serve the cause of greater visible unity. Küng's essay is an important reminder that the dialogue reports ought also both to reflect more overtly the fruits of critical scholarship and to be expressed in language which takes more overt cognizance of what he calls the horizon of contemporary human experience.

In the other direction, the dialogue process is important to Küng's proposals in two ways. First, these dialogues are at present one of the most important media by which individual theological perspectives are examined, balanced and given a hearing at official levels of the respective churches. Some of the creative angularity of the individual participants is often submerged in the larger process and final reports, but this is to be expected and is actually a positive thing if their individual contributions are to get into a form which is convincing to those who must act upon them officially. Second, most of these dialogues have quite consciously been informed by and reflect a critical yet positive reappropriation of patristic sources and, above all, the trinitarian and christological dogmas of the first four ecumenical councils. Küng does indeed allude to the patristic *resourcement* carried out by people like Danielou, DeLubac and Von Balthasar; and he rightly calls for an historical-critical hermeneutic of those sources to match that of the Scriptures if we are to understand their original meaning and contemporary relevance. But he appears to take these sources far more seriously in his earlier work (I think of the appendix to his *Justification*) than in his later work (I think of his Christology in *On Being a Christian*). In this essay, at any rate, he is so aware of the uncritical, positivist abuses which are often made of these ancient dogmas that he seems to minimize their constructive role in the advances made in Vatican II, their function in re-confessing the apostolic faith in a liberating way such as we find them used in Gutierrez's *Theology of Liberation*, and their belonging to any future consensus which is more fully ecumenical.

Those who are engaged in serious ecumenical dialogue must view with anxiety the recent actions of the Vatican's Congregation on the Faith toward Schillebeeckx and Küng. At the time of this writing, it is not clear exactly for what Küng was not only censured but directed to give up his teaching office. I know that, in one sense, those of us who are not Roman Catholics should respect the internal affairs, as it were, of Roman Catholics; and I am aware that Professor-Father Küng has gotten the bone of infallibility in his jaws and refuses to let it go, just at a time when otherwise the exact meaning of infallibility might be left in flux in an extremely difficult period of transition for the post-Vatican II Church. Nevertheless, internal affairs do have an effect on foreign affairs. Or, to be more accurate, all Christians today must be concerned about the order and vitality of all the churches to which we are tied by a mutual bond of love; the internal-foreign affairs analogy is not finally applicable in the ecumenical movement, for the health of one member of the body of Christ is, literally, of vital importance to every other member. That is why some distinction needs to be made clearer in the Curia's action on Küng. Was it taken because of his recalcitrance to be obedient as the Curia defined obedience, because of his particular teaching about infallibility, or—and here is the most serious question—because a decision was made to throw a blanket over his teaching as a whole? I simply cannot bring myself to believe that a global censure of Küng's teaching was intended, for, by far, the main features of Küng's doctrine are not that extraordinary, and surely those main features do not constitute a minority report or a private opinion. They are widely shared by theologians who have a zealous love for the Church, who understand their critical scholarship as a Christian vocation, and who recognize in Küng a Roman Catholic voice which those engaged in ecumenical dialogue cannot afford to ignore.

HISTORICAL THINKING AND DOGMATICS

Paul M. van Buren

If Hans Küng's essay signals a developing consensus in Roman Catholic theology, it can be greeted by theologians of more or less reformed branches of the Catholic Church, albeit with some reservations. If our Roman colleagues want to take the Bible seriously enough to attend with care to the work of biblical exegetes, we welcome them to the common task. And if they now see that every theologian and exegete, because he or she lives at a particular time in history, has no alternative but to speak the language and think in his or her own time, then that too seems a wise concession to what many of us have long since seen to be unavoidable. I know of no Archimedean point from which to judge whether 1980 is a better time in which to do theology than 1280 or 1580, but if theology is to be done at all today, I see no alternative to doing it as a human activity of our own time. On both counts, then, Küng's proposed consensus for Roman theology can be welcomed.

Küng proposes parenthetically, however, a consensus for ecumenical theology and at this point I have doubts. More than doubts they cannot be, for at each crucial point Küng writes with such vagueness as to leave his meaning ambiguous. The issues therefore remain unclear and it is not possible to tell from his essay whether there is an ecumenical consensus on the matters at hand. The issues in doubt all center in what it is to think historically. I see no grounds for speaking of a consensus until we can agree on clearer answers than Küng has given to the following four questions which his essay raises:

1. What is *"historical*-critical research?"
2. If there is no such thing as uninterpreted experience or uninterpreted history, what sense has the distinction "from above"/ "from below"?
3. What is meant by "the history of Israel"?
4. Is the difference between our modern "world of experience" and that of the New Testament authors itself historical?

I shall discuss briefly these four interrelated questions.

1.

Küng thinks that historical study can enable us to follow "the mental journey" (whatever that may be) of the first disciples from the baptism of Jesus to his death and even derive from this a comprehension of their confession of Jesus, after his death, as the living Christ. I should have thought that biblical scholars had warned us, by their newer methods of redaction criticism, not to

94

speak of their recent efforts to apply sociological methods of analysis to the texts, against any such project as attempting to trace the "mental journey" of Jesus' Galilean disciples. There was a time in the last century when, with a sense of history and historical research hardly possible to sustain today, attempts were made to discover a "Jesus of history" or even "a historical personality" of Jesus. Küng seems to think—I can't be sure—that this nineteenth-century project is still viable, that some way has been found to carry out this enterprise which does not make the "history" in question that of the exegete. The Jesus of history which the nineteenth century discovered was, as we can now see, a Jesus of their own nineteenth century. I have a shade more trust in more recent discoveries of a first-century Palestinian Jew of a more or less Pharisaic tendency, but we are still learning so much these days about Judaism in the first century of the Common Era that I hardly want to base my faith on such tentative hypotheses. Biblical scholars have taught me to be cautious about their tentative conclusions. Since Küng never mentions redaction criticism and speaks only of "historical-critical research," I have no idea whether he is proposing a position about which there can be an ecumenical consensus.

2.

The second and more puzzling question is raised by the way in which Küng speaks of the relationship between revelation and interpretation. At several points he quotes Edward Schillebeeckx in words which point to what might indeed become an ecumenical consensus. In each case, however, he proceeds to sum up the point in a way which leaves it unclear whether he has understood his Dutch colleague. Schillebeeckx believes, as Küng quotes him, that "the interpretive experience is an essential element in the concept of revelation." I agree. Does Küng? His own summary is: "Thus we have the image of revelation coming 'from above,' from God, but continually experienced, interpreted, verified and then made the object of theological reflection from below by humanity." Does Küng think he is saying the same thing here? In the first formulation, there is no possible room for an "above" and then a "below." There is only the single reality to which we give the name revelation. That single reality is an interpreted experience, the implicit assumption being that there is no such thing as an uninterpreted experience. Revelation, like history, is just an event or situation interpreted in a certain way. Neither revelation nor history exists first of all "out there" or "from above." "From above" and "from below" are only misleading ways of describing two different experiences. On this view of the matter, a "Jesus of history" is every bit as much of an interpretation as is "Jesus the incarnate Word of God," and "Jesus as the self-revelation of God" is no more an interpretation than "Jesus the first-century Pharisaic rabbi."

It is not clear to me whether Küng could agree to this. In his summary, revelation refers to what comes "from above," or from God, to which is added the experience and the interpretation. Just how one is to conceive of this sort of revelation is not explained. It appears that that which for Schillebeeckx is essentially one and can be analyzed into its constituents is for Küng two, which then must be unified conceptually. Is there then really a consensus in Roman Catholic theology?

Again, Küng quotes Schillebeeckx as affirming that "the interpretive explication is an inner moment of the experience itself." Küng explains this by saying that "every experience is already accompanied by elements of interpretation." Once more he seems to be struggling to unify elements which Schillebeeckx never thought of as separate.

Behind this subtle difference lies an issue of utmost importance for the future of theology: whether we shall say that revelation, in order to be revelation, must always be at least a human activity, whether we can recognize that, apart from the human contribution, there is no reason to speak of revelation at all. That contribution has always in the past taken the form of a reinterpretation of Israel's tradition. Redaction and canon criticism have taught us to see this. Ever new reinterpretations of Israel's tradition built the Hebrew Scriptures, and our New Testament consists to a remarkable extent in a further reinterpretation of those reinterpretations. This says something not only about revelation but also about the God who so chooses to involve creatures in Self-revelation.

Resistance to seeing and saying this in Christian theology has its roots in our traditionally insufficient attention to the doctrine of creation, to the commitment made by God to that which was established in freedom, and to God's commitment to Israel, which we must assume to be still as valid as our conviction that God is faithful. The passages quoted above appear under a heading which defines as a standard of theology "God's Revelational Address in the History of Israel and the History of Jesus." May I call attention to the total absence in the section so entitled of any mention of the "history of Israel"? Nor do we hear one word about creation. May we conclude that neither has a constituent role in Küng's proposed consensus? This may provide a hint about the roots of his talk about revelation "from above" and its interpretation "from below." It may also throw light on how it is possible for him to search for a "Jesus of History" so totally abstracted from the continuing reality of God's Israel. Evidently he has not reflected on the fact that Second Isaiah's faith that Israel's Redeemer is Israel's Creator has remained so central in Israel's faith to our day. These are just some of the prices that must be paid if one wishes to undercut historical thinking in theology by such unhistorical categories as "from above" and "from below."

3.

Our second question has already opened up our third. Why did Küng include "the history of Israel" in his first source or standard for theology, since he obviously had nothing to say on the subject? On this matter, the Vatican and Roman bishops are still way out ahead of Roman theologians. Küng himself doesn't discuss even the history of ancient Israel, much less Israel's history over the past nineteen centuries, and of course Israel's history over the past staggering forty years goes unmentioned. He cannot mean seriously that all this is a source and standard for his own theology. He is evidently one of those remaining theologians who still think one can simply go on doing theology after Auschwitz as it was done before. He is, of course, hardly alone in this, yet he ought to see, given his proposal, that until this question is settled, there can hardly be serious discussion of a consensus in theology, Roman Catholic or otherwise. What is baffling is not that he does not take sides. The issue is extremely difficult and, as Roman and non-Roman official statements have stressed, its resolution has fundamental consequences for every aspect of our faith and theology. What is so unsettling is that he does not even seem to see the problem and so can propose a consensus for theology, touching explicitly our understanding of Christian origins, without so much as mentioning the Jewish locus of those origins and apparently unaware of the question posed for the church by the living reality of Judaism, especially after Auschwitz. How seriously, then, are we to take his call for a *historical* reading of the New Testament? Does he understand what that would involve?

I ask this question in part because Küng quotes Schillebeeckx on a related matter without comment. Speaking of our contemporary experience and expectations, Schillebeeckx is quoted as saying that these "must also undergo the scrutiny of the expectation of Israel *as* it was fulfilled in Jesus." Looking the victims of Hitler in the eye, just *how* does Küng think Israel's expectation of deliverance from oppression was fulfilled in Jesus? Will he continue the ancient de-historicizing, de-politicizing, spiritualizing of Israel's still living expectation so as to affirm its "fulfillment" in Jesus? Has Jesus' own cry of dereliction from the cross been answered satisfactorily for Küng by the church's faith? Or will he say that our traditional triumphalist interpretation of Easter "fulfillment" stands under the judgment of that cry? I do not know because he does not say, but can there be serious talk of a consensus in theology today when we have not come to one mind about this hardly secondary matter?

The lack of consensus here can hardly be overcome, as Küng implies, by calling theologians to listen to the exegetes. They too are sharply divided over this question. That should not surprise us, for the issue is precisely what it means to read a text historically. From a fuller exposition of the matter published elsewhere ("Wie sind die Apostolischen Schriften heute auszulegen?" *Freiburger Rundbrief* 30 [1978]: 83-89), I offer one answer: "First, we Gentiles Christians shall exegete the Apostolic Writings historically by seeing them as witnesses to the beginning, and only the beginning, of our God-given way through history. Second, we shall exegete them historically by seeing them as a part of the complex reality of Judaism in the first century of our Common Era. Third, and most importantly, we shall exegete them historically by learning from them to listen and respond, as their authors did, to major events in the history of the Jewish people, of which those in the first century were hardly the last."

4.

Finally, I wonder what Küng—or Schillebeeckx, whom he quotes—means when he says that the New Testament authors had "a completely different world of experience" from that which we have. The difference could not be complete, for if it were, we would not be able to understand them at all. Granting a considerable difference, however, in what does it consist? Once more, the crux of the matter is left in doubt. Is it that they employed certain "images" that were once but are no longer "meaningful"? How is this vague assertion to be tested? No doubt such expressions as "Lamb of God" and "Word of God" are not common in our "world of experience," but is it clear that they were in theirs? Did these expressions require no interpretation then? Or is the difference, with Bultmann, that the biblical authors spoke of God in terms of this world? But since we have no terms at all but our own, and so "of this world," what is the alternative? Abstract, existentialistic, or transcendentalist terms are just as much those of human conceptuality as any used by Paul or Matthew or John.

The difference between the authors of the New Testament and ourselves is considerable and important, but to define the difference by comparing our worlds of experience or our conceptualities is, I suggest, a-historical. Historically conceived, the difference between the author of Matthew, for example, and ourselves is the nineteen-hundred years that lie between us in which so many important developments have taken place. After the death and so obviously not possibly part of the "world of experience" of Matthew and the other New Testament authors, but certainly part of our past and so of our "world of experience," have occurred such events as the fact that the Evangelists' genera- tion did indeed "pass away" and still "all these things" (Mt. 24:34) did not take place and have still not taken place; that the church of Jew and Gentile of the author of Ephesians became an almost totally Gentile church that persecuted the Jews; that Judaism under rabbinic leadership underwent a renaissance that has kept the Jewish people alive to our own day; that the church's growing hostility to Jews fed a spirit of anti-Judaism which helped a baptized "Catholic" dictator to orchestrate the murder of one-third of all the Jews in the world; and much more. When we read the New Testament, we read it with all that history between us and it and so as part of our "world of experience." That is the difference between ourselves and the biblical authors conceived historically.

I see no evidence that Hans Küng sees the difference in this way. On the contrary, he appears to think in essences and universals, abstracted from the historical reality of God's creation. Thus he lists ten criteria for doing theology which define as a "determining" criterion "the Gospel, the original Christian message itself," as if a real message could ever be a message "itself" rather than *someone's* message, human words—whatever more we may trust them to be—available for us from a particular date and situation, and only available to us through our human understanding.

Küng says that a theology pursued according to his criteria "would be a Christian theology for contemporary humanity." Are we to understand that he means to include the Jews within his universal "contemporary humanity," and specifically the survivors of the Holocaust? Does he also include the Muslims? If he wants to do theology historically, should he not say "a Christian theology for contemporary Christians"? Once more, I cannot tell.

***

"Exegesis that is grounded in the historical-critical method calls for a dogmatics that is likewise historically-critically grounded." So Hans Küng. If only I could believe that he means this with full seriousness, I would say that we are in agreement on the most fundamental level. But until we come to a far more carefully defined agreement about what it is to do both exegesis and theology *historically*, it is I fear too early to talk about a new consensus in Catholic theology, whether Roman or Ecumenical.

AN ORTHODOX CONTRIBUTION TO CONSENSUS

Nikos A. Nissiotis

If consensus has not yet become clearly manifest amongst the historic confessional families it is however a reality amongst their theologians regarding, especially, theological method and the concern for theological renewal in their common task of interpreting the Gospel message to the world of today. Reading Prof. Küng's paper commenting on Schillebeeckx's two recent books leads one to agree almost entirely with his main thesis, regardless of one's own confessional adherence. This is because the concerns of both the prominent Roman Catholic theologians are equally those of all systematic theologians desiring a dynamic presence of church and theology all over the world.

The author detects the burning issues in systematic theology today in the works of Prof. Schillebeeckx and suggests to his readers methods of theological reflection which are valid in a transconfessional context. An appropriate method in systematic theology presented in this consistent way does not simply refer to the function of theology, but also to the content of the Christian message presented in a renewed spirit in order to facilitate its human experience within a world dominated by positivistic ideologies. Traditional methods and confessional differences become secondary when one grasps the issue of the relevance of theological thought in the university and society of today. The uniting factor of all Christian theological traditions in our days is to be found primarily in its "Sitz-im-Leben."

The understanding of the function of Christian dogmas as introducing an open system of thought, the appreciation of the historical-critical method in the research on the historical Jesus, the importance of human experience for a deeper reflection on Christian revelation, the necessity of a theology which takes into serious consideration as an indispensable element of theological reasoning the problem of faith of modern humanity and its doubts—all these subjects take a new priority over comparative theology and confessional dialogue. Theology in ecumenical perspective is practiced more efficiently when we all focus on our task of renewing the framework of theology beyond our scholastic formulations of confessional disagreements.

Certainly, this kind of "theological communion" will take place only if all kinds of renewed interpretations, of new methods, and even of radical approaches are deprived of liberal one-sideness and extremist positions. Hans Küng, in conjunction with Schillebeeckx's thought, offers us an example of a well-balanced presentation in the most crucial issues. He is persuasive that a consensus within an authentic catholic-ecumenical theology need not negate essential elements of doctrine, or revolt against theological links with the past, or make the world's situation or doubt in matters of faith a unique criterion for systematic theology.

That is why I find it very difficult to criticize such a paper from a particular confessional standpoint, for I am afraid that by doing this I risk falling back into my confessional ghetto, thus negating my remarks about the need for renewing theology as the primary ecumenical task today. Consequently, my response consists first in raising some further questions in the same direction and, second, in trying to contribute some complementary ideas from my own theological tradition. I dare to believe that in these cases Hans Küng would perhaps remark that most of my observations are implicit in his paper.

I

The first area proposed by Küng as crucial for theological method is the fundamental issue of the relationship between divine revelation and human experience. I understand the latter as something deeper and broader than a simple answer of faith. It comprises both recognition-knowledge as well as will and feeling. In the paper we are given two kinds of experiences: the first is the one of a theologian who has passed through a conscious decision of faith in the objective reality of divine revelation in Christ, and the second is the one expounded in the later part of the paper, referring to "daily experiences" in the world, i.e., social problems which betray a religious dimension of human existence.

With the first kind of experience both Schillebeeckx and Küng remind us of the reciprocity and mutual interpenetration of revelation which does not originate in subjective human experience and reflection but can only be perceived in and through human experiences. This justified effort underlines the importance of the subjective appropriation of the objective reality of divine revelation. They affirm both on equal footing, though they reserve an essential priority to the latter as originating from God. The "givenness" of the revelation is encountered by the subjective human reality (recognition-reception and reflection) without which there is no transcendental event to deal with.

While fundamentally in agreement with this position, I am tempted to raise the question whether we are not given here a framework of reference which overemphasizes the subjective human role in the matter of the whole concept of revelation. My concern is that divine revelation is directly connected with the individual human experience. Küng states that "divine revelation and human experience are not simply antithetical. Rather divine revelation is only accessible through human experience."

How are we to understand this "human experience"? Experience is also a way of perception or knowledge of objective reality. The subject perceives the object in order to assimilate it by using cognitive categories based on the law of immanence and logical proof with universal approval which renders this cognitive operation valid. But is this kind of experience possible with reference to divine revelation? Is it not a risky operation if we understand it as the gaining of the human knowledge of an object through its total possession by the knowing subject in order to use or exploit it according to human will and purpose? I hope that Küng would agree that in theology we have this experience only by *sharing* in the objective reality in our particular case, i.e., revelation, which cannot be entirely objectivized like all other objects, because an act of God in history can never become a mere object of human intellect.

If I may be permitted an appraisal of human experience of divine revelation according to Eastern Orthodox tradition, laying an emphasis on *Logos* theology, which is a participatory theology, i.e., a thinking of how one shares in the incarnate Word of God, then I would have to observe that the relationship between revelation and human experience first cannot be a direct one, and second, cannot be only or even primarily a process of individual subjective cognitive operation, but rather a process of life comprising all of the areas of consciousness, knowledge, will, and feeling.

What I miss in this context—I hope that it is there implicitly—is any mention of the community of faith, i.e., the fact of co-experiencing divine revelation. In other words, I miss the ecclesial character of the experience, which is of its essence as an "objective reality" *sui generis*. Christ is never directly related to my experience and my experience is never purely subjective. It is rather an inter-subjective reality which makes my relationships with Christ a communal event, in a double sense, i.e., a sharing with others the same experience and a communicating personally (and not individually) with Christ.

What I explicitly miss in this understanding of experience is a clear, most necessary reference for Christian theology, to the operation of the Holy Spirit. Without this operation there is no human experience of divine revelation. It is the Spirit which renders the objective an intrasubjective reality, making it possible for it to share in the divine revelation. The pentecostal event, i.e., the foundation of the church, is the *conditio sine qua non* of a human experience of divine revelation.

It might look as if I were introducing here an impossible category of thought in theological method, perhaps reminding Western theologians of mystical trends. On the contrary, I find that this pneumatological and therefore ecclesial character of human experience excludes any kind of "antithetical" relationships between revelation and human experience and that it keeps theology watchful and alerted against the threats of an individualistic rational and intellectual one-sidedness.

II

With reference to the other kind of experiences, the daily or worldly ones which betray religious trends, and the very correct appeal of Küng to all theologies to take them seriously, as well as the doubts of others about the person of Christ, in order to investigate more deeply the main issue of theology in modern times, I have nothing to object. But again this operation of theological method is not possible unless through an ecclesial pneumatology one professes the cosmic Christ in world history as a basic presupposition for modern theology. *Logos* theology as an ecclesial (participatory) one has a cosmic dimension and the church is regarded as a *pars pro toto*. It is not again because we, as individual theologians, find in contemporary doubts and unbelief hidden or subconscious religious experiences and decide to use them methodologically for adapting our theological thought to modern reality. We are not attempting an "Anpassungstheologie" by theological reflection adapted to modern needs. Rather, we detect the world-universal-catholic dimension of Christ's event as operating for the whole of humankind, intentionally and potentially saved, by virtue of the incarnation, cross, and resurrection.

In the same spirit I would like to offer some reflections on the main issue of Küng's paper, namely, to take seriously historical-critical research and to concentrate on the life of the historical Jesus "as the living Jesus of history, the source, standard and criterion of Christian faith." I again whole-heartedly join this appeal and I am in agreement that there can be no hope for a renewed theology without this honest reference to Jesus of history. But at the same time I would raise a question about the motive and purpose of this reference. If it is made for the sake of rendering Christology more rationally accessible to modern positivist thinking I would express uneasiness, but if it is suggested for the sake of taking historical reality more seriously, including worldly religious experiences, then I will fully follow the suggestion.

Küng gives this suggestion a central importance in his paper. Therefore, I would like to comment further on this point, for it looks as if this issue has created a definite and unbridgable gap—unduly—between biblical and systematic theologians. Without underestimating the paramount value of research on the historical Jesus, I want to comment on his phrase, "can a serious systematic theology that seeks to deal responsibly with Christian origins ground itself in anything other than the biblical findings attained through historical-critical exegesis?" Certainly I agree, provided that we remind ourselves of the ecclesial character of faith and the necessity of approaching Christology only through pneumatology, which is totally absent from the paper.

As with the case of "human experience," the historical Jesus is not accessible directly by theology. The man Jesus of history, deprived of any hallow and glory of traditional Christology, is communicated to us not simply and directly through the scriptural evidences given by the text. This would be either a biblicist's or an historicist's point of view and I am sure that Küng does not share either. The "Jesus of history" has been revealed in the Spirit and within the Ecclesia as the Christ of God. That is why a possible clash between the historical Jesus, as he is investigated by critical biblical research, and the Christ of God, as he is experienced by the ecclesial faith and communal consciousness, is unthinkable for a theology of participation over against a rational theology.

Of course, "the recognition of Jesus as the Christ always remains a venture of faith and trust of metanoia," as Küng appropriately writes. But this is so because the individual faith in Jesus as the Christ of God is rationally entirely impossible. The seeking of a way to him by a single pilgrim with reason alone is a vain venture, indeed. It is not the concept of the historical Jesus which will help us out in modern positivist times. It is the nature of such a recognition which excludes a direct identification between the historical Jesus and the Christ in human reflection which respects human categories of rational thought. The Jesus of history can be perceived, received, and shared as the Christ of God only as a communal, participatory, and therefore ecclesial event. Alone and directly no one comes to authentic Christology. Faith in Christ is personal, i.e., relational and not individualistic-subjective. This is so not because of the narrow limitations of human reason, but because of the nature of the divine revelation and of the person of Christ who is the Jesus of history, who as the Word of God has assumed human nature, being at the same time the concrete historical person Jesus from Nazareth. Both things are identical, because the one cannot be perceived without the other and the one conditions the other.

One risks falling into a schizophrenic situation by affirming the one and neglecting the other. Christology is not, therefore, something detached from the reality of the historical Jesus, added *a posteriori* as a church faith and therefore of another nature of transcendental knowledge due to human interpretation. Christology has to be, right from the beginning, possible only as an ecclesial event which leads to church confession. In the creed we confess equally faith in God, in Christ as the only begotten Son, in the Holy Spirit, and finally we confess to believe the church. Without believing the church (*credo . . . ecclesiam*), no confession of faith in the divine revelation is possible. Faith in the historical person of Jesus as the Christ of God is ecclesial by nature.

Are these remarks outside of the circle of the problems that Küng is raising? Are the hermeneutical question and biblical exegesis in relationship with the person of "Jesus of history" a problem *a se*? Perhaps with my criticism of the lack of pneumatology in Küng's paper I abandon the area of his immediate hermeneutical and exegetical concerns. I dare to think, however, that regarding biblical Christology one should not neglect the reference to the operation of the Spirit precisely on the basis of the whole of the Bible, i.e., the Synoptics, John's gospel, and Paul's epistles. The Synoptics attribute the proof of the messianic role of Jesus to the operation of the Spirit chrismating Jesus for his mission (Lk. 4:18).

In the gospel of St. John we read that it is expedient that Jesus departs from this "historical life" so that the era of the Holy Spirit can begin, because it is the Spirit of Truth as the Paraclete who will guide the disciples into all truth and remind them of all that Jesus has commanded them (Jn. 16:13-16). St. Paul, finally, gives us the most important reference dealing with New Testament Christology by clearly stating, "that no one can say that Jesus is the Lord but by the Holy Ghost" (1 Cor. 12:3). I will not give other specific references concerning biblical pneumatology, for I want to point only to texts pertaining to

Christology—in which case, of course, one should mention these texts referring to the biblical witness that it is the Spirit which incarnates Jesus as the Christ of God (Lk. 1:35) and that it is the Spirit which raises him from the dead (Rom. 8:11).

Are we not, therefore, obliged, when we deal with the exegetical problem of the "Jesus of history," to include in our problematic biblical pneumatology as well? Christian theology is a difficult discipline of knowledge because the operation of the Spirit, which "blows where it listeth . . . but canst not tell whence it cometh and whither it goeth" (Jn. 3:8), cannot be easily grasped and expounded. Theology in its deepest, most difficult function is a commentary on this operation of the Spirit recorded in the Bible. Consequently, a dry scientific approach to the biblical text for detecting the "historical Jesus" is not easily possible, does not do justice to the whole of the *authentic* biblical text, and does not suffice to give us the full image of Jesus as a person and his messianic nature and mission. But it is thanks to this operation of the Spirit that theology and all of its particular branches, including biblical hermeneutics and exegesis, cannot become a closed scientific system like some other historical or positivist sciences sometimes risk becoming.

III

With this remark we enter into the third area of problems raised by Küng's paper. They are problems related to the renewal of Christian theology. One cannot but rejoice at all of the suggestions made by the author and also his "ten guiding principles for contemporary theology," as well as the three requirements for theology so that "it would be a Christian theology for contemporary humanity," i.e., first, the analysis of the contemporary empirical world; second, the investigation of the constant elements of the fundamental Christian experience in the New Testament and later tradition; and third, the critical relating of "both sources," thus expressing his full agreement with Schillebeeckx's main thesis. Again Küng shows us the way toward a consensus in trying to adjust theological method to the demands of our times. In the same direction I would like to suggest one more problem which is not directly raised and some complementary thoughts to his "decalogue."

The main issue, perhaps, in this area is the fact that, due to the nature of theological knowledge related to the personal revelation of God in history, our theology has to be mainly of a *deductive* nature. The "Logos became flesh" proposition is a basic and total statement which obliges us to a global and "holistic" vision of reality. I gather that Küng expresses this same fundamental notion by saying that Christian "tradition can be normative . . . but only on a derivative manner, i.e., as a norm that is itself validated by the Gospel (*norma normata*)."

The validation of theological reflection by the Gospel does not save theology from its deductive nature and modern biblical exegesis even in its most radical form cannot overcome this difficulty. The character of Christian theological reasoning has to be "derivative" anyway. The main issue, therefore, should be the delicate question of how theology can also adopt an *inductive* method which is not immediately possible by its origin grounded in the event of revelation as recorded in the Bible. Certainly, this task is rightly envisaged by Küng and Schillebeeckx by the above-stated three "requirements of critical correlation."

The major issue for theology, however, remains: To what extent can it really become inductive and contextual, giving priority to the world's situation by its involvement in the struggle for a free, just, and participatory society? The notion of the "historical Jesus" and the revelation of the dynamic person of Christ as identified with the poor and with those fighting for liberation has helped contemporary theology to renew its method and its concerns, and to define more fully its task in the modern world. Scientific and school theology is seriously challenged in this respect. Contextual theology has to become the counterpart of the deductive, derivative method of theological discipline, but in all cases it should not replace the unique criterion, which is the Gospel, and the basic priority given by the event of God's personal revelation in history.

This is the most difficult task of theology today, and Küng is making a significant contribution by facing this problem. He is sufficiently radical in not allowing himself to become a unilaterally deductive theologian, and he is sufficiently deductive in his approach in not allowing himself to become a unilaterally inductive secular revolutionary. His phrase, "that path lies in the middle between ecclesiastical opportunism and secular separatism," shows clearly his fully justified and well-balanced concern for contemporary theology.

In the light of Küng's remarks, I feel called upon to reflect on my own tradition's theological education in order to correct some trends in it. I will presume to repeat here some remarks I made in a paper regarding "Orthodox Theological Education," published in the "Annals of the Theological Faculty of the University of Athens of 1978." I referred there to the following dangers threatening our theology: first, a one-sided sacral overtone; second, a super-developed academism; third, an historicism and dogmatism; fourth, a conservatism which reflects a hesitation to change; and fifth, an esotericism by using ideas and language cut off from our milieu. It seems to me that such a self-criticism is necessary for some theologies today if we are honestly to seek together to renew our theological thinking and methods so that theology in a progressive way can converge more and more toward the fulfillment of its threefold task, which can be described as follows: *quality*, that is to say, intense and genuine scholarship and study; *authenticity*, that is to say, theology combining ancient wisdom with an open attitude toward new streams of thought and new patterns of action in today's world; and *creativity*, that is to say, reasoning with a view toward renewed action by the church in the field of the struggles for justice and liberation and an appropriate witness by a faithful *diaconia* of the Gospel in church and society.

Now, I would like to return to the "ten guiding principles for contemporary theology" proposed by Küng. I am sure that no one can disagree with the concerns expressed clearly by them, that theology should not defend narrow confessionalism, ecclesiastical systems, and polemic attitudes against contemporary ideologies, but become a really interdisciplinary, uniting, credible theory with livable practice, ready for a critical dialogue which leads neither to a hostile confrontation nor to an indifferent coexistence with contemporary trends.

I would like, however, to question his expression: "the Gospel should not be proclaimed in biblical archaisms nor in *hellenistic scholastic dogmatisms*" (principle No. 8). I understand what he wants to reject in school theology and I agree, but the expression "hellenistic scholastic dogmatism" is a contradiction in terms for me. It is the misuse and abuse of the hellenic philosophical and cultural inheritance by the medieval scholastics and the modern confessionalists which has given us this neo-orthodox dogmatism. I hope that Küng uses this term in this sense, for I am a bit hesitant to adopt the attitude that "hellenistic" is to be regarded as a negative educative element together with "scholastic" and in identity with "dogmatism."

It is difficult to know what Küng wants to signify by the term "hellenistic" here. Those who have studied classic philosophers are aware of the careful use that the early church Fathers have made of them, when this use proved to be necessary to give a deeper and reflective expression of the biblical message—which also presupposes this hellenistic background in its terminology. The usual opposition between Jewish and hellenistic elements in the Bible set up by some exegetes is to a certain extent a too easy generalization, which does not do full justice to the positive contribution of this culture to Christian theology as a whole. The use of Aristotle, especially, in Western theology in the past and in neo-orthodoxy in the East should not be regarded as the only and definitive one that theology can make of this philosophy, which is far more flexible, free, dynamic, and creative than Christian scholastic dogmatism succeeded in making of it by using it for apologetic and confessionalistic purposes.

I am conscious that I refer to a well-known, old, and complicated subject and I know the dangers of mixing up Greek and Christian elements in theology without a critical and delicate discrimination between the two, but I nevertheless wish to question the term "hellenistic scholastic dogmatism" as it has been used by Küng in his paper. Perhaps he has other things in mind in formulating this problem in this way. It remains, however, an important issue for Christian theology today because it concerns its own presuppositions and its genuine indigenization in new cultural environments.

Let me now return to the main theme of the renewal of theological method. What I miss in the "decalogue" of Küng is a whole dimension which I think is not only proper and characteristic to the Eastern Orthodox theological tradition, but is equally biblical and Western. Certainly, *Logos* theology has emphasized not only participation and communion but also the Resurrection connected always with the Cross of Jesus, while in Western theology the problem of redemption has dominated theological work and led to the very profound theology of grace. However, it is a fundamental characteristic for both of them that theology in its highest and most authentic appearance is praise to God and a reasonable thanksgiving. Perhaps this trend is more evident in the East because of the closer connection of theology with the ancient liturgies which center around the event of Resurrection, but I would also wish to claim that it is not entirely absent from Western theological thought either.

Küng, because he is so exclusively—and rightly—preoccupied with the renewal of theological thinking and method, has neglected to include in his "decalogue" the doxological dimension of theology and therefore also its eschatological nature, which for me, however, has great importance precisely for theological renewal today. *Theologia crucis*—another one-sidedness of some contemporary radical historical-critical biblical scholars—cannot become the only Christian theology, dictating a narrow "scientific" theological method. *Theologia gloriae*, on the other hand, should not be understood as opposed to it, but rather both of them together should be seen as comprising the same theology of the whole biblical message, and thus should inspire a more "catholic" approach to the Gospel. When we speak of a doxological dimension in theology we do not mean any kind of triumphalistic theology or visionary speculation. We simply mean theology as a commentary on the kerygma of Jesus as crucified and risen, the Jesus-Victor, i.e., the crucified Jesus who as the Risen Lord will come back in full glory at the end of time.

Without the *doxa* of the Lordship of Christ in the world there is no right eschatological hope, i.e., just as the historical reality here and now, so also theology would be empty and crippled. We should not forget that the root of the word *doxa* is the same as the verb *doko*, i.e., "I think." Dogma, therefore, also has a doxological dimension in Christian theology; it is an act of praise and reasonable thanksgiving to God. Without this element theology risks becoming inflexible, confessionalistic, lacking grace, and neglecting its charismatic nature. The modern world expects from theology not only redemptive reflection on the misery and suffering of humanity, but also a sober celebration, praise, and doxology at a period of world history when technocracy has dried out our thoughts and made life a machine-like operation. Amidst the suffering and on the basis of the sacrifice of Jesus modern humanity wants to know how to celebrate in God's creation. If Christian theology will not respond to this request, which other discipline of knowledge can?

In concluding, I have to express once more my thanks to the author of the initial paper. It is always very refreshing to read Küng because he honestly struggles for a theological renewal, without which an authentic ecumenical movement cannot exist, and the necessary changes in the life of the church communities in the modern world will not come about. I trust that my criticism of some of his expressions and my suggesting some complementary points concerning method in Christian theology and its presuppositions have not distracted from his excellent and challenging attitude concerning the essential and crucial issues that he rightly raises for us all regardless of our particular theological traditions.

SIX JEWISH THOUGHTS

Jacob B. Agus

1) I find myself thoroughly in agreement with Hans Küng's way of developing ecumenical theology. We have to render our specific historical tradition transparent to the comprehension of those raised in other traditions, especially within the Judeo-Christian family. In the case of Judaism, dogmas are not ranked as highly as in the Christian tradition. The law, *halachah*, created the consensus needed for the maintenance of the community. The awareness of *not knowing* the nature of God and God's will was intimately associated with the assurance that Torah, both the written and the oral, contained God's revealed Word. Philo claimed that God is "unknowable." The Talmud envisaged God saying, as it were, "I wish they had neglected Me, but kept my Torah." Nevertheless, some basic dogmas were implicit in the observance of the Law. Therefore, modern Jewish theology needs to grapple with problems that are essentially similar to those described by Küng. *Orthopraxis* cannot be completely separated from *orthodoxy*.

2) The interpretation of dogmas "as official aids, guides and warning signs" corresponds to the Maimonidean position in Jewish theology. He distinguishes between ideas that are true in themselves and those that are "necessary" for the maintenance of communal unity and stability. The latter may be characterized as dogmas; they are justified experientially and pragmatically, not logically (Guide of the Perplexed II, 28).

3) Modern Jewish theologians deal with "two sources" of religious guidance, namely, the traditional experience of the Jewish heritage and the contemporary human experience of Jews and non-Jews. The awareness of this duality characterized the interpretive labors of Philo. Looking at origins in the distant past, the Palestinian Sages speak of the revelation of Noachide principles; looking forward to the eschaton, they speculated about the "New Torah" that the Messiah will reveal to all humanity. Paul wrote as a disciple of Gamaliel when he maintained that God and God's will should be clear to all human beings (Romans 1:20).

Küng speaks of "the contemporary human experiences of Christians and non-Christians." As Jews, we recall God's precept to Abraham, "that all the families of the earth may be blessed through you" (Genesis 12:3). We are so constituted that our most distinctive experiences are, when transposed in other cultural contexts, most significant to others. The unique and the universal form a polarity, which is inwardly one.

4) The interpretation of revelation as "the human word engendered in an interpreted context from the experience of the Word of God" is a view that I share. The Sages of the Midrash state this truth indirectly when they assert that God employed "the voice of his father," when speaking to Moses. The divine is

mediated to us through our education and upbringing. It is through the critical recognition of the human element in the divine-human encounter that the intent of the divine can be discerned.

5) The return to history which Küng advocates is in keeping with the prevailing trend in Jewish thought. In a sense, this insistence on historical authenticity reflects the intention to root theology within the actual course of events. Since we are all the passive products of history as well as its co-creators, to an infinitesimal degree, the message of an earlier generation caught in a similar paradoxical situation is altogether relevant. The "historical-critical" method does more than "protect the community from faulty interpretation." It is first of all a reaffirmation of loyalty to objective truth even in the most subjective of all domains of spiritual life. It is also a reminder of the limits of human knowledge. The human condition is as little served by absolutism as by its polar opposite, radical relativism. We do possess a core of truth, but its exact application in all instances eludes us.

As a Jewish theologian, I applaud the return to history as an attempt to confront the realities of Jewish life in the first century. While some Protestant Bible critics in the nineteenth century managed to inject a heavy dose of antisemitic venom in their ponderous studies of "Jesus of history"—we recall the taint of the Aryan myth in the work of even so luminous a scholar as Ernst Renan—the progress of research is on the whole self-correcting. The common pursuit of historical truth is the best antidote against the myths of communal narcissism.

6) We have learned from recent philosophers as well as from bitter historical experience that certain words denote several layers of meaning. We must judge beliefs by their consequences, not alone by their inner truth. I agree with Küng's assertion, "Indeed, we can only employ the word 'God' in a meaningful sense when it represents a liberating response to the genuine problems of life."

This statement is congenial to Jewish thought. The first of the Ten Commandments identifies God as the source of national freedom. Philo regarded personal freedom as "the image of God" in humanity. The Sages in *Avot* assert that the Law makes possible true freedom. But freedom connotes a positive assertion as well as the rejection of a foreign yoke.

It implies the inner capacity to discern worth and to assign values. In both dimensions, the range of freedom in human life is necessarily limited. The history of humanity can be written as a record of failures in the quest of the fullness of freedom. "Seven times the righteous fall, but they rise again." It is the task of theologians to gather the "sparks of holiness" under the ashes of all these historic and contemporary failures, and to generate faith in the holiness of the quest itself.

A MUSLIM REFLECTION ON RELIGION AND THEOLOGY

Seyyed Hossein Nasr

The observations and commentaries on Hans Küng's lead essay in this volume made here below come not from the point of view of a particular school of Islamic theology, but from that of the Islamic tradition itself, and in fact of tradition as such. To have lived and experienced any religion fully is in a sense to have experienced all religions. To have meditated on the basic intellectual problems concerning a particular religious community is to have confronted these problems as they face people of religion everywhere. The unity of the human race and the universality of the intellect as it functions in human beings are such as to permit the followers of one religion to think about and comment on the theological perspectives of another religion, especially in a world such as ours where traditional barriers between various civilizations have been lifted.

Yet, precisely because it is religion which actualizes the potentialities of those who follow it and provides an objective cause for the functioning of that inner revelation within humanity, which is the intellect—in its original rather than debased meaning—particular problems of each religion remain its own. In commenting upon Küng's theses, I am therefore fully aware that I have no right to deal with the specific religious and dogmatic problems of Catholicism and might be accused of being simply an intruding outsider were I to deal with specific issues of the Catholic faith and practice in a purely Catholic context. Still, it is amazing how religious issues in one religion are also confronted by other religions and how the weakening or floundering of a particular religious universe can affect others. It is with full awareness of these factors and in humility as an outsider to the scene of present-day Catholic theology that the following comments are offered.

At the beginning of his essay Küng writes, "However, the Second Vatican Council demonstrated that this [neo-scholastic] theology was unable to deal effectively with the contemporary problems of humanity, the church and society." The question to ask is whether the neo-scholastic theology, which is a revival of Thomism, is unable to deal with contemporary problems because of innate flaws in Thomism, or because its principles have not been applied to contemporary problems or because these problems are for the most part pseudo-problems brought into being as a result of ill-posed questions. Is Thomism true? If it is true, that is, if it is an expression of metaphysical truth in its Christian form, then it cannot cease to be true. Its language might need modification but its message and content must continue to possess validity. And if there are other forms of theology necessary in the present context, are these other forms of theology different ways of explaining the eternal message of Christianity in a particular historical context with full consideration of the contingent factors involved, or are they no more than theologizing about passing and ephemeral experiences or so-called scientific "truths" which often cease to be of any great relevance from a theological point of view by the time the theologians have finished theologizing about them?

Truth must always come before expediency and even timeliness, especially as far as theology is concerned. Theology is after all literally "the science of God." It should explain the temporal with reference to the Eternal and not the Eternal in the light of temporality which is made to sound very *real*, central, and important by being baptized as the human condition, the modern world, or urgent human problems. There is no more urgent a human problem than the task to distinguish between the real and the Eternal on the one hand and the illusory and ephemeral on the other. The plurality of theologies is valuable only if it means different paths opening unto the same Truth, as it was in fact the case in early Christianity, and not of relativizing the Absolute and positing pseudo-philosophies based upon the confusion between the Eternal and temporal orders alongside authentic forms of theology which remain conscious of the basic mission of theology as the study of God and of creation in the light of God and God's Wisdom and Power.

Küng is not even satisfied with post-Conciliar theology because, in his words, "since modern exegesis was generally neglected in otherwise productive movements of theological renewal, such as the patristic-oriented 'ressourcement' (H. De Lubac, J. Daniélou, H. U. von Balthasar) as well as the speculative-transcendental mediation of Karl Rahner, their insufficiency became more and more apparent." Would a theology inspired by St. Augustine and Origen be insufficient because it does not take into account modern exegesis, by which is usually meant the so-called "higher criticism"?

This issue is quite sensitive from the Islamic point of view since Islam is based wholly on a sacred book. For it, "higher criticism" can only mean the unveiling of the inner meaning of the sacred book (*ta'ūīl* or the *kashf al-mahjūb* of the Islamic esotericists). Moreover, this process can only be achieved through the use of the higher faculties of humanity associated with the Intellect which resides at the heart or center of humanity's being. It implies an inwardness and drawing within the "book" of one's own being in order to reach the inner meaning of the Sacred Book. It certainly has nothing to do with archaeology or rationalistic analysis of texts and documents. The so-called "higher criticism," which in fact reduces the really "higher," which can be nothing but revelation, to the level of human reason, is based on the twin error which in fact characterizes so much of modern historicism and also science.

These two errors are, first of all, the presupposition that that for which there is no historical document did not exist, and secondly, that there is a kind of "uniformitarianism" in the laws and conditions of human society and the cosmos similar to what is posited as the key for the interpretation of the past by geologists and paleontologists. According to this thesis the systems, laws, and relations between cause and effect must have existed in days of old, let us say at the time of Christ, in the same way and mode that they can be observed today.

To walk on water must be "understood" and explained away because no one can walk on water today. There is no better way to kill the inner meaning of a sacred text and the very elements which allow the human mind to ascend to higher levels of being than the so-called "higher criticism" whose result is the death of the meaning of sacred scripture as revealed meaning and the gate to the spiritual world.

Neither "higher criticism" nor the exegesis of sacred scripture, based on the common experience of a humanity which has been cut off from spiritual nourishment and lives in a world of ugliness, which stultifies the heart and the mind, can cause a theology based on the eternal truths of any religion to fail. If such a theology does exist and it appears to have "failed," the failure must be laid to those who have not succeeded in uderstanding it rather than to the theology itself, provided the theology in question is a veritable "science of God." It would be better to have a true theology understood by just one person than a diluted or distorted theology based on compromising the truth but expressed by the multitude. Surely in the question of religious truth it cannot be numbers that reign, otherwise what could one say concerning the lives and actions of that very small minority known as the early Christian martyrs?

The author believes that the only theology that could survive the future would be one which blends the two elements of "a 'return to the sources' and a 'venturing forth on to unchartered waters' or . . . *a theology of Christian origins and center enunciated within the horizon of the contemporary world*." We could not agree more with the author concerning the doctrine that God is at once the origin and the center, the beginning and the "now." Therefore, theology must obviously be concerned with origins and the "now" which is the only reflection of eternity in time which binds humankind to the Eternal. But religion is also tradition. It is a tree with its roots sunk in heaven but also with a trunk and branches and a law of growth of its own. Also, like a living tree, a living religion is always amenable to a revivification and rejuvenation. Every "back to the roots" movement which negates the existing trunk and branches, the long tradition which binds the particular person or community wanting to return to the roots to the origin, only weakens the tree as a whole. There are many examples of this phenomenon in nearly all the major religions of the world, and their result is almost always a much impoverished version of that religion which resembles the origin outwardly but is never actually able to return to it. An awareness of Christian origins and center is exemplified most positively in the history of Christianity by a St. Francis of Assisi who was called "the second Christ." If by returning to the origin and center such an event or reality is implied, then certainly what it would produce would not only live through the future but in fact shape and make the future. What it needs, however, which is most difficult to come by, is another St. Francis.

As for the "uncharted waters," as a result of the rampant secularism of the Western world, the water is first charted by more religious forces and then religion is asked to take the map of a secularized cosmos and navigate through it.

From the traditional point of view, however, it is religion itself which must lead the way and chart the course. Theology as the intellectual expression of religion must be able to *make* the future and not simply follow the secularized disciplines with the hope of guaranteeing some kind of survival for itself by placating the "enemy" or even ceasing to call a spade a spade. Today there are many physicists who wish theologians would take theology a bit more seriously and modern science somewhat less as far as its biological implications are concerned.

It is in the light of this statement that Küng's agreement with Schillebeeckx on the "two sources" necessary for the creation of a "scientific theology" must be examined. These sources are "the traditional experience of the great Judeo-Christian movement on the one hand, and on the other the contemporary human experiences of Christians and non-Christians." First of all in the term "non-Christians" two very disparate elements are covered in an indiscriminate fashion. A non-Christian can be a Muslim, Hindu, or Buddhist or he or she can be an agnostic or atheist, who in fact is, to say the least, as far removed from the followers of other religions as she or he is from Christianity and Judaism. There are then three groups or "sources" to consider rather than two: the Judeo-Christian tradition, the other religions, and modern secularism. There is no doubt that the time has come for serious theology in the West to take cognizance of the religious and metaphysical significance of other religions, whose presence in a less mutilated and secularized form than much of contemporary Christianity is in a profound sense a compensation sent by heaven to offset the withering effect of secularism and pseudo-religious ideologies. A veritable dialogue in the spirit of an ecumenism which would respect the totality of each tradition and not reduce things to a least common denominator would certainly be a great aid to future theological formulations among Christians. The writings of such figures as Frittijof Schnon have already made accessible the remarkable richness of this perspective.

But as far as the experience of the secular, or even modern science itself, is concerned, we do not believe that this can be a "source" for theology. Rather, it must be an element which contemporary theology must seek to explain in the light of its own principles. It is not theology which must surrender itself to modern science and its findings. Rather it is modern science which must be critically appraised from the metaphysical and theological points of view and its findings explained in this light. As the basic role of religion is to save the human soul from the world and not simply to carry out a dialogue with the "world," the role of theology is to cast the light of the Eternal upon the experiences of humankind's terrestrial journey. If modern humanity has experienced the void and nihilism, theology can explain the reason for such an experience and the meaning that such an experience can have in bringing humanity back to God, for as Meister Eckhardt has said, "The more they blaspheme the more they praise God." But this experience of the void or despair or injustice cannot be a "source" of theology without doing grave injustice to theology and destroying the sacred which alone can render meaning to human life.

There are a few other particular points in Küng's statements of agreement with Schillebeeckx which need to be commented upon in a few words. Küng states, "*divine revelation is only accessible through human experience.*" "Human experience" yes, but not ordinary human experience. There is more to consciousness than what we usually experience. There is a hierarchy of consciousness as there is a hierarchy of experience leading to the concrete experience of the spiritual world. Genuine revelation is certainly an experience but not on the same level as everyday experience. It has been said of the messenger of divine revelation in Islam, namely Muhammed, that he was a man among men but not an ordinary man. Rather, he was like a jewel among stones. For Christianity, which is based on the doctrine of the incarnation and the God-man, surely divine relevation cannot be reduced to the level of ordinary human experience, especially in a world where the higher modes of experience available to a human as a theomorphic being have become so rare.

As for revelation coming, in Küng's terms, "in a lengthy process of events, experiences and intepretations and not as a supernatural 'intrusion,'" what is meant by revelation here is the disciples' faith in Christ and not Christ himself who *is* the revelation in Christianity. But even on the level of the apostles, this secondary mode of "revelation" was not necessarily always a lengthy process. It could certainly have been an immediate "intrusion" and illumination if the substance of the disciple in question were already prepared. For people living today it is hardly conceivable to imagine what it would mean actually to encounter a great saint, not to speak of the Abrahamic prophets or Christ himself.

Closely allied to this assertion is the second point of agreement between Küng and Schillebeeckx, namely that revelation is always reached through the human experience which is never "pure." This would negate the "supernaturally natural" function of the Intellect in humanity which is able to know objectively and to discern between the absolute and the relative. It would also negate the possibility of "annihilation" or what the Sufis call *al-'fanā'*, through which the soul becomes "nothing" and removes itself as the veil, allowing the Supreme Self within to say "I." If humanity could not know the truth in itself, truth would have no meaning as either the source of objective revelation or that inner revelation which is the illumination of humanity's inward being. To say that there is no such thing as "pure experience" of the truth is in a sense a negation of his very thesis. We must first accept that there is such a thing as pure experience unveiling the truth in its pristine purity in order to decide that our experience is not pure experience in comparison with this pure experience—of which we must have had some kind of knowledge if we were going to compare something with it.

The third point of agreement between Küng and Schillebeeckx involves the significance of the "*living Jesus of history*" as "*the source, standard and criterion of Christian faith.*" While not at all questioning this distinctly Christian position, we would only like to add that one cannot at the same time forget or neglect the central significance of that trans-historical Jesus who said, "I am before Abraham was." Islamic Christology, which emphasizes the trans-historical Jesus, is more akin to certain early forms of Christology rejected by the later councils. It is strange that, now that there is so much attention paid to the "origins" and patristic-oriented theology, contemporary theologians do not emphasize more the Christ as the eternal *logos* to which in fact many young Christians in quest of the rediscovery of integral Christianity are strongly attracted.

Finally, a comment must be made on each of the ten "guiding principles for contemporary theology" which Küng had formulated in his *Existiert Gott?* and which he repeats in the essay under review.

1. "Theology should not be an esoteric science only for believers but should be intelligible to non-believers as well."

Comment: First of all every living tradition *does need* an esoteric science which, however, is not usually called theology. As for theology, it should of course be written in such an intelligent manner that even the intelligent non-believer would be attracted to it. But it would be better for theology not to lead believers to unbelief in its attempt to be intelligible to unbelievers.

2. "Theology should not exalt simple faith nor defend an 'ecclesiastical' system but strive for the truth without compromise in intense scholarly fashion."

Comment: Certainly the goal of theology must be the truth, but if current scholarly methods are sufficient to attain the truth, then what is the difference between theology and humanistic and rationalistic scholarship? The role of theology cannot but be the defense of the truth as revealed in God's religion. Then there is the basic question of what guarantee there is in each religion for the protection of the truth. Each religion has a different response. In Christianity it has always been the *magisterium*. How can one prevent the truth from becoming reduced to mere individualistic whim and fancy if the authority of the *magisterium* is denied?

3. "Ideological opponents should not be ignored or hereticized, nor theologically co-opted. Rather their views should be set out in a fair and factual discussion and interpreted *in optimam partem* as tolerantly as possible."

Comment: Views of opponents should certainly be studied factually and objectively without passion. But truth is one thing and charity another. We must love other people, but that does not mean that we must be indifferent to the truth. Where truth is no longer of any consequence, the question of agreement or opposition is of little importance. It is easy to be tolerant when there are no immutable principles for which one stands. The situation becomes much more difficult when we have faith in a particular form of the truth which we call our religion and then either see those who possess other forms of truth which also come from God (a tree is judged by the fruit it bears), or simply live in error from the point of view of the truth we accept as truth. It is this much more delicate problem that all "living theologies" of today and tomorrow face and will face not only in Christianity but in all other religions.

4. "We should not only promote but actually practice an interdisciplinary approach. Along with a concentration upon our own field, we must maintain a constant dialogue with related fields."

Comment: This is indeed sound advice provided it is not carried out from a position of weakness and with an inferiority complex and that theology remains faithful to its own nature, mission, and genius. Physicists should also follow the same advice, but that does not mean that tomorrow they will go into the laboratory and study subatomic particles through theological methods, even if they draw theological conclusions from their physical studies.

5. "We need neither hostile confrontation nor easy co-existence, but rather a critical dialogue especially between theology and philosophy, theology and natural science: religion and rationality belong together!"

Comment: This is certainly true but it can come about only if theology stops its retreat before the onslaught of both philosophy and natural science. Dialogue is possible only among equals or those nearly equal. Theology has as much a right to study nature and the mind as do science and philosophy. Each discipline has a different approach and hence reaches different aspects of the truth which in its wholeness can only be seen by the science of the whole or of the totality, which is metaphysics in its original sense.

6. "Problems of the past should not have priority over the wide-ranging, multi-faceted dilemmas of contemporary humanity and society."

Comment: It is mostly as a result of neglecting the past as a source both of tradition and of experience for humankind that so many problems face present-day humanity. Of course, theology must deal with contemporary dilemmas, but always in the light of the truth, which *is* and does not *become*, and the profound aspects of human nature, which despite appearances remains remarkably the same. It is in the light of this permanence that apparent change should be explained.

7. "The criterion determining all other criteria of Christian theology can never again be some ecclesiastical or theological tradition or institution, but only the Gospel, the original Christian message itself. Thus, theology must everywhere be oriented toward the biblical findings analyzed by historical-critical analysis."

Comment: Without in any way denying the central role of the Gospels we cannot but be astonished at how this Holy Book could serve as the source for the truth of the Christian faith without the church, the oral teachings, the traditions and all that in fact connect a human being who calls her or himself Christian to the origin of this religion. If the Gospels sufficed, how could there be so many different schools all basing themselves on the same book? Although the phenomenon of the proliferation of schools and "sects" is the same in all religions, nowhere has it been as great as in Christianity when the Gospels became considered by certain schools as the main source for Christianity. But even in most of these schools, until now, certain other aspects of Christianity as a historical reality have also been accepted. If the Gospels were to be taken as the sole source of theology, again the question would come up as to what guarantees the truth of the religion and what is the origin of the faith in the light of which the Christian reads the Gospels.

8. "The Gospel should not be proclaimed in biblical archaisms nor in Hellenistic scholastic dogmatisms nor in fashionable philosophic-theological jargon. Rather, it should be expressed in the commonly understood language of contemporary humanity and we should not stay away from any effort in this direction."

Comment: We disagree completely with this thesis. The so-called commonly understood language of contemporary humanity is itself no more than a debased jargon, influenced by the mass media and often deprived of the beauty of the language in question. Sacred books are too sublime to be cast in the molds of a language form by the lower psyche of a humanity which is being dragged downward by the very "civilization" it has created. Religious texts have always been elements of beauty which have adorned human life, and today humanity is in need of this saving beauty more than ever before. Why should the words of God sound like the outpourings of a football announcer? In other religions such as Islam where the Sacred Book is couched in the immutable beauty of a sacred language, the unchanging nature of the language has certainly not made people any less religious over the ages, even people whose mother tongue has not been Arabic. The experience of Islam should be of some value for those who believe that catering to contemporary jargon will somehow draw people more to religion and the study of the Gospels. Let us not forget that even on the American frontiers the Bible survived in the language of Elizabethan England and was probably more widely read than many of its Americanized descendants are read by the "more-educated" descendants of those cowboys.

9. "Credible theory and livable practice, dogmatics and ethics, personal piety and reform of institutions must not be separated but seen in their inseparable connection."

Comment: We could not but agree with this thesis, for in all religions method and doctrine must go hand in hand. But as far as reform is concerned, it is most of all the reform of ourselves that is at stake. Modern humanity wishes to reform everything but itself. That is why so many of its reformations become deformations.

10. "We must avoid a confessionalistic ghetto mentality. Instead we should express an ecumenical vision that takes into consideration the world religions as well as contemporary ideologies: as much tolerance as possible toward those things outside the Church, toward the religious in general, and the human in general, and the development of that which is specifically Christian belong together."

Comment: Expressing an ecumenical vision in the sense already mentioned, by all means, but joining world religions and contemporary ideologies, which are the products of a secularized West, is really an insult to those religions. The much more logical position would be to place all the religions, including

Christianity, in one world or camp before which stand the forces of agnosticism and secularism. In fact Christianity, already scarred by several centuries of battle against humanism, secularism, and rationalism, has the choice of either returning to the universe of religion as such, to the sacred cosmos which Islam, Hinduism, Buddhism, etc. still breathe, or attempt to bring about some kind of a wedding with secularism, which itself was born from a void created by the loss of the all-embracing Christian vision in the West. For the sake of humanity, let us hope that the first alternative will be followed and that the West will rejoin the rest of humankind, for from the marriage with secularism there cannot come into being anything but those beasts which shall lay the earth in ruin and to which the *Book of the Apocalypse* has referred so majestically.

I feel somewhat embarrassed criticizing a well-known Catholic theologian, but perhaps this exercise can be seen as a counterpart to the voluminous works written by Orientalists on the present and even future of Islam and even Islamic theology. In contrast to some of these works, however, my intentions have derived not from hatred but love for Christianity and the followers of Sayyidnā Īsā, as the Quran has called Christ. Moreover, an aspect of the experience of contemporary humanity necessitates a universal perspective on religion and an awareness of the interrelated nature of the spiritual destiny of all of humankind which made an interest in other religions imperative for a Muslim concerned with the future of his own religion as well as religion as such.

A HINDU SELF-REFLECTION

Kana Mitra

Hans Küng's essay very clearly highlighted the weaknesses of Catholic theology, and thereby stimulated my self-reflection about the problems of Hindu theological thinking. Theological thinking in the Hindu tradition is different from Denzinger-type Catholic theological thinking. Since the coherence of scripture (*Sruti*), reason (*Yukti*), and experience (*anubhava*) is the standard criterion of Hindu theological thinking, neither the new knowledge in biology, psychology, or physics, nor a renaissance in general posed problems for Hindu theology the way they did for Catholic dogmatic theology. In the nineteenth and twentieth centuries, when Hinduism encountered the West and modernity, the then-practiced Hinduism, which for all practical purposes was not different from a system of rituals and taboos based on the caste system and its laws, became unacceptable to many Western-educated Hindus. Various reform movements began. Yet all the reform movements were directed against the social systems and practices and did not generate any radically different theological thinking with the exception of that of Sri Aurobindo. One of the important reasons for this is the congeniality of Hindu thought with the findings of modern science. Some contemporary Hindu thinkers often feel and exhibit a certain triumphalism about Hindu thought because of this congeniality. Writings of the monks of the Ramakrishna order can clearly indicate this attitude, e.g., *Ranganathananda* (Science and Religion) (Calcutta: Advaita Asrama, 1978).

Again, although most of the classical Hindu thinkers belonged to the *Brahmin* caste, which was the overseer of Hindu tradition, in Hinduism there never has been any official hierarchy or "ecclesiastical system," as in the Vatican, to test the authenticity of a doctrine or dogma. Actually in Hinduism there is no dogma as it is found in Catholicism. In Hinduism the absoluteness of truth is proclaimed. However, the perception or apprehension and explication of that truth by humans are considered relative. In other words, the fact that theological thinking about the absolute is done by humans is always recognized and, therefore, although different Hindu thinkers vie with each other to prove that their perception and presentation of the truth is the most adequate one, they are tolerant and careful listeners to other presentations of it also. Hence in Hinduism *anathema* is itself an *anathema*. Hans Küng's proposal in the field of Catholic theology that ideological opponents should not be ignored or hereticized or theologically co-opted has been observed in Hindu theological thinking as a matter of methodological procedure and has been its strong point. In traditional Hindu theological thinking the statement and understanding of opposing views is the first step; the second step is analysis and refutation of those views; the third step is the statement of one's own view. The classical Hindu writings, therefore, have an encyclopedic character.

The factors like emphasis on faith in dissociation from reason, intolerance of opposing ideologies, absolutization of an "ecclesiastical system," etc. are undeniably the constituent factors of weaknesses in Catholic theology. The absence of these factors provides strength to Hinduism. This reinforces Küng's conclusion. However, to emphasize only the negative qualities of these factors and to neglect their positive value might lead to throwing away the baby along with the bath water. The factors which constitute the weaknesses of Catholicism also act as its strength, and conversely, the absence of these factors which constitute the strength of Hindu theology are also its weakness. Dissociation of faith and reason is not acceptable in the post-Enlightenment era, yet over-emphasis on reason also may lead to blunders or sophistry in the name of sophistication. That has actually happened in the history of Hindu theological thought. Many post-Samkarite *advaitins* offered pure dialectic in the field of theological thinking but, although their systems may be the acme of logical skills, they could not serve as the basis of a livable practice. Thus, as a classical rebound the *vais nava* doctrine of pure faith was developed, and consequently we have, e.g., the Began saying, "Visvāse milaye Krsna tarke vahn dur" (by faith one has *Krsna*, but by logical argument he is kept far away). Reasonableness of belief can justify faith, as is argued in Thomas Aquinas's writings as well as in Hans Küng's *Does God Exist?* But reason can produce neither belief or disbelief by itself—it has to be accompanied by experience or existential choice.

Ignorance and intolerance of ideological opposition are unacceptable these days. Ignorance and intolerance of opposing ideologies are not justified because of the transcendence of truth and the finiteness of the human endeavor. However, because the human perception of truth is relative, absolute relativism cannot be justified. If relativism is absolutized then anything can be said in the intellectual realm, and the distinction between truth and falsehood becomes meaningless. If something is true *only* within one universe of discourse, then the different universes of discourse would become like Leibnitz's monads—closed systems. The only choice left would be the co-existence of the different systems with mutual ignorance, indifference, or disregard. That is what is happening in contemporary Hindu thinking. After Sri Aurobindo, who died in 1950, hardly any Hindu thinker considers the different opposing views with any seriousness and tries to analyze, refute, or integrate them with Hindu thought. Present-day Hindu elites are proud of their tolerance. But that tolerance is producing either self-complacence or syncretistic co-existence with mutual ignorance and indifference. Doors and windows can be closed because of dogmatism, but absolute tolerance in the sense of "everything is O.K." can also lead to virtually closed systems.

The absolutization of an "ecclesiastical system" would virtually amount to an esoteric theology which could be understood only by the initiate and not by others. The "ecclesiastical system" has acted as a cohesive factor for the Catholic community. However, when this becomes insensitive to the changed awareness in the community, it begins to act as a disintegrating factor. In Hinduism pluralistic patterns of thought existed side by side and did not act as cohesive factors; the caste system fulfilled this function. In the contemporary awareness of the Hindu community the caste system is becoming more and more unacceptable and thus is losing its power to act as a cohesive factor. However, Hindu thinkers are not coming up with any alternative social structure which is practical.

Hindu thinkers are proud of the trans-historical character of Hinduism. Hinduism emphasizes the perennial truth which is not bound to any historical person or event. However, Hindu thinkers are not aware of the fact that any religious tradition, including Hinduism, is bound to history and hence is historical. For example, the practice and realization of the values that are described in the Bagavad-Gita, although they have their universal implications, are nevertheless very much related to the caste-structured society of Hinduism; *sva-dharma* means one's own nature is to be realized, but *sva-dharma* is presented in terms of the caste system.

In the modern period when the caste system is becoming increasingly unacceptable, and hence unaccepted, the cohesiveness of Hindu society is also disintegrating. To the Western observer India appears as a sapless, hopeless, soulless country! Hindus inside and outside India do not have any sense of direction other than some romantic notion of the Hindu ideals. They do not have any consciousness of what it means to be a Hindu. At the present time, on the one hand, there are Hindu leaders who maintain that the protection of the cow or the prohibition of alcohol or even using the cow's urine as the only medicine (Morarji Desai) can cure Hindu problems. On the other hand, there are technologically and scientifically sophisticated and sometimes completely Westernized Hindus who think that following the West (sometimes it amounts to aping) is the only cure for Hinduism.

Hindu theological thinking has its strength in being universal, in emphasizing trans-historical truth. But it also has to show how this trans-historical truth can best be reflected or realized in the concrete historical situations of human life. Hindu thinkers emphasize the idea that the problems of history cannot be solved in history. Yet that should not create an attitude of carelessness about what is happening historically. Even Samkara, who is considered by many as an illusionist, indicated that our starting point is history—the concrete human situation—and to be born as human is one of the boons of human life.

A human being's religious quest, according to Hinduism, is an individual quest. It is the journey of the alone to the alone. Yet the individual is the part of the society—is born in a particular historical situation. However, many forms of society in a particular historical situation are not conducive to the individual's quest for the absolute. A monk may take the vow of poverty, yet that would not be healthy for masses as such. Vivekananda has aptly pointed out that one cannot pursue the religious quest on an empty stomach. The Upanisads stated *annam Brahman*, or food, is *Brahman*. One is rooted in the concrete conditions of life.

Traditional Hindu theologians were thinking within, and thus for, the cohesive structure provided by the caste system. Within this social condition the quest for the absolute could be perceived realistically. To contemporary consciousness the caste system is anachronistic. However, no alternatives have yet been thought through. Hindu thinkers have not yet come up with any concrete picture of the ideal society which is practical. *Rame Rajye* and the way of realizing it is too romantic. In reality Hindu thinkers are not making any conscious effort to understand what it means to be a Hindu in the present concrete situation of history. For most of the Hindu elites, to be a Hindu does not mean anything more than following liberal human ethical values. The non-elites are still, almost mechanically, following the traditional practices of their forebears and are not changing with the altered conditions of our present-day life. There is need for conscious reflection by Hindu theologians about what it means to be a Hindu in contemporary history of humankind. Dialogue with other worldviews and with the findings of the social sciences, as well as cross-cultural and cross-disciplinary reflection, may in the case of Hindu theological thinking also provide some positive clues.

CHRISTOLOGY WITHOUT JESUS OF NAZARETH IS IDEOLOGY: A MONUMENTAL WORK BY SCHILLEBEECKX ON JESUS

John Nijenhuis

In 1974, the year that he celebrated his sixtieth birthday, Edward Schille-beeckx saw the publication of his monumental book on Jesus.[1] Within a year the book went through two more editions, with some clarifications added in the third edition. The book was hailed as "a voluminous ecumenical present," and this for two reasons. The first reason is "the fact that a theologian from a church which in the past never excelled in biblical studies now leads us, Protestants, in exploring the sources of the story of this Living One." The second reason is that the writer wrote for "the many Christians in the churches who cannot fall back any more on those mystifications which, under the guise of 'mystery of faith,' enabled us to escape the customary examination of critical scholarship."[2]

Schillebeeckx considered his book as the fulfillment of his life's dream.[3] Nevertheless, he states that this book is only a prolegomenon or, as in the subtitle, "an experiment in Christology,"[4] and that its inner dynamics demand a complement that will deal with redemption and grace, "partly with 'liberation theology' in mind" (pp. 35 and 669). This second book was published in 1977 as *Justice and Love: Grace and Liberation*.[5] Since then Schillebeeckx has published a smaller book, *An Interim Report about Two Jesus Books*,[6] and has announced

---

[1]*Jezus, het verhaal van een Levende* (Bloemendaal: Nelissen, 1974), 622 pages, fl. 67.50, and *Jesus, An Experiment in Christology* (New York: Seabury Press, 1979), 767 pages, $24.50. The references in the body of the article are to the English-language edition and are meant to be illustrative, not exhaustive.

[2]A. Geense, "Jezus, het verhaal van een levende: een volumineus oekumenisch geschenk (Jesus, The Story of a Living One: A Voluminous Ecumenical Present)," *Kosmos & Oekumene*, vol. 8, no. 7 (1974), pp. 180-183; the article is abstracted in the *Journal of Ecumenical Studies*, vol. 3, no. 3 (Summer, 1975), pp. 446-447.

[3]Joep Spitz in an interview with Schillebeeckx, *Kosmos & Oekumene*, vol. 8, no. 7 (1974), p. 184.

[4]The subtitle of the English edition is explained on p. 35. "Experiment" appears to be the translation of "proeve" in the Dutch edition (which has for its subtitle "The Story of a Living One"). It would seem that the Dutch word "proeve," in contrast with the similar "proef" (experiment) has the connotation of a "tentative treatment of a subject offered to one's scholarly colleagues for scrutiny and critique" (cf. the German "Probe" and French "essai," meaning: "sample, trial"). Apart from some such phrases, the translation as a whole reads as well (or with as much difficulty) as the original Dutch text.

[5]*Gerechtigheid en liefde: Genade en bevrijding* (Bloemendaal: Nelissen, 1977), 903 pages, fl. 125.

[6]*Tussentijds verhaal over twee Jezusboeken* (Bloemendaal: Nelissen, 1978), 144 pages, fl. 19.90.

the possibility of a third big book which would deal with pneumatology and ecclesiology.[7]

The first Jesus book consists of four parts: the first is a survey of the various criteria and methods which are used today in interpreting the New Testament writings. The second (and longest) part discusses the life and message, the death and resurrection of Jesus of Nazareth. The third part attempts a reconstruction of the earliest (intratestamentary) Christian interpretations of who Jesus was and is: while he lived on earth and as he is now with God and actively present among his followers. The fourth part marks the beginning of an attempt to answer the question, "Who do you say that I am?" in a manner that will speak to the mature contemporary Christian (cf. p. 673).

Main Motifs

The book is characterized by a curious mixture of three types or styles of writing. On the one hand, there are many beautiful passages written in a warm, personal, and moving style and, on the other hand, there are many intricate discussions of an exegetical nature, and then there are, as Schillebeeckx himself admits, various deep and difficult speculations of a theological and philosophical nature, for which (in Part Three) "some effort may well be needed."

The beautifully written passages may have contributed to the events behind Schillebeeckx' report that he has received about thirty letters from alienated Christians telling him that they had been "converted" by his book.[8] Indeed, in a sustained and subdued manner Schillebeeckx paints an image of Jesus that is so "attractive" that one cannot help being drawn close to this very real, human Jesus offering salvation-from-God.

One of the most striking motifs of the book is Schillebeeckx' almost obsessive preoccupation with the presence of evil and suffering in the world, then and now.[9] Whereas in the recent past the phrase "salvation history" appears to have become the hallmark of modernity, Schillebeeckx sees—and more realistically—an all-pervading intrusion of evil into the entire history of humankind. He often speaks, in entire sections (pp. 19-26, 172-178, 612-625) and in numerous passing references, of the "history of evil," of a "negative history of

---

[7]Cf. E. Schillebeeckx, "Op weg naar een christologie (Toward a Christology)," *Tijdschrift voor Theologie* vol. 18, no. 2 (April-June, 1978), p. 153.

[8]In the article "Verrijzenis en geloofservaring (Resurrection and Faith Experience)," *Kultuurleven* (January, 1975), p. 81.

[9]Schillebeeckx returns to the problem of suffering in "Mysterie van ongerechtigheid en mysterie van erbarmen: vragen rond het menselijk lijden (Mystery of Iniquity and Mystery of Mercy: Questions about Human Suffering)," *Tijdschrift voor Theologie*, vol. 15, no. 1 (January-March, 1975), pp. 3-25. A similar concentration on the mystery of evil is also found in Hans Küng, *On Being a Christian* (New York: Doubleday, 1976); there is also a similarity of approach in other areas, such as "death as non-Utopia" and "Man's cause as God's cause."

violence, injustice and suffering" (p. 270). He does this in a play on words such as is possible in Dutch: "on-heil," literally "un-salvation."[10] He emphatically rejects any attempt to find a rational "solution" to the eternally mysterious question of evil.[11] All one can do is to fully trust, as did Jesus, that "the Father is greater than all our suffering and grief" (p. 625):

> Jesus brings the message "from God" of God's radical "no" to the continuing course of man's suffering. The whole point of history, although only the *eschaton* will make this clear, is peace, laughter, total satisfaction: the "final" good of salvation and happiness (p. 177).

> . . . even now the poor, the hungry and grief-stricken may rise up in hope, to say: but all the same . . . Laughter, not crying, is the deepest purpose that God wills for man (p. 178).

As stated above, the ecumenical significance of the book was seen to lie in the fact that, now in Schillebeeckx' words, "hardly any theologians but very many exegetes are cited" (p. 40). The amount of exegetical background reading by the author is impressive, if not overwhelming. This fact is worthy of mention in itself but becomes even more important when we hear of the purpose to which this biblical scholarship is put: a new "Quest for the historical Jesus." The term "historical Jesus" is used to mean "that which the methods of historical criticism enable us to retrieve of Jesus of Nazareth, that is, the 'earthly' Jesus" (p. 67). It is possible to discover "a relatively coherent picture" of the historical Jesus out of the "kerygmatic Jesus of faith" of the early Christians. This is also imperative because "Jesus is the revelation, in personal form, of God" and "there are no ghosts or gods in disguise wandering around in our human history" (pp. 33-34). Schillebeeckx would agree with the Dutch Protestant theologian H. Berkhof who writes that there is today "a rather surprising consensus about the words and deeds of the historical Jesus."[12] For phrases such as "the hard historical centre" (p. 389) and "the memory still at work behind the gospel stories" (p. 386) abound throughout the book. Thus he sees his initial working hypothesis confirmed: "Broadly speaking, the New Testament is a true to life (faith-motivated) reflection or mirroring of the historical role enacted by Jesus of Nazareth" (p. 515). Christians need such a reminder, for

> whereas God is bent on showing himself in human form, we on our side slip past this human aspect as quickly as we can in order to

---

[10] Another peculiarity of the Dutch (and German) language is that the word "heil" has not such an exclusively religious connotation as has the English "salvation" (cf. the Nazi slogan "Sieg heil"—with apologies). The Dutch word can therefore suggest that "(un)salvation" covers also the secular domain and touches men and women in their concrete daily existence. This play on words gets inevitably lost in the English translation where such words as "the ill," "calamity," and "calamitous" have been adopted.

[11] Notably in "Mystery of Iniquity," pp. 10 and 14.

[12] *Christelijk geloof* (Nijkerk: Callenbach, 1973), p. 290. This book of 596 pages was competing with Schillebeeckx' *Jezus* on the Dutch theological marketplace!

admire a "divine Ikon." . . . Thus we run the risk simply of adding
a new ideology to those which mankind already possess in such
plenty: that is to say, Christology itself! (p. 671)

"Salvation in Jesus coming from God" or some very similar phrase is the
recurring description of the message of Jesus. Schillebeeckx originally intended
this to be the title of his book (p. 557). "Salvation" was the topic of the day:
"Jesus' time was full to bursting with an assortment of hopes regarding some
good thing to come" (p. 20). It was in such a context that Jesus preached the
message of a God who, in another recurring phrase, is "bent upon humanity."[13]

Several theologians speak of a "break(age)" in the history of Jesus and
regard the death (and resurrection) as this point. Schillebeeckx however
repeatedly insists that the great break was an event in the earlier, historical life
of Jesus, viz., the painful discovery that his message was being rejected (pp.
294ff., 638, 642-643). This break-motif is intimately linked up with the
question whether Jesus, whose mission was a "historical failure" (p. 625), died
for an illusion, whether he was wrong (pp. 269-271, 302-312, 542-543), and
with the lesson which this seeming failure contains for us (pp. 636-639):

> Was his life then something Utopian and an illusion, even the saddest
> proof of all, that positive hope of a better world and a better
> mankind turns out to be impossible? (p. 271)

To this question Schillebeeckx returns again and again.

What Jesus Proclaimed and How He Lived and Died

The second part of the book is an attempt at reconstructing the life of the
earthly Jesus, who is "the norm and criterion" of Christianity, another of those
phrases which occur throughout the book. The first thing which can be known
about Jesus with historical certainty is his baptism by John. The historical core
of the Gospel reports of this event is that the meeting with John the Baptist
"must have been for Jesus a disclosure experience" (p. 137), by which he
became aware of his mission to preach "salvation on its way from God" (cf.
p. 115).

The notion of the Reign of God is "the basic impulse behind the message
and preaching of Jesus" (p. 140). Amply documented discussions of the parables
and the beatitudes highlight Jesus' idea of God's humane intentions for men and

---

[13]The word "humanity" is taken in one of its dictionary senses: "The quality of being
humane, benevolence, kindness, mercy" (*The American Heritage Dictionary*). Schillebeeckx'
usage of the word seems to be inspired by Titus 3:4, where the Latin text has *humanitas* for
the Greek "philanthropia." The translation misses this point in the heading "God's rule
directed at mankind" (p. 140), where "bent (or: intent) on humanity" would have come
closer to the original meaning of the Dutch text.

women. Schillebeeckx describes Jesus' manner of life as a "caring and abiding presence among people, experienced as salvation coming from God" (p. 179).

The theme of the disciples' "non-fasting" in the living presence of Jesus must have been a particular recollection of the disciples who had not forgotten that "being sad in Jesus' presence was an existential impossibility" (p. 201). This facet also reveals why Jesus expressed his idea of "joyful commitment to the living God" (p. 200) in "eating and drinking with his fellows" (p. 201), a custom of Jesus' put into unusual relief by Schillebeeckx (pp. 206-213); Jesus himself as host is a copious gift from God (pp. 213-218). The "God of Jesus" inspires Jesus to act as "man's liberator from a constricting view of God," which is the heading under which Jesus' attitude toward the Law is expounded (pp. 229-256).

When Jesus stood face to face with death, he gathered his disciples for a final fellowship meal. Schillebeeckx, in trying to reconstruct how Jesus interpreted his own death, rejects the common assumption that Jesus' message "took its meaning only from his death" (p. 306); death is an entirely negative event (p. 648).[14] At the same time Schillebeeckx is at pains to make clear that Jesus did not believe that he would die for an illusion, that his mission had been a failure. A detailed analysis of what happened at the Last Supper leads to the conclusion that Jesus "has come to proper terms with his death, which he evidently does not feel to be an absurd miscarriage of his mission" (p. 309). "Jesus stands open to God's future for man" and "gives God the final word" (ibid.), phrases which are explained as meaning that

> Jesus felt his death to be (in some way or other) part and parcel of the salvation-offered-by-God, as a historical consequence of his caring and loving service of and solidarity with people. (p. 310)[15]

Some passages could create the impression that Schillebeeckx is one of those theologians who hold that Jesus had (earlier) counted on some "empirical" intervention by God, through some celestial "son of man."[16] But so great is

---

[14]The negativity of death is again emphasized in "Mystery of Iniquity," p. 16, and in "Resurrection and Faith Experience," p. 92 and n. 4. From note 4 it would appear that Schillebeeckx has a running battle with Karl Rahner who, says Schillebeeckx, "ascribes to death a positive meaning (besides the negative meaning)—and this is still incomprehensible to me." The reference is to Rahner's *Theological Investigations* (New York: Seabury, 1974), vol. 4, "Dogmatic Question on Easter," pp. 127-128.

[15]In a section on "The death of Jesus as interpreted in early Christianity" (pp. 274-294), three complexes of traditions are examined: the contrast-scheme of the eschatological prophet-martyr, the scheme of salvation-history, and the soteriological scheme. The first scheme "ascribes no salvific implications to the death of Jesus itself" (p. 275). Mark's reference to the "ransom for many" (Mk. 10:45, and not 14:24, as is found in both the Dutch and English edition), which is discussed under the third scheme, may well have "its historical basis in a saying or gesture of Jesus, as even then he interprets for himself his coming death" (pp. 293-294).

[16]E.g., John Macquarrie, *The Faith of the People of God* (New York: Scribner's, 1972): "Jesus himself seems to have believed that the end of the age was imminent" (p. 167; cf. p. 96).

Schillebeeckx' piety toward Jesus that when this interpretation was mentioned to him he vigorously rejected it: "Jesus left everything 'open,' trusting God unto death."[17]

The Easter Experience

The starting points for a reconstruction of what happened after Good Friday are the following two "historical facts": the group of disciples, after betraying Jesus, disintegrates; reassembled in Jesus' name they proclaim, a while after Jesus' death, that this same Jesus is alive, or that he is risen (p. 380). What took place between Jesus' death and the proclamation by the Apostles? (p. 331) The answer cannot be: the "resurrection" itself, which is nowhere recounted in the New Testament, nor an "empty tomb" which, as also holds true for the resurrection, presupposes belief in the resurrection (p. 380). The answer has to be found in the fact that "anyone who has at first taken offence at Jesus and subsequently proclaims him to be the only bringer of salvation has of necessity undergone a 'conversion process'" (p. 381). The content of this conversion and its subsequent development is elaborated by Schillebeeckx in a complex if not tortuous manner; the main structural elements seem to be: Easter experience, resurrection terminology, the appearance stories, the empty tomb.[18]

After the arrest of Jesus the disciples fled back to Galilee. Then, "a while after Jesus' death,"[19] it was Peter who underwent a double experience: he experienced forgiveness, a "renewed offer of salvation in Jesus," and the call to go forth preaching that God was still offering salvation in Jesus (pp. 381, 390).[20] Peter then was the intermediary for the other disciples (so that they might also) undergo the same experience of "forgiveness and call-to-preach" (p. 389). Schillebeeckx emphasizes that this experience was felt by the disciples to be "an act of sheer grace on God's part," a "sovereignly free initiative of Jesus" (p. 390).[21]

---

[17]Personal communication to this writer, May 26, 1975. The emphasis is by Schillebeeckx who also suggests regarding the phrase "Jesus himself" in the quote submitted to him: "himself: *delete*."

[18]Something like this seems to be the "logical" if not also chronological order in which these elements came into existence in the early Church. In the book these elements are discussed in a different order, beginning with the "(empty) tomb" (cf. pp. 332-334). The resurrection theme features also in several systematic discussions in Part Three (pp. 518-544) and Part Four (pp. 640-650).

[19]Küng suggests that Luke's fiftieth day may have for its historical kernel the actual memory of the approximate time elapsed between the disciples' flight to Galilee and their return, after the conversion experience, to Jerusalem to await the glorious return of Jesus (*On Being a Christian*, p. 354).

[20]The reasons for ascribing this role to Peter are the several references to a certain "primacy" ("protophany") of Peter in the New Testament, for which there must have been a "hard historical centre" (pp. 388-390). In a similar vein, some women must have played a role in this gathering together of the disbanded disciples, because of several references to women in the stories of the appearances and the empty tomb (pp. 344-346).

[21]Schillebeeckx does not seem to succeed in giving us a clear picture of how this divine

This reassembling of the disciples is what Schillebeeckx calls the "Easter experience," which marks the beginning of the Church (pp. 357-358, 387). The concrete shape which the Apostles' preaching originally took was that Jesus himself was now regarded as the Son of Man who would soon return as the "Judge of the World" (pp. 409-411, 472, 539).[22]

Initially the Apostles did not ponder the manner in which Jesus had been brought from the realm of the dead, so convinced were they of the imminent *parousia* (p. 411). One early way of explaining the manner was the notion of resurrection (along with the perhaps earlier and more widespread notion of exaltation), which was soon formulated in some communities but came into general use at some later date (pp. 396-397, 538-539).[23]

When Schillebeeckx discusses the "appearances of Jesus," he is conscious of going against a long tradition, but adds that only if his reasoning has been shown to be deficient will he retract (p. 710, n. 119). He sees them strictly as "stories,"[24] and therefore has no use for "pseudo-empiricism," a "crude and naive realism," which raises all sorts of false problems, such as whether it was

---

"initiative" took place; he comes closest to it on p. 382. Küng seems to present a more "intelligible" account by referring to the transcendental immanence of God in creatures (*On Being a Christian*, p. 377).

[22]There would only be "a very brief interlude" (p. 411).

[23]Since "resurrection" appears to be a "derivative" notion, the seemingly radical question could be raised, viz., whether it would be profitable for the correct understanding of the "Easter" event to drop the "resurrection" terminology and, instead, refer to Jesus "to whom Easter has happened" as the "Living One," as Schillebeeckx does in the subtitle of the Dutch edition (pp. 391, 396).

Support for such a radical proposal is present in W. Marxsen, "The Ressurection of Jesus as a Historical and Theological Problem," in C. F. D. Moule, ed., *The Significance of the Message of the Resurrection for Faith in Jesus Christ* (London: SCM Press, 1968): "We speak thoughtlessly of the appearances of the *Risen One* without bearing in mind that he who was seen, namely Jesus, could be designated as the Risen One only as the result of reflection." The question can be raised "whether we ought not to speak more correctly of the appearances of *Jesus*" (p. 34), and this may entail that "I need no longer accept the concept of 'the Risen one' unreservedly, but must speak of the 'Living one'" (p. 40) author's emphasis). In the *Gospel of Thomas* Jesus is indeed designated as the "Living One." (See J. M. Robinson and H. Koester, *Trajectories through Early Christianity* [Philadelphia: Fortress Press, 1971], p. 173.)

Finally, it is a little puzzling that few theologians, when writing on the "(Risen) Living One," do not mention more incisively that the experience of Jesus' being alive was indeed great good news for the (Jewish) disciples, because of the then prevailing uncertainty about "life after death" (cf. *Jesus*, pp. 518-523).

[24]Schillebeeckx has bitterly complained that his view of the "resurrection" has been misinterpreted, as if it meant only a subjective experience of the disciples and not something that objectively happened to Jesus ("Resurrection and Faith Experience," p. 89, and "Mystery of Iniquity," pp. 19-20). He attributes this in part to his own inconsistency in writing sometimes simply "appearances," although his intention is to treat them as "stories," or "accounts," or "traditions," or even "experiences" of appearances ("Resurrection and Faith Experience," p. 90, n. 1, and "Mystery of Iniquity," p. 21, n. 28). To avoid such misunderstandings, he has made some clarifications in the third Dutch edition, specifically by adding a new section, "The intrinsic significance of Jesus' resurrection for salvation" (*Jesus*, pp. 644-650). In the two articles Schillebeeckx specifies that "appearances" and "resurrection experience" are identical, while admitting that discussion is

"objective" or "subjective" seeing (ibid., and p. 346). He does not see in the recounted "Christ appearances a sort of condensation of various pneumatic experiences within the primitive local congregations" (p. 382), let alone with the Apostles themselves. His reason is that "in the gospel accounts the apostles have already come together *before* the appearances" (p. 385), so that in equating the "appearances" with actual events one is "postulating what has to be demonstrated," one is already "presupposing the existence of the 'gathered congregation'" (pp. 382, 538).

Similarly, the accounts of the empty tomb assume the fact of the reassembled community. The story of the visit to the empty tomb "points to a practice of venerating the tomb of Jesus at Jerusalem." Although the tomb motif is a rather early datum, the story of the (visit to the) empty tomb must therefore be of a more recent date (pp. 334-337).[25]

Eschatological Prophet and Later Christological Definitions

In Part Three Schillebeeckx energetically chooses for the thesis that the early church (in its quest for the identification of Jesus, the Crucified-and-Risen One) found a model in which "they recognized a full reflection of Jesus," viz.,

---

possible about the *original* content" of the "appearance experiences." Cf. *Jesus*: "The New Testament suggests an undeniably intrinsic connection between Jesus' resurrection and the Christian, faith-inspired experiences at Easter, expressed in the model of 'appearances'" (p. 645). The words "stories," "accounts," etc. (and other words too) are often italicized in the Dutch edition, because in Dutch writing italicizing is quite customary, but this is less often done in English, as in the present English edition. With a view to the subtlety with which Schillebeeckx treats the issue of the "appearances"(!), it may be regrettable that the Dutch word "verschijning" is translated as both "appearance" and "manifestation"; the switch is made even within one and the same sentence, as on p. 382, lines 3 and 4.

[25]It is striking how little attention is given by the "respectable" new theologians to the question which is burning on the tongue of the ordinary Christian: "What happened to the body (corpse) of Jesus?" By their silence they seem to deny that "resurrection" means "*bodily* resurrection." Their main concern seems to be the "negative" one of rejecting the Jewish notion of a "re-animation of a body" (cf. *Jesus*, p. 336). Re-animation would fit into the "objective" interpretation of the appearance stories, one which is rejected by Schillebeeckx. Nevertheless another issue seems to be overlooked, viz., that of the preservation of the body of Jesus, which body had been (is?) instrumental in our salvation (cf. St. Thomas, *Summa Theologica*, part three, question 51, article 3; cf. ibid. q. 19, art. 1). An interesting solution is offered by John A. T. Robinson, in *The Human Face of God* (Philadelphia: Westminster Press, 1971), pp. 135-141, who speaks of the body disappearing because of its not being sustained anymore by the "spirit" of Jesus. A more intelligible solution (because the body is preserved) is found in Xavier Léon-Dufour, *Resurrection and the Message of Easter* (New York: Holt, Rinehart and Winston, 1974): "The body placed in the tomb does not simply return to the universe . . . but is wholly taken up by the living Christ who transforms the universe by integrating it to himself" (p. 241). This theory could be made more "concrete" by seeing the "beyond" as consisting of "unknown dimensions or perspectives within a universe of which we apprehend only the one aspect which is in tune with our own organo-psychic structure" (Gabriel Marcel, *Mystery of Being*, 2 vols. [Chicago: Regnery, 1960], vol. 2, "Faith and Reality," p. 176).

that of the "eschatological prophet" (p. 473). The thesis that in his life on earth Jesus soon became viewed as the "eschatological prophet" is "one of the basic propositions of this book" (p. 245).[26] The notion of the "eschatological prophet" came into Jewish circulation shortly before the time of Christ (pp. 480-482). This "latter-day prophet" was thought of as one who is filled with the Spirit of God, bringing glad tidings to the poor, according to the lines of Ex. 23:20-23 (pp. 441 and 486). Several indications of the "historical" correctness of this view are listed (pp. 475-480).

The discussion of the eschatological-prophet theme was preceded by the presentation of four early credal modes which came to be merged in the canonical gospels, viz., the so-called *Parousia, Theios anèr,* Wisdom, and "Easter" Christologies; each expressed a facet of the life of the earthly Jesus (pp. 403-440). Common to all these creeds is "their identification of Jesus with the latter-day prophet—the basic creed of all Christianity" (p. 440).

It is also from the notion of eschatological prophet that the three main titles ascribed by the early Church to Jesus were deduced as if by a process of logical reasoning, viz., Lord, Messiah (Christ), and Son of God. These titles had been bestowed before upon figures in Jewish history, "figures from the dim and distant past," but all this is now "being said at a moment when many friends and companions of Jesus are still living" (p. 474). First, it was a Jewish tradition that any prophet or messenger who had faithfully delivered the word of God, had eventually the name proper to God bestowed on him, viz., *Lord* (pp. 487-491). Second, the eschatological prophet who was filled with the Spirit of God ("anointed") could be called *Messiah,*[27] in Greek: the *Christ* (pp. 491-497). A third traditional Jewish term used to designate the faithful prophet-messenger was *Son of God* (pp. 491-499). Schillebeeckx carefully explains, however, that it was not this title by itself which eventually gave rise to the dogma that God and Jesus are related in an ontological Father-Son relationship (cf. p. 557).

So far, we have seen Schillebeeckx giving us a Christology "from below" (p. 570), and it all makes "logical" sense; it is "intelligible" (cf. p. 33). Readers who favor such a "low" Christology of the "intratestamentary" time (p. 35) are in for a surprise when they find Schillebeeckx, further in Part Three (pp. 545-571) and in Part Four (pp. 626-669), wholeheartedly embracing the "high" Christology of Nicea and Chalcedon. Schillebeeckx does admit that the defini-

---

[26]The identification of Jesus with the eschatological prophet is "most likely—though perhaps only as a question ('Is he the coming One?')—a pre-Easter datum" (p. 440). In view of the centrality of the notion of (eschatological) prophet, it seems "wrong, therefore, that in many exegetical surveys of Jesus' titles that of 'Jesus as prophet' is often brought in at the end, is usually put low on the list and furthermore is regarded as somehow defective or inadequate" (p. 479).

[27]In another section Jesus is presented as the "messianic son of David," whereas the Christian interpretation is shown to have rejected "the dynastic messianism of the house of David" (pp. 499-515; cf. pp. 450-459). But "when the title 'son of David' is applied to Jesus, this does not derive from remembered facts or genealogical trees, whether of Joseph's family or of Mary's" (p. 502).

tions of these councils are based on one particular strand in the New Testament, namely, the Johannine, and that this constitutes a break with pre-Nicene Christological pluralism (pp. 436, 570). But he adds that this indeed one-sided development, once it had taken place, cannot be undone (p. 571).

In a later article Schillebeeckx assures us that such a reader's surprise is legitimate.[28] He informs us that the Christological section of Part Four was indeed added to the book as what he calls a "systematic insert."[29] He did this as a temporary measure in order not to disturb the faithful and before he could explore more fully a historico-genetical Christological project in a second (and perhaps) third book. Stating that the question of the "divinity" of Jesus can be, but need not be, a wrong question, he now seems basically to repeat a passage in *Jesus* as being the proper description of who and what Jesus is:

> Human pro-existence (or shared humanity), but proceeding from God and to the praise of God. To that end Jesus is filled with God's Spirit and his very existence as a man is wholly the work of God's Spirit.
>
> Whatever new name (or names) we can and may think up for Jesus, those two aspects will have to be in them, if we still want to be talking about the Jesus of the gospels, and thus, having regard to the conspicuous fidelity of the gospels to the norm and criterion of the earthly Jesus, about the historical Jesus of Nazareth—him and none other. (pp. 557-558)

In the later article Schillebeeckx claims that such a view "may not be taken as Christological agnosticism."[30]

In a similar vein the present writer expressed his surprise to Schillebeeckx, after the publication of the Dutch edition, about the fact that the (Holy) Spirit is introduced without any previous discussion of the biblical data, so that the "classical" doctrine of the Trinity can then simply be presented (p. 661). In this instance, too, Schillebeeckx shows his desire not to deviate from tradition (unless he has the occasion to explain such a move more fully!). He did this in answering the following question:

> Would a "binity" of Father and Jesus, the Son, be more "acceptable," and not all that untraditional when we keep in mind, on the one hand, the biblical usage which mainly speaks of the Spirit of Jesus who is the Spirit of God, the Father, and, on the other hand,

---

[28]"Toward a Christology," pp. 152-156.

[29]Section Three: "Jesus, parable of God and paradigm of humanity," ch. 1: "God's saving action in history" and ch. 2: "The Christological problem" (pp. 626-669). One section in ch. 2 (pp. 644-650) was added in the third Dutch edition; see n. 24.

[30]One wonders whether, as the translator would have put it, a Nicean-cum-Chalcedonian believer (cf. the headings in the English edition on p. 450 and p. 456) will be able to accept this.

the Augustinian explanation of the Spirit as the bond of love
between the Father and the Son—so not so much a "third"[31] as an
in-between"?

Schillebeeckx replied:

> "Binity" has indeed something in its favor. But both Binity and
> Trinity continue to have their problems. There I wished simply—in a
> sensible way—to remain faithful to the "great Christian tradition."
> I do not speak of an essence-trinity of *persons* BEFORE the Incarna-
> tion! But [I do maintain] that this name (Trinity), which can be
> used exclusively from the time of the Incarnation, has *something*
> corresponding to it IN God, which we cannot name *as such*![32]

Unique Universality of Jesus

The first two sections of Part Four, under the possibly misleading title
"Who do we say that he is?" examines very critically the "unique universality"
of Jesus.[33] If Schillebeeckx himself could think that "some effort may well be
needed" to follow sections of Part Three, what must one think, then, of the
style of writing in these two sections, of which a chapter heading such as this
one is fairly representative: "A conjunctural horizon of ideas and non-
synchronous rhythm in the complex transformation of culture" (p. 576)? The
solution offered to safeguard both the uniqueness and universality of Jesus and
of Christianity is very "ecumenical" toward the non-Christian religions, a feat
which is accomplished by introducing the notion of the *humanum* (p. 606).
Schillebeeckx is further true to form regarding his idea of the primacy of the
"history of evil" when he writes in this context:

> So the question of the universal significance of Jesus of Nazareth
> finds its proper context within the universal horizon of understand-
> ing which, although in itself resistant to theorizing, is included (as a
> logical implication) in negative contrast experiences and in particular
> experiences of meaning . . . (p. 619).[34]

---

[31]Cf. Thomas Aquinas: "The (three divine) persons are not formally distinct as persons
but as in origin antithetical relations" (p. 663). For references, see p. 657 and p. 735, n. 58.
See also *Summa Theologica*, I, q. 30, art. 1, ad 4; art. 2, ad 5; art. 3, and 2.

[32]Personal communication (see n. 17); the various emphases are the author's.

[33]The title seems to have been influenced by the "Christological insert," which has been
added to this Part.

[34]"Contrast experiences" are the "negative" experiences of evil and suffering (p. 20).

Jesus' Abba *Experience*

In regard to the Christian's attempt to "understand" Jesus Schillebeeckx places a great value on what he calls Jesus' "*Abba* experience." This idea is discussed in two separate places, in Part Two (pp. 256-269) and in Part Four, where it forms a part of the (added) Christological "insert" (pp. 652-669).

The first discussion is a respectful attempt at reconstructing a "psychology" of Jesus, with the help of many exegetical data. "Jesus' familial expression for God, *Abba*, points to a religious experience of deep intimacy with God" (p. 263), who is "bent upon humanity" (p. 267). This *Abba* experience is "the soul, source and ground of Jesus' message, praxis and ministry as a whole," as it was given "substantive content by Jesus' actions and way of life" (p. 266). The deepest reason why Jesus adopted such an attitude was that he apprehended God as the "power of the benevolent 'anti-evil' one who says no to all that is bad and hurtful to human beings" (p. 268). Here and elsewhere Schillebeeckx heavily emphasizes that Jesus was not a mere humanitarian, because his "motivation" for "doing good" was derived from his *Abba* experience: "That is why trying to delete the special 'relation to God' from the life of Jesus at once destroys his message and the whole point of his way of living" (ibid.).

In the second discussion, which is of a more speculative nature, the *Abba* experience is regarded as explaining Jesus' creaturely status:

> The human being aware of his creatureliness apprehends himself to be pure gift of God. Because of the totally unprecedented depth of Jesus' experience (of himself as gift of God, the Father) the faith of the Church . . . proceeded to call Jesus 'the Son,' thereby specifying Jesus' creaturely relation to God. (p. 655)

The "historical" ground for speaking like this is found in the gospels which show Jesus transferring the epicenter of his life to God, the Father (p. 655), and as "constitutively 'allo-centric': orientated upon the Father" (p. 658). From this the "theological" conclusion is drawn:

> Jesus' unique turning to the Father in absolute priority is "preceded" and supported by the absolute turning of the Father to Jesus: and this self-communication is precisely what early Christian tradition calls "the Word." (p. 666; cf. p. 658)

How to Be an (Ecumenical) Christian

The Ecumenical Christ

Schillebeeckx' original intention with his book was "to bridge the gap between academic theology and the concrete needs of the ordinary Christian" (Foreword). He admits defeat in this respect when he expresses the hope that others will "translate" his pastoral intentions (p. 40).[35] A good Jesus-book for the ordinary Christian would be an ecumenical gift of the first order. For if Christianity is based on the historical Jesus of Nazareth, then any book presenting the so-called "authentic" Jesus (cf. p. 34) can function as the most fundamental ecumenical statement of unity. If Christ is the one foundation of all Christian churches, then:

> the ecumenical and institutional recognition of "one Christian faith" is a primary and pressing stipulation—recognizing oneself in a differently constituted but real Christianity. And then—remembering the plural yet fundamentally one Christianity of the "New Testament"— I think that we cultivate and cherish divisions where to judge from the New Testament they are no longer tenable. (p. 672)

For Catholics in particular this would require that they stop talking about their renewed Vatican-II Church and go a little further back, beyond Trent, to the historical Founder of Christianity. Moreover, recovery of the one authentic Jesus will appeal, as was mentioned in the beginning of the article, to alienated Christians and to the many "anonymous Christians" who are "to be found primarily within the churches" (p. 672). Recovery of the authentic Jesus will also purify the churches themselves, for

> I must persist in putting it on record that, through a lack of well-grounded information, a lot of people fall into an "overbearing" style of Christian belief, overbearing and even un-Christian in its absolutist claims, so alien to Jesus and his gospel. Much passes for "Christian" that for anyone conversant with the New Testament in a spirit of study and prayer turns out to be essentially un-Christian (pp. 35-36).

It would be a daring ecumenical venture to have a movie made about the authentically human Jesus (but who is also a Jesus intimately close to God), as portrayed by Schillebeeckx and Küng,[36] instead of the "insipid trivialities which are offered under the guise of 'religious films.'"[37] This would be "daring," for anyone familiar with the level of "intelligible" Christological discourse in most churches will ask the God of Jesus to have pity on the priest or preacher who proclaims the unabbreviated "Jesus and his gospel." This is the paradox of present-day Christianity: scholars are beginning to discover the authentic Jesus who is so much more inspiring than the "celestial" Jesus of the churches;[38] yet

---

[35]Bas van Iersel, "Onontbeerlijke prolegomena tot een verhaal over Jezus (Indispensable Prolegomena for a Story about Jesus)," *Kosmos & Oekumene*, vol. 8, no. 7 (1974), p. 179, and Gabriel Smit in the Dutch daily *De Volkskrant*, September 7, 1974.

[36]A challenging highpoint in such a film would be to portray Küng's masterful dramatic description of Jesus' abandonment on the cross (*On Being a Christian*, pp. 339-342).

[37]Cf. Michael S. Bird, "Film as Hierophany," *Horizons*, vol. 6, no. 1 (Spring, 1979), p. 91.

[38]The terms "unabbreviated (Jesus)" and "celestial (Jesus)" are used in "Resurrection and Faith Experience," pp. 81 and 82.

proclaiming this Jesus, the Crucified One, will be considered radical, dangerous, because it may offend (disturb?) the ideological sensibilities of many Christians.

God's One Message in Jesus

In his ecumenical Jesus-venture Schillebeeckx wanted "to look critically into the intelligibility for man of Christological belief in Jesus, especially in its origin" (p. 33). To this end we are invited to look for "traces in the life of Jesus that, for us as for the disciples, could constitute an invitation to assent in faith to what is indeed God's great work of salvation in Jesus of Nazareth" (p. 258). In this enterprise we have to admit to ourselves that "why, in the end, anyone should put their trust in a given person is a mystery" (p. 673). Nevertheless, our act of believing trust in Jesus and in "the authentic non-illusory reality of Jesus' *Abba* experience," although not deriving from "reasonable" motives, can yet adduce sufficient "rational" motives.[39] Searching the book for some such motives, perhaps even the fundamental motive, we discover that two events which for most Christians constitute the "proof" of their faith, fall by the wayside, viz., the "resurrection" itself and the "empty tomb." Whatever legitimation value the resurrection of Jesus has, says Schillebeeckx, it is "totally eschatological," meaning:

> Just as Jesus did, the Christian takes the risk of entrusting himself
> and the vindication of his living to God; he is prepared to receive
> that vindication where Jesus did: beyond death. (p. 643)

The perhaps fundamental motive we are looking for in *Jesus* takes its cue from the paradoxical statement: the "very *Abba* experience was the grand illusion of Jesus' life" (p. 260). But how, then, can this Jesus still be "God's great act of salvation in this world" (p. 258)? Schillebeeckx seems to suggest the final answer in the form of a dilemmatic question, the second half of which appears to be answered in the affirmative throughout the book:

> The question is whether the visible presence of God, to be tested by
> empirically registrable facts, is the final word, or whether God does
> not mean to give us his ultimate message through Jesus' ultimate
> acceptance of his life's destiny and reconciliation to it. (pp. 317-
> 318)

For when Jesus "came face to face with death—not comprehending it, perhaps, but as a heartfelt conviction" (p. 542), at "the moment also of God's own silence" (p. 643), Jesus gave

---

[39]The Dutch edition has two different words ("redelijk" and "rationeel"), which are rendered by the same English word "rational" (p. 637). Cf. p. 639, where two different Dutch words with a similar meaning are appropriately translated as "rational" and "rationalistic"; the latter word would come closer to the sense intended by Schillebeeckx with his use of "redelijk" (reasonable).

the last word to well-being and goodness, because the Father is greater than all our suffering and grief and greater than our inability to experience the deepest reality as in the end a trustworthy gift. (p. 625)

For Christians who believe but do not see, this "is the heart of the Christian message" (p. 639); this is "God's message in Jesus" (p. 636; cf. pp. 143, 301). A *theologia crucis* (a theology *of* the cross) is replaced by a *theologia ex cruce*, a message *from* the cross. Jesus invites and inspires all "to put one's trust gladly in God" (p. 204).[40]

Orthopraxis

Jesus preached and, prepared in prayer, put into practice what he preached. Christians are to follow after the full Jesus. Ortho*doxy* alone is not enough. This applies also to theologians, says Schillebeeckx in *The Understanding of Faith*:

> When a theologian such as Paul van Buren, for example, says . . . that Christ is our unique rule of life, then the really orthodox meaning of his statement . . . is partly dependent on the influence that it has on his actual life.[41]

With regard to the church as a whole Schillebeeckx is not overly optimistic: "what a rare event among Christians, even, is the consistent praxis of the kingdom of God," he writes in one of the last pages of the book (p. 673).

Schillebeeckx puts the question: "What do Jesus' message and praxis have to contribute to the overall effort to liberate humanity in the full sense of the term?" (p. 623). This would mean, to mention a more specific area, that, to say the least, one must be aware of and concerned about the socio-economic reality of the world, of one's own country. The "socio-political relevance of the gospel"[42] is one of the main thrusts of his *Justice and Love*. In a recent article he accuses Western society of "utilitarian individualism" and implicitly condemns the (American) Protestant ethic which he calls the "Nixon Myth."[43]

In *Jesus* Schillebeeckx repeatedly mentions Jesus' association with the outcasts and the oppressed. Who are the outcasts today in the U.S.A.? In Schillebeeckx' Christological thinking this question has to be asked, and answered: therefore, let the theologians lay aside their academic tomes for a moment, let the church-goers close their hymn-books, and let all come down to the wretched of the country, as did the Son of God. One example has to suffice, made in America where according to some statistics ten million people go to bed

---

[40]The motto in the book opposite the title page is 1 Thess. 4:13: "That you may not grieve as others do who have no hope" (cf. p. 639).

[41](New York: Seabury, 1974), p. 69.

[42]"Toward a Christology," p. 149.

[43]Ibid., pp. 146-147.

hungry and an additional twenty-five million live in real poverty.[44] Is this so because, since they live in "the best of social structures" (cf. p. 624), it must be their own fault? Of is the political system such that, if Adam Smith is still correct, "for one very rich man, there must be at least five hundred poor"?[45]

Christians who refuse to face this issue are requested by Schillebeeckx not to read his book, which he intends to have "practical and critical effect," as we read in the concluding paragraph of the whole book (p. 674). To give one concrete example (the gospel is concrete): how many Christians know that the implication of a proposed welfare reform aimed at bringing all families to at least sixty-five percent of the poverty level is that the really needy will get a little over half of what they minimally need? American Christians, even more so than the Athenians in Isocrates' time, should, in what should be perhaps the most urgent ecumenical concern, come to regard "poverty among their fellow-citizens as their own disgrace."[46]

What would the "Jesus of Schillebeeckx" say when he would see hunger in one (perhaps the only one) of the richest countries of the First World? Schillebeeckx himself, who would be as stunned as are many Americans on hearing about the extent and cause of "Poverty U.S.A.,"[47] would undoubtedly have a one-word exclamation: "un-Christian" (cf. p. 36), a total abdication of Christian ecumenical responsibility.

---

[44]Theological journals find it apparently unacademic to discuss these subjects, which were very crucial to Jesus. A notable exception is the *Journal of Ecumenical Studies*, vol. 14, no. 4 (Fall, 1977): John C. Raines, "Religious Liberty and Social Inequality" (pp. 677-680).

[45]*An Inquiry into the Nature and Causes of the Wealth of Nations*, quoted in *Reflections on Inequality*, ed. Stanislav Andreski (New York: Barnes & Noble, 1975), p. 53.

[46]*Isocrates* (Cambridge: Harvard University Press), 3 vols., vol. 2, *Areopagiticus*, no. 32.

[47]Cf. Mariellen Procopio and Frederick J. Perella, *Poverty Profile USA* (New York: Paulist Press, 1976).

ON BEING A CHRISTIAN

Werner H. Kelber

At one point in this massive study the author recollects Pope John XXIII who, when addressing Catholic canonists, suggested digging a tunnel through the mountain of theological interpretations and ordinances which had come to stand in the way between God and humanity. In his new book, *On Being a Christian* (translated by Edward Quinn [Garden City: Doubleday, 1976], 720 pp.), Hans Küng has fulfilled the wish of Pope John.

This book constitutes a summary presentation of Christian history, faith, and life in the light of modern culture. In the first part Küng places Christianity against the horizon of post-Christian humanisms and world religions. Against secular one-dimensionality he expounds the God question, forging a middle road between natural and dialectical theology. In the second part the author develops the distinctive feature of Christian faith, i.e., the activation of the memory of Jesus. The third and major part is devoted to Jesus. Set apart from Sadducean establishment, Zealotic revolutionaries, Essene emigration, and Pharisaic compromise, Jesus is seen as an itinerant preacher and charismatic healer above all party politics. As representative of lawbreakers and outlaws he raised fundamental questions about religion, without founding a new religion, let alone a church. Among the numerous aspects discussed in this part are the ethics of poverty, miracles, Kingdom message, execution, resurrection, Pauline interpretation, demythologizing, Spirit, Mary, Trinity, and Church. Overall, part three demonstrates the transition of a Christology "from below" to Christologies "from above." In the fourth part Küng outlines the implications of Jesus' life and death for modern people. Jesus' message of "a God with a human face" (p. 308) is developed into a program designed to restore the humanity of human beings.

In a work of such magnitude it is not difficult to single out flaws. One may regret that the author has not explored more deeply the significance of myth in the New Testament. The historical concreteness of Jesus is exploited to the detriment of myth, and the issue of myth and history is as unresolved as ever before. Should not a book preeminently concerned with the redemption of humankind have given more space to modern women's struggle for justice and dignity inside and outside the churches? One wonders whether Küng has not underplayed the political implications of Jesus' life and death. Now that we have acknowledged the kerygmatic nature of the gospels, most and quite possibly all of which were composed after A.D. 70, it seems indeed plausible that their authors camouflaged the politically most disturbing aspects of Jesus. One feels uneasy about Küng's explanation of the juridical trend of Latin Western theology in terms of "a re-Judaizing process in the name of Christianity" (p. 421). One wonders why the social encyclicals are not consulted, and one is amazed at the absence of any reference to, or appropriation of the work of, Bernard Lonergan.

Yet none of these points can seriously affect the stupendous achievement of Küng's latest work. It is cause for rejoicing without end. One appreciates his unflinching support of biblical, historical, and theological inquiries, of a critical questing in which he has proved himself a courageous and creative leader. One respects his careful attention to questions asked by conservatives and his frequent impatience with the answers provided by the progressives. He correctly observes the inadequacy of the traditional Protestant triple-office Christology in view of the christological pluralism in the New Testament. His relentless criticism of Roman authoritarianism and ecclesiastical paternalism is as much to the point as his rebuke of Luther's anti-Judaic, Reformation fanaticism, Protestants' indifference toward their churches, and "the dogmatic repression of the problem of religion by Karl Barth and 'dialectical theology'" (p. 111). A deep concern for social justice and a moving reflection on the conditions of South America are combined with a sober reservation toward political theologies and uncritical modernism. This latter point, unmistakably derived from Karl Barth's political ethic, will not win Küng the approval of radical theologians, but it is prudently designed to prevent Christianity from lapsing into the trap of ideologies. Throughout, Küng calls the Church and the churches away from the exercise of power as domination and back to "the exercise of power as service" (p. 487), reminding hierarchs and theologians that it was and is the humble folk who are likely to uphold the faith. The application of justification by works to the modern achievement and consumer society (pp. 581-590) is a piece of exquisite brilliance. After Auschwitz and Hiroshima one reads with keen interest the section on "God and Suffering" (pp. 428-436). Showing the limitations of philosophical and theological theodicies, including Jürgen Moltmann's recent inner-Trinitarian thesis, Küng reflects on Jesus' "senseless" death as the paradigm of suffering which encompasses—rather than explains—the sufferings of humankind.

Throughout this book Küng exhibits a rare mastery over biblical criticism and New Testament theology, philosophical and historical theology, church history and ethics, and the history of religion and cultural history. The result is a composition of systematic coherence and intrinsic plausibility. Unlike conventional theological ambition, however, Küng has had the courage not to give us another great system. All data are placed at the service of a reactivation of the biblical message for twentieth-century man and woman. He returns us to the New Testament which "remains (fortunately) the unchangeable norm for all later proclamation and theology in the Church" (p. 466), and he refreshes our memory of what Christianity was meant to be. The *proprium Christianum* is not the Christ of higher christological mathematics, but the Jesus of Nazareth, the Galilean killed in the capital, a man "not backed by any party or authorized by any tradition" (p. 278), who paid the ultimate price for his scandalous message and demonstration of humanity.

Küng's work is remarkably free of such habitual vices as cheap apologetics, unreflected skepticism toward the sciences, or theological sleight of hand. There is not a trace of faddism—a rare feat in our time and culture. A profound sense of honesty and humanity permeates this book from start to finish.

Reference must also be made to the artistic quality of this work. This reviewer has read the book in both the German and the English versions. Küng's German is brisk, lucid, and of unpretentious clarity. One further acknowledges Walter Jens, his colleague in Tübingen and a nationally known author and professor of German literature, who has given extensive advice on matters of style and substance. Last but not least, there is the unsung hero in our modern communications world, the translator. Edward Quinn deserves our warm congratulations for a faithful and beautiful rendering accomplished within a very short time.

On Being a Christian is not only one of Küng's masterpieces, but it will rank among the theological classics of the twentieth century.

DOES GOD EXIST?

Leonard Swidler

If there needs to be a clinching argument that all serious students of religion must know German, Hans Küng has just provided it with his latest book, *Does God Exist?*,[1] published Spring, 1978. (This 878-page book—first printing: 100, 000 copies—is not to be confused with the 394-page book *Nothing but the Truth*[2]—first printing: 50,000 copies—published three weeks earlier.) It is a magnificent analysis of the fundamental issues surrounding the question of the existence of God and their far-reaching implications.

As in his book *On Being a Christian*, Küng clearly takes the problems generated in modern times extremely seriously. The reader gets the distinct feeling that the conclusions were not foregone when Küng started wrestling with these issues—and s/he is right. Küng ends up agreeing with many of the central criticisms of modern thought on the God question. The reader also senses that here is a sure guide who has gone through the modern circle of flame surrounding God, one who, like all thinking men and women today has also been struck at the very core of his being by the arguments of contemporary thought and science against the existence of God, but who, unlike most of us, by dint of a penetrating analysis and massive research has grappled with those problems—and solved them.

But on top of that—and this is one of his greatest strengths—Küng has an incredible ability to communicate his analyses and resolutions in limpid clarity that is also utterly convincing. Time and again this reader found himself saying: "Yes, yes! But of course! Absolutely! So that's what that means; now I see it!" and the like. By an often neglected key touchstone I would judge this book to be *good* theology for it "makes sense" to me as I experience contemporary human life. It rings true to life. It helps to explain my experience to me, rather than provide some formulas from the outside that are supposed to "explain" reality, but really do not—if I am honest with myself.

But such clarity, such empathetic power with modern women and men is not, strangely enough, seen by everyone as an unmixed blessing. With the prodding of Rome the German bishops have been hounding Küng in the wake of his similarly clear and empathetic book *On Being a Christian* (over 160,000 German copies sold). The giveaway remark was made by Cardinal Hermann Volk: *Das Buch ist mir zu plausibel!* (To me the book is too plausible!)

Anyone who reads the acknowledgements and the footnotes (ninety-one pages) in *Does God Exist?* will see how untiringly Küng has worked at the almost overwhelming task of research he set for himself, including engaging in extensive discussions, colloquia, and seminars with colleagues in a great variety of disciplines, including biochemistry and astrophysics. In fact, it is due to one

---

[1]*Existiert Gott?* (Munich: Piper Verlag, 1978).
[2]*Um Nichts als die Wahrheit*, ed. Walter Jens (Munich: Piper Verlag, 1978).

of Küng's most valuable—and rare—talents that he was able to accomplish this massive undertaking: the ability to organize and direct research. Most American professors would be exhausted simply by trying to keep the nine persons mentioned in Küng's acknowledgments busy. Küng obviously reverses the process and arranges things so as to release his energies to do what only the scholar-author can: absorb information, think, and write.

But no one works as hard as does Küng himself. Not only does he read, think, discuss, and finally write every word himself, he re-writes his text frequently to produce not only the desired overall structure and conceptual clarity but also the most felicitous style. This latter is terribly important, much more than most plodding professors are aware of, or at least are willing to admit. It is a significant reason why Küng's ideas reach and influence so many people. It is also a significant reason why serious students of religion should learn German. The German of *Existiert Gott?* (and *Christsein*) is conceptually and rhetorically beautiful. Naturally no translation can capture the total power of that beauty. It is also the easiest-to-read scholarly German I have ever come across—so, religion students of German, take heart.

Like all good contemporary theology *Does God Exist?* is presented within an historical matrix, focusing on the major thought patterns of modern Western history as exemplified in break-through thinkers, starting naturally with Descartes, and moving on through Pascal, Spinoza, Kant, Hegel, Feuerbach, Marx, Nietzsche, Freud, Adorno, Horkheimer, Heidegger, Wittgenstein, and others. Important personal, social, and intellectual historical information is painstakingly presented after obviously thorough-going research. In fact, as someone who has spent many years formally studying and teaching intellectual history I find this dimension of Küng's work extremely insightfully done and immensely helpful. Küng clearly penetrated very sympathetically to the heart of the thought of these giant thinkers—no mean feat—and equally clearly and sympathetically presented and analyzed their thought, carefully drawing out its significance for the question at hand—the God question.

After presenting each thinker's ideas *in optimam partem*, affirming and absorbing everything in them he can find that is helpful, negatively or positively, Küng also poses fundamental questions about problems, lacks, misperceptions, and contradictions he may discern therein. He does not set up straw figures to demolish with preconceived ready answers. He enters into the mind of each of his interlocuters and is often much persuaded by them—which of course he should be, lest we are prepared to call the world that was so influenced by them fools—a presumptuous position too many theologians, and others, have been willing to take. However, at the same time Küng is never simply swept along with the latest idea or hero. Everything is sifted very precisely and purposefully before it is accepted in whole or part or rejected.

Does God Exist? is divided into two large parts. The first half of the book is devoted basically to an historical presentation and analysis of modern thought and its problems concerning the understanding of God and whether or not God exists, and whether that existence, or ultimately anything else in the world, can be known by humans. The second half of the book is basically Küng's—affirmative—response to the fundamental questions: Can we know reality? Does God exist? But even in the latter half of the book Küng also systematically deals with the great post-Nietzsche thinkers of the twentieth century.

Küng starts his analysis of the modern God question with the seventeenth-century Descartes, whose thought he sees as a "Copernican turning point," whereby "the locus of foundational certitude is shifted from God to humanity. That means, no longer the medieval movement from the certitude about God to the certitude about one's self, but rather the modern movement from certitude about one's self to certitude about God!"[3] Descartes placed reason, the *cogito*, "clear and distinct ideas," etc. at the basis of all human knowledge—massively influencing all subsequent Western thought and the posing of the God question.

Whereas Descartes believed he proved the existence of God with his own reasoning, his younger contemporary and similarly brilliant mathematical genius, Pascal, argued that reason alone was incapable of *proving* the existence of God but was capable only of showing the reasonableness of *believing* in God's existence—hence his famous recommendation that it is wise to *wager* in favor of the existence of God. Put in other terms, Descartes argued that at the basis of our knowledge is reason, whereas Pascal said belief was at its ultimate basis: I understand so that I can believe (*intelligo ut credam*), or I believe so I can understand (*credo ut intelligam*).

This profound epistemological argument between the exponents of reason and of belief, between rationalists and fideists, or existentialists, continued into the present, reaching a kind of nadir on one side in Friedrich Nietzsche who expounded the ultimate anti-rational position in radical epistemological nihilism: we have no ineluctably persuasive basis for affirming the validity, the reasonableness of reality, of "being"; why should reality not be seen as ultimately meaningless, absurd, "nothingness" (hence, "nihilism")?

Küng faces this fundamental, and frightening, option squarely; he does not, for example, try one of the short-circuit ploys such as saying: Of course reality is reasonable, otherwise how could you reason that it is unreasonable? Rather, Küng starkly states:

> Nihilism is *possible*. The pervasive questionableness of reality itself makes nihilism possible. . . . *Nihilism is not disprovable*. There is no necessarily convincing argument against the possibility of nihilism. It is even at least possible that this human life is ultimately meaningless, that accident, a blind fate, chaos, absurdity and illusion rules the world, that everything ultimately is ambiguous, meaningless, worthless, nothing.[4]

---

[3]Küng, *Existiert Gott?*, p. 36.
[4]Ibid., pp. 467-468.

That is unflinchingly looking ultimate terror in the eye. However, Küng coolly adds that *"nihilism is not provable.* There is no rational argument for the necessity of accepting nihilism. It is even also possible that this human life is ultimately not meaningless, that not only accident, fate, absurdity and illusion rule the world, that by no means is everything ambiguous, meaningless, worthless, and ultimately nothing."[5]

Granting that neither rationalism nor nihilism can logically force the acceptance of its position, we are nevertheless not left with the luxury of shrugging our shoulders, of not making a decision. This is one of those situations where not to decide is to decide: either we accept the meaningfulness of reality—or not. "Here it is *a matter of trust or mistrust* in which without certainty and guarantee I put myself on the line. . . . Either I hold reality to be trustworthy—or not."[6]

Though allowing that a "no" to reality is humanly possible, Küng finds at least three basic reasons which incline men and women toward a "yes" to reality: (1) Humanity is neither oriented toward a "no" to reality nor is it indifferent before the decision: human inclinations, the pull of experience, etc. all draw humanity toward affirming the trustworthiness of reality—though it does not force such an affirmation. (2) An act of basic trust of reality opens one up to reality so that "despite all the ambiguity we experience we see beyond it a hidden identity: reality as 'one'; despite all the senselessness we experience a hidden meaningfulness: reality as 'true'; despite all worthlessness we experience a hidden worth: reality as 'good.' "[7] (3) Unlike a basic mistrust of reality, a basic trust can logically be carried out in practice without self-contradiction. Thus Küng *decides* in favor of basic trust in reality.

However, Küng wishes to find a way to sail between the Scylla of epistemological rationalism and the Charybdis of epistemological irrationalism, existentialism; neither simply reason nor belief is the sole ultimate basis of our knowledge. Rather,

> if I in a consistent manner do not close myself to reality, but rather open myself to its working, if I do not withdraw myself from the light of being but rather dare to give myself over to it, I will thus perceive—*neither before, nor only afterwards,* but in the very act itself—that I am doing the right thing, indeed, "the most rational" thing. For what beforehand is not subject to proof or experience . . . I experience *in the act of trust itself.*[8]

Thus Küng does not opt for a "critical rationalism," a la Karl Popper, who said, "the decision for rationalism cannot be grounded through argument and experience. Although one can discuss them they ultimately rest on an irrational

---

[5]Ibid.
[6]Ibid., p. 485.
[7]Ibid., p. 494.
[8]Ibid., p. 496.

decision, on a belief in reason."[9] Rather, Küng chooses what he calls "critical rationality" in which his fundamental "yes" to reality is

> neither something rationally provable nor irrationally unexaminable, but something more than rational, namely, a *supra-rational* trust which is precisely so rationally responsible that it is not something irrational but rather a thorough-going rational wager—which always remains a wager. There is consequently a way between an irrational "uncritical dogmatism" and an ultimately likewise irrationally-based "critical rationalism": the way of critical rationality.[10]

Having thus established a solid basis for human knowledge in a critical rationality founded on an act of basic trust in the meaningfulness of reality, Küng is prepared to address the question of the existence of God. Like the fundamental question of nihilism, this basic question of whether there is an ultimate source and goal for all reality is treated with utter honesty by Küng. He places the discussion within the historical framework in which the modern manifestation of atheism developed from the Age of Enlightenment and then especially the nineteenth century forward, dealing sympathetically with all significant figures involved in modern atheism, particularly Feuerbach, Marx, and Freud.

Of these three intellectual giants of atheism Feuerbach is the most fundamental. Marx and Freud largely follow and refine Feuerbach, who in turn is based on the greatest genius of them all, Hegel (to whom Küng devotes over a hundred pages—down from his 704-page analysis of Hegel's Christology[11]), but in converse form. Küng notes, "It can be seen with Feuerbach how terribly dangerous Hegel's identification of the finite and infinite consciousness, of humanity and divinity, was for belief in God and Christianity. One only need to change the standpoint and everything appears turned around."[12] For Feuerbach "the consciousness of God is the self-awareness of the human being, the knowledge of God is the self-knowledge of the human being. . . . The consciousness of the infinite is nothing other than the consciousness of the infinity of consciousness."[13] In short, God is a psychological projection of the human mind and heart.

Küng accepts the seriousness of the Feuerbachian claim of the human dimension of the God image. But he is not persuaded by the ungrounded reductionist approach of Feuerbach:

> It likewise cannot be excluded ahead of time—contrary to the simple assertion of the atheist—that all these needs, wishes and drives in fact

---

[9]Karl Popper and Herbert Marcuse, *Revolution oder Reform?* ed. F. Stark (Munich, 1971), p. 38.
[10]Küng, *Existiert Gott?*, pp. 498-499.
[11]*Menschwerdung Gottes* (Freiburg, 1970).
[12]Küng, *Existiert Gott?*, p. 231.
[13]Quoted in ibid., pp. 231, 233.

correspond to something real. . . . I can also psychologically derive my experience of the world, but that says nothing against the existence of a world that is independent of me as the correspondence point of my experiences. And I can psychologically *derive my experience of God*, but that *says nothing against the existence of a God that is independent of me* as the correspondence point of all my needs and wishes. In short: my psychological experience can in reality quite well correspond to something real; the wish for a God can quite well correspond to a real God.[14]

In fact, Küng justly turns Feuerbach's analysis back on its author and asks, "Could there not be precisely in Feuerbach's interest (for many understandable reasons) in a decisive atheism the wish that is the father of the thought? Atheism itself the projection of humanity?"[15] The conclusion of the analysis of Feuerbach: "Are perhaps belief in God as well as atheism both incapable of disproof, but also incapable of proof?"[16]

Here *in nuce* is the result of Küng's lengthy, insightful, and appreciative analyses of all the arguments against the existence of God—philosophical, economic, psychological, sociological, and anthropological. They all combine to discredit the logical necessity of the arguments in favor of the existence of God, but at the same time cannot sustain the logical necessity of the atheist position either:

All proofs or demonstrations of the significant atheists are sufficient to make the existence of God questionable, but not sufficient to make the non-existence of God unquestioned: neither a philosophical-psychological (Feuerbach) nor a social-critical (Marx), nor a psychoanalytical (Freud) interpretation of the belief in God can decide about the existence or non-existence of a reality that is independent of our thinking, willing, feeling, of psyche and society. . . . The ever again varying individual or social psychological argumentation that religion is a projection is based methodologically and substantively on an ungrounded postulate: Feuerbach's projection theory, Marx's opium theory, and Freud's illusion theory are incapable of proving that God is only a projection of humanity or only a self-interest-conditioned consolation, or only an infantile illusion. Statements of "only," or of "nothing but," are to be met with mistrust.[17]

As with the fundamental question of the meaningfulness of reality or not, Küng finds the question of the existence of God also one that not only can be neither proved nor disproved, but also that ultimately cannot be avoided, for,

---

[14]Ibid., p. 243.
[15]Ibid., p. 244.
[16]Ibid.
[17]Ibid., pp. 369-370.

"the no to God means an ultimately ungrounded basic trust in reality. . . . Whoever denies God does not know why ultimately s/he trusts reality."[18] As with the meaningfulness of reality, one affirms the existence of God by a free act of reasonable *trust*:

> But as with basic trust so also is the God-trust in no way irrational. If I do not close myself to reality, but open myself to it, if I do not withdraw myself from the primal and final ground, sustainer, and goal of reality, but rather dare to give myself over to it, I will thus perceive—*neither before nor only afterwards*, but *in the very act itself*—that I am doing the right thing, indeed at bottom "the most rational thing." For what *before hand* is not subject to proof I experience in the carrying out, in the act itself of acknowledging knowledge.[19]

Though for Küng and other believers, there is light and resolution in this reasonable God-trust grounded in a basic trust of reality, there can be no complacent setting aside of the God question: "The belief in God vis-à-vis atheism is never made securely unassailable and free of possible crises by rational arguments. The belief in God is always threatened and vis-à-vis pressing doubts must always be realized, persevered in, lived and grappled with in renewed decisions."[20]

Now, with the existence of God affirmed—though ever to be re-affirmed— Küng proceeds in another hundred pages to analyze the concepts of God presented by the world religions, particularly Christianity. For one in a religion department with many non-Christian colleagues it is gratifying to watch Küng's knowledge and sympathetic appreciation of the other great world religions grow and deepen with each of his books, e.g.: "other world religions can also be paths to salvation."[21]

The presentation of the Christian understanding of God is largely a distillation of Küng's book *On Being a Christian*, with some further precisions concerning the nature of Christ. Küng writes, "Jesus 'functions' for me not only as the Word and Son of God, he *is* it, and he is it not only for me, but also in himself."[22] Such *ought* to satisfy the German bishops, who so harried Küng to make such a statement about Jesus *being* the Son of God. But it may well not, given the ultra-conservative mindset of Cardinal Höffner of Cologne, the President of the Conference of German Bishops and chief episcopal antagonist of Küng's, for nowhere does Küng say that Jesus *is* God. But of course he should not, cannot, logically. To say that Jesus is God except in the most analogical (in this case, really metaphorical) sense is either blasphemy or nonsense (or both), for it is to

---

[18]Ibid., p. 627.
[19]Ibid., p. 630.
[20]Ibid., p. 631.
[21]Ibid., p. 686.
[22]Ibid., p. 750.

speak of God (Being) as if s/he were *a* being, and/or of *a* being (Jesus) as if he were Being. To so speak, teach, and preach today (if it was not always) is utterly misleading and a gross disservice to the Gospel of Jesus.

Küng himself sums up the thrust of *Existiert Gott?* in his prefatory remarks:

> Does God exist? We are putting all our cards on the table here. The answer will be: "Yes, God exists." And as human beings in the twentieth century we can certainly reasonably believe in God, even in the Christian God. And perhaps more easily today than a few decades or even centuries ago. For, after so many crises, it is surprising how much has been clarified and how many difficulties in regard to belief in God have been cleared up—even though some people are still not aware of the fact. . . . Some time ago an English Nobel Prize winner is supposed to have answered the question whether he believed in God: "Of course not, I am a scientist." This book is sustained by the hope that a new age is dawning when the very opposite answer will be given: "Of course, I am a scientist."[23]

As this book was in press a new reference to *Existiert Gott?* appeared in print. It was a brief but pertinent statement by Bernard Häring, the world's most renowned Catholic moral theologian, who was not only the teacher and retreat master of popes but also for decades has taught in Rome as well as all around the world. He wrote: "The most recent study on atheism is that of Hans Küng, *Existiert Gott?* . . . It is one of the most profound treatises from a philosophical, psychological, and theological point of view, and perhaps the best of Hans Küng."[24] Such a judgment exists not only in the "free" world, but also in the Communist, for *Existiert Gott?* is translated, read and discussed in Russia,[25] and in the latter half of 1979 Küng, at the invitation of the Chinese government, delivered a lecture on the main theses of the book before the Academy of Science in Peking.[26]

---

[23]Ibid., p. 19.

[24]Bernard Häring, *Free and Faithful in Christ*, vol. II, *The Truth Will Set You Free* (New York: Seabury Press, 1979), p. 378, n. 1.

[25]Heinrich Fries, "Hans Küng–ein Zeuge des christlichen Glaubens," *Süddeutsche Zeitung* (Munich), December 24, 1979.

[26]Hans Küng, "Nine Theses on Religion and Science," *The Kennedy Institute Quarterly Report*, vol. 5, no. 2 (Fall, 1979), pp. 22-26.

EXISTIERT GOTT?

Karl-Josef Kuschel

I

In the near future we can expect the English translation of Hans Küng's most recent book, an extensive 878-page study of the question of God: *Existiert Gott? Antwort auf die Gottesfrage der Neuzeit*. Many readers of Küng's books, including those in America, will ask themselves: How is it possible so soon after the large volume *On Being a Christian* to write another still more extensive book on the question of God? Simply from the technical side, how can it be done? Even Küng's Catholic critics, despite all their misgivings on the content, acknowledge with or without envy, "Küng's book, provided with ninety pages of fine-print scholarly documentation, is first of all an impressive performance. Just the physical strength that stands behind the compilation and conception elicits respect" (Karl Lehman).

In the past not a few critics assumed that in order to write all that he does Küng must employ a whole string of "Research Assistants" whose contributions he then as it were needed only to compile into bulky tomes. Or, bluntly, while Küng acts as if he were the author of his books, they are in fact the work of his assistants—the work of a collective, so to speak.

The facts? As one such Research Assistant who collaborated on the books *On Being a Christian* and *Existiert Gott?* perhaps I can be helpful in preventing misunderstandings and innuendoes and in "disclosing the truth" by reporting on the working technique Küng used in writing his most recent books. Granted that this way of considering a theological book may be somewhat odd—for supposedly it is only the spirit and ideas which are significant, not such earthly and profane matters as writing technique and organization of work—yet why should the question of technique and organization, long considered reasonable in reference to "secular" authors, not be properly directed to theological authors? Moreover, it can be quite fascinating for theologians who have written or plan to write books to have a glimpse behind the scenes of a "prolific writer."

The Catholic critic above was correct, and anyone who was involved knows of what he speaks: the mere physical strength which Küng invests in writing books demands respect. Küng's workday is eighteen or nineteen hours long, and when it is a matter of finishing up a book, the last reserves are mobilized. Nor can we contradict the critic when he says, "A university teacher who besides his daily obligations accomplished such a task in three years not only needs iron energies but also wishes to fulfill a mission." In fact Hans Küng does endure the rigors of writing books principally in the conviction that he must somehow write the book, *must write it now*, at this hour. It is not the fun of being a prolific writer (with books of this scope that "fun" quickly disappears), but rather the conviction that people "outside" both within and without the church await his response, a response which at bottom only he can give, that makes him return again and again, day in and day out, to his desk and perform his "damned duty and obligation."

In this Küng demands much of his co-workers (three academic co-workers and one secretary) in their daily contribution, but most of himself. In writing *Existiert Gott?* the following plan was usually followed. Before a large chapter was begun the entire concept was deliberated upon and the design, execution, and construction of the chapter analyzed and discussed by the circle of co-workers. Then Küng began to write. For many months—from Spring, 1975, till the end of August, 1977—Küng constantly worked from nine in the morning until late at night with one assistant (in this case myself) and a secretary (Dr. Margret Gentner), who was primarily responsible for the typing of the manuscript. My task essentially consisted in commenting critically on and revising the various manuscripts of Küng's work from the viewpoints of literary style and content.

Even before the first typed draft (and only that was presented to me for revision) Küng had written out for himself two or three hand-written drafts in which he gave the first shape to the material which was based on primary and secondary literature. Here lay the real creative process of writing; the various stages of this process can be understood by outsiders only with difficulty and can be described adequately only by the author himself. This hand-written draft was then dictated by Küng into a dictaphone so that the secretary could produce the first typed draft. For Küng dictation is not only a technical expedient in the production of the manuscript; it also has an important function in relation to language and content. The flowing style of Küng's books (and the ease with which they can be understood) is due not least to the "oral testing" of the text by reading it aloud. Again and again Küng and I read the manuscript aloud to one another and through that very process of "listening" were able immediately to pick out complications of both a stylistic and a substantive nature.

This first typed copy was then thoroughly revised and discussed by Küng himself and me for content and language, with Küng deciding which of my corrections he would adopt. Then the secretary made the second typed copy. This copy then as a rule went to the other two academic co-workers, who were also in constant personal contact with Küng. Furthermore, one of them had also taken on special tasks such as communication with libraries for special literature or checking the extensive documentary section of the book. After this, if necessary, a third typed copy was produced.

That all this demanded of the secretary incredible patience—retyping books of more than 700 or 800 pages over and over—cannot be acknowledged sufficiently. Hans Küng has the good fortune to have had such a secretary for many years.

Yet even after all this revision procedure, Küng was still not satisfied. In certain chapters where the systematic theologian ventured into a specialized area foreign to him, the counsel of specialists was sought. As he had done already in *On Being a Christian*, Küng gave parts of the manuscript to his university colleagues from natural science, philosophy, and biblical studies to check. Although this only seldom resulted in major alterations to the text, it sometimes led to important corrections of details. After this, and after several re-readings by Küng himself, the manuscript was sometimes typed for the fourth time.

Several things can be concluded from all this.

1. Hans Küng is a *hard worker*. His books do not drop out of the blue but are the result of day-by-day hard work. The ease of his style and the brilliance of his success should not conceal the fact that Küng works like a galley-slave in writing. Küng forces himself to write his book methodically from the beginning to the end, even if that is often burdensome, in order not to lose the integration of the whole.

2. Küng, with all the audacity of his ideas, is a *careful man*. He writes quickly; formulating his ideas gives him no trouble, but he is a careful "editor." He always declares his manuscript finished only with hesitation; he is not content until all possible objections and doubts, aspects and distinctions of a problem in the text have been considered. Again and again everything is re-examined and then reexamined once more with the help of other literature.

3. Hans Küng has the ability—and not everyone has—to *work with a team*. Of course he can with right and reason claim that he has written his books himself from the first to the last line, but he makes use of constant checking by the co-workers who are his daily dialogue partners from the very beginning. He is able to delegate work (e.g., the literature which must be taken into consideration for a particular problem), but ultimately he retains supervision and control. However, co-workers are not simply presented with completed manuscripts for stylistic-cosmetic operations or for general approval; rather they are responsibly involved in the work process from the very beginning and candidly urged to criticize. This makes collaboration fascinating, but of course exhausting as well; yet no co-worker is able to say that he or she and their opinions were not taken seriously. Criticism and corrections are accepted by Küng with no ifs, ands, or buts if they seem objectively justified; long haggling about formulations he finds tedious, and manuscripts are not "sacred texts" to him but constantly open to revision. When a book is finished, Küng often proudly speaks within the circle of co-workers of "our book," but it is certain that some people will misunderstand the phrase.

4. The *readability and clarity* for which many readers have often praised Küng's books is neither accident nor literary inspiration, but the result of constant self-correction and stylistic struggle. To be sure, Küng—unlike others of his profession—was never a complicated thinker who crammed complicated thoughts into a still more complicated grammar; from the beginning his style was free and flowing. The fact, however, that a published manuscript has gone through at least three, and often four or five, typed versions, to say nothing of the handwritten, is an expression of Küng's additional effort at constant

linguistic-stylistic control. There are many—especially in Germany, where a book must be difficult to read to be considered scholarly—who dismiss this as "journalism," showing that they understand nothing of journalism or of writing. For Küng there is no opposition between scholarship and good style. Complicated sentences make him nervous, abstract theological jargon irritates him, but behind his efforts for style lies a primarily pastoral motive: he wishes theology not only to be read but also to be understood. As a theologian he believes he is responsible to the people for explaining the Christian message clearly to them in their language.

II

Was *Existiert Gott?* necessary? How did it originate? What is its relation to *On Being a Christian*? Many people are unable to suppress a question: "What an odd series! First Hans Küng writes a book *On Being a Christian* and then one on the question of God. Isn't it necessary, if one is a Christian, to presuppose the existence of God?" Well, *Existiert Gott?* was in fact never planned that way by Küng. It —like most of his work—arose out of an "accident," or, to put it better, out of the necessity of unburdening *On Being a Christian*. Küng had originally planned the debate with atheism and nihilism, that is especially with Feuerbach, Marx, Nietzsche and Freud, in Part A II of *On Being a Christian*: The Other Dimension. This part—in the final draft—encompassed about eighty or a hundred pages. But when we read over Part A once more in its entirety, we suddenly noticed (as Prof. Walter Jens had drawn to our attention) that this part was much too long as an introduction. Even without this section it had over a hundred pages, though still conceived as merely an overview of the present economic, social, political, cultural, and religious situation. We saw that it would simply take too long for the reader to push through Parts A and B to the central chapter C on the message of Jesus. For *On Being a Christian* is not intended primarily to offer a discussion of atheism and the question of God but to reply to the quesiton, What is specifically Christian? Who is Jesus Christ? What is Christian behavior? We then decided to withdraw this longer discussion of atheism from *On Being a Christian* and to publish it separately as a small paperback (as an appendix, as it were, to the larger book) under the title *Existiert Gott?* And, in 1974, we hoped to do that in the following year, 1975.

That this was our sincere intention is vouched for in *On Being a Christian* itself. The footnote can still be found in the spot where we took out the section on atheism, p. 611, n. 5: "For the discussion with nihilism, omitted here because of pressure of space, See H. Küng, *Existiert Gott?* Munich 1975" (cf. likewise notes 40 and 50 in the same section). From a little paperback the manuscript grew into a large book, from eighty pages it became 880 pages, from 1975 the publication was moved to 1978. What was to be merely an appendix to *On Being a Christian* developed into an independent book.

Why, for heaven's sake, could Küng not leave it at eighty or a hundred pages? Why did he have to write another such thick volume? The answer is simple: it depends on what plane, on what level, and in what depth one wishes to pursue the debate on atheism and nihilism. It depends on one's degree of readiness to take stands on complex philosophical and theological problems. Thus when in Spring 1975 we began to make preparations for the publication of the little paperback and reviewed the manuscript once again, it seemed to all of us too superficial, too inadequate, too unsubstantiated. The greatest atheists cannot be discussed adequately in twenty pages apiece. And what of the presuppositions and consequences of atheism in intellectual history? What of Kant and Hegel, Darwin and Comte, Heidegger and Whitehead? What of analytic philosophy and critical rationalism? The reader would like to know how all of these fit together. So we decided to revise the start developed in *On Being a Christian* and to give it a deeper foundation from the perspective of intellectual history. In this we wished to present the question of God in its development, and in order to do this, we had to begin where, at least since Hegel, the intellectual history of the modern era begins: with Descartes and Pascal in the seventeenth century. Küng's goal: to elaborate and present coherently everything possible in philosophy, sociology, psychology, and natural science that has anything to do with the question of God in modern times.

Can all this be accomplished in two years? Only if one, first of all, knows what one wants to do, and, secondly, can fall back on preparatory work. In other words, an intuition of the whole was crucial for Küng before he had written the first line; already at the beginning he saw the complete book before him, as perhaps a composer sees a symphony or an architect a relatively complicated building. For Küng the question "Does God exist?" was no longer an open question. The book is concerned with the grounding of the existence of God within the horizon of modern thought, and with the elaboration of the previously discovered constructive solution to the problem. This "solution" of the question of God, however, was for Küng much different from a merely cognitive intellectual process which a theologian might think out after suitable study of other writers. This "solution" grew out of a decades-long personal experience in which he was entirely engaged, mentally and emotionally. The crucial turning point for Küng came in the final years of his study in Rome, 1953-1955, when he discovered for himself a new solution to the relationship of reason and belief, one between natural and dialectical theology. It became clear to him then that the "solution" of the problem consists in a "belief" before belief, that is, in something like a "basic trust," and this became the crucial theological foundation of the book *Existiert Gott?*

In Paris, where he studied from 1955 to 1957 at the Sorbonne and the Institute Catholique, Küng was impressed by lectures he attended on Descartes and Pascal, in which he found the relation of reason and belief again reflected, without discovering anything crucial to his "solution." It was indeed no accident that as a young professor at the University of Tübingen in 1960 Küng began his very first lecture with a comparison of Descartes and Pascal (thus discussing again the faith-knowledge question), just as eighteen years later he also began the book *Existiert Gott?* logically, from the perspective of intellectual history, with these French thinkers.

Likewise it had already become clear to Küng in his years in Rome that God must be thought of dynamically, in terms of becoming and dialectic, an approach which after long years of preparatory work in the 1950's was elaborated both theologically and philosophically in 1970 in his book on Hegel's Christology (*Menschwerdung Gottes. Eine Einführung in Hegels Philosophie als Prolegomena zu einer Künftigen Christologie*). The chapter on Hegel in *Existiert Gott?* can thus presuppose the large volume on Hegel, which, though it has not yet appeared in English, is at present being translated. In this book German idealistic philosophy (Kant, Fichte, Schelling) is also sketched in outline form, along with philosophical currents of the twentieth century, as, for example, the philosophy of Martin Heidegger—likewise an important preparation for *Existiert Gott?* When it seemed objectively justified to him, Küng did not hesitate to refer to and sometimes even quote from earlier books and works, not to spare himself further work but to show the inner continuity of his books more clearly. Thus Küng was proud that for the presentation of his ecclesiology in *On Being a Christian* (1974) he was able to take much from his book *The Church* (1967) without alteration, and that in *Existiert Gott?* the christological section in the final chapter contains parts of *On Being a Christian*.

Since 1970 Küng has given lectures regularly on the question of God in which he has especially dealt with an analysis of the atheism of Feuerbach, Marx, Nietzsche, and Freud and developed the solution (basic trust and basic distrust) in a broad theological-systematic fashion which he then presented in writing for the first time in *On Being a Christian*. In the course of his studies for these lectures Küng found himself corroborated by the American psychoanalyst Erik H. Erikson, in whose work the concepts of basic trust and basic distrust play an important role. Küng continued to work with the problem in numerous seminars, even during the writing of the book; he held one on Ernest Bloch's *Atheismus im Christentum* (Bloch in celebration of his ninetieth birthday participated in one session along with Jürgen Moltmann), one on positivism and critical rationalism, one on theology as a science (discussion of the Vienna Circle, Popper, Habermas, Gadamer), and, not least, a seminar for doctoral candidates on the process philosophy of Alfred North Whitehead.

All this makes it clear that when Küng began to write *Existiert Gott?* in 1975 he was well prepared; he did not need to work out everything suddenly from the beginning but could presuppose much from his own earlier publications and his own teaching activity. Above all—to repeat—Küng had an intuitive conception of the nature of the book: he knew what he wanted. Many details naturally still had to be elaborated, many things had to be studied at much greater depth, others had to be attacked from the beginning, but the crucial inspiration and even a not insignificant positive working-up of the material had already taken place twenty-five years before the final writing of the book. If, like Küng, one has the crucial themes and constructive solutions, the working out of the various parts of the "symphony" is of course always hard work, but the "artist" has already at bottom passed the crisis before the first note was written.

How does one write a book like *Existiert Gott*? Only, I think (for despite all my involvement I remain an outside insider), if many things come together simultaneously for the author: existential, even spiritual, prior decisions; a clear idea of the goal during the writing process; a precise conceptualization; decades-long studies; one's own scholarly preparatory work; enthusiam for the subject which carries one through all frustrations; totally engaged co-workers capable of loyal criticism; a secretary who types up even the tenth version patiently without protest; and, not least, the unshakeable conviction that there are innumerable people within and without the church, whether in Europe or America, to whom this book can provide an orientation for life but also for death.

Translated by Arlene Swidler

WHY I REMAIN A CATHOLIC

Hans Küng

Why do I remain a Catholic?

This is not an easy question to answer in the midst of a time- and energy-consuming controversy, when it becomes almost unbearable to write at all. After an unjust and unfair procedure on the part of the highest ecclesiastical authorities, I was deprived by decree of the title of "Catholic theologian" and an attempt was made to drive me out of my faculty of Catholic theology after twenty years of teaching there and to thrust me—without being overscrupulous about methods—to the margin of my Catholic Church very shortly after I had completed twenty-five years as a priest and celebrated my jubilee. In the face of harassments and threats, is it possible to offer declarations of loyalty or to make professions of faith?

Under these circumstances, why do I remain a Catholic? From thousands of letters, telegrams, telephone messages, the same depressing question faces me, raised in sadness, anger and despair in a variety of ways by innumerable Catholics throughout the world. Many are wondering if the wheel of history is to be turned back in our Catholic Church to the time before John XXIII and the Second Vatican Council. Are the new open-mindness, readiness for dialogue, humanist and Christian spirit again to yield to the triumphalism disavowed by the Council? Are Roman authorities again to abolish the freedom of theology, to intimidate critical theologians and to be allowed to discipline them by the use of spiritual power? Are bishops to be merely recipients of orders and to be obliged to carry out the Roman policy on those who are under their care? And, despite fine ecumenical words and gestures, is the ecclesiastical institution with its unecumenical attitudes and deeds to become once more an unfriendly, inhospitable, unfruitful "fortress" in this modern society of ours?

This latest development has in fact driven some already to formal secession from the Church and many others to a final emigration. This indeed is the most disastrous feature of the present ecclesiastical policy: The silent mass withdrawal from the Church will continue. Precisely those who as pastors, chaplains, and religion teachers on the grass roots level have to dish out the soup that the hierarchs have cooked up for them, those therefore who at their wit's end seek for arguments which will make the measures taken by Rome somehow "reasonable" in the face of the critical questions people raise—they will wish to know the answer to the question: Why still remain a Catholic?

A Personal Question

It is not any liking for theoretical problems which makes me raise this question, but the necessity of defense. For the doubts about catholicity are not mine, they are raised by certain authorities and hierarchs. Why then do I remain a Catholic? The answer will first of all be for me, as for many other people: I do not wish to allow that to be taken away from me which throughout my life has become valuable and dear to me. In the first place, I was born into this Catholic Church: baptized, it is true, into the much larger community of all those who believe in Jesus Christ—nevertheless, born at the same time into a Catholic family which is dear to me, a Swiss Catholic parish to which I am always glad to return: in a word, into a Catholic homeland which I do not want to lose, which I do not want to abandon. All this I feel precisely as a theologian.

At a very early stage, I became acquainted also with Rome and the papacy, and—despite all calumnies—I do not cherish any "anti-Roman feeling." How often am I to continue saying and writing that I am not against the papacy nor am I against the present Pope, but that I have always contended inside and outside the Church for a Petrine ministry—purged however of absolutist features—on biblical foundations! I have continually spoken out for a genuine pastoral primacy in the sense of spiritual responsibility, internal leadership and active concern for the welfare of the Church as a whole: a primacy which might then become a universally respected authority for mediation and conciliation in the whole ecumenical world. It would of course be a primacy not of dominion but of unselfish service, exercised in responsibility before the Lord of the Church and lived in unpretentious brotherliness. It would be a primacy, not in the spirit of a Roman imperialism with religious trimmings, such as I came to know quite closely under Pius XII during my seven years of study in Rome, but a primacy in the spirit of Jesus Christ, as it was illustrated for me in the figures of Gregory the Great and—as a Council theologian I was able to observe him at close quarters—John XXIII. These were Popes who expected not servile submissiveness, uncritical devotion, sentimental idolization, but loyal collaboration, constructive criticism and constant prayer on their behalf: collaborators of our joy, not masters of our faith, to adopt a saying of the Apostle Paul.

At a very early stage, too, I came to know the Catholic Church as embracing the whole world and in it I was able to receive and learn an immense amount from innumerable people—many of them friends—everywhere. From that time onward, I have become more clearly aware that the Catholic Church must not become confused simply with the Catholic hierarchy, still less with the Roman bureaucracy.

But above all there was Tübingen, Protestant Tübingen with its Catholic faculty. Here as professor from 1960 onward, I have increasingly become a part of this faculty which, from its foundation, has had a great history, not only of success, but also of conflict. How many Catholic theologians in Tübingen, including some who are still alive and teaching, have been admonished, put on the Index, harassed and disciplined! There is nothing new under the Tübingen sun.

It was from this Catholic faculty of Tübingen, in the free air of Tübingen, that both my books and the books of my colleagues emerged and without which they would scarcely have been possible or at any rate only in another form. In continual discussion with colleagues and students it was possible for a Catholic theology to emerge here, which—unlike the former controversial theology—has a truly ecumenical character and seeks to combine two things: loyalty to the Catholic heritage and openness to Christendom—in fact, to the ecumenical world as a whole. Discussion, particularly with Protestant colleagues, was of decisive importance, not in order to disparage the Catholic reality, still less to squander it, but in an ecumenical spirit to throw new light on it from the Gospel and to gain a deeper understanding of it. Seeing this task as my duty, I was able in 1963 to switch over in the Catholic theological faculty to the recently established chair for dogmatic and ecumenical theology. This position was combined with the direction of an Institute of Ecumenical Research which worked systematically for the convergence of divergent theologies without attempting to avoid questions hitherto regarded as taboo. Under these conditions, can a theologian be blamed for defending himself with all legitimate means against the pressure to get him out of this faculty of his?

Why then do I remain a Catholic?

Not merely because of my Catholic *origins* but also because of this *life task* of mine which is grasped as a great opportunity and which as a Catholic theologian I can fulfill appropriately only in the context of the Tübingen faculty of Catholic theology. But now the question must be asked: What, properly speaking, is this Catholic reality for the sake of which I want to remain a Catholic theologian?

Who Is a Catholic Theologian?

In accordance with the original meaning of the word and with ancient tradition, anyone can describe her/himself as a Catholic theologian if s/he is aware of being obliged in her/his theology to the "Catholic"—that is, to the "*whole*," the "universal, comprehensive, total"—Church. This catholicity has two dimensions: temporal and spatial.

First, *catholicity in time*: A theologian is Catholic if s/he is aware of being united with the whole Church—that is, with the Church of all times. S/he will therefore not describe from the outset certain centuries as "un-Christian" or "unevangelical." S/he is convinced that there was in every century a community of believers who heard the Gospel of Jesus Christ and attempted to live it, sometimes with success and sometimes not, as is always the case with human fragility and fallibility in translating intentions into deeds.

Protestant radicalism on the other hand (not to be confused with evangelical radicality) is always in danger of wanting unhistorically to begin at zero and so to pass from Jesus to Paul, from Paul to Augustine, and then in a great leap to pass over the Middle Ages to Luther and Calvin, and from that point to leap across one's own "orthodox" tradition to the more recent church fathers or, better, heads of schools.

The *Catholic* theologian, by contrast, will always start out from the fact that there was never a time when the Gospel was left without witness and will try to learn from the Church of the past. While insisting on the necessity of critical scrutiny, s/he will never overlook the boundary posts and danger signals which the Church in former times, in its concern and struggle for the one true faith, often at times of great distress and danger, set up in the form of creeds and definitions to distinguish between good and bad interpretations of the message. S/he will never neglect the positive and negative experiences of his/her predecessors and colleagues in theology, those teachers who are her/his older and more experienced fellow students in the school of sacred Scripture. It is precisely in this critical scrutiny that the Catholic theologian is interested in the *continuity* which is preserved through all disruptions.

Second, *catholicity in space*: A theologian is Catholic if s/he is aware of being united with the Church of all nations and continents. S/he must therefore not orient her/himself only to the regional Church or to a national Church and will not isolate her/himself from the Church as a whole. S/he is convinced that in all nations and on all continents there is a community of believers which ultimately does not wish to be anything other than his/her own Church, is impelled no less by the Gospel, and which has something to say to her/his own Church and theology.

Protestant particularism on the other hand (not to be confused with evangelical congregational attachment) will always be inclined to orient itself to the locally restricted church, its faith and its life, and to be content with a theological (occasionally intellectual, highly cultivated) provincialism.

The *Catholic* theologian will always start out from the fact that the Gospel has not left itself without witness to any nation, any class or race, and s/he will try to learn from other churches. However deeply rooted s/he may be in a particular local Church, s/he will not tie his/her theology to a particular nation, culture, race, class, form of society, ideology or school. Precisely in his/her specific loyalty, the Catholic theologian is interested in the *universality* of the Christian faith embracing all groups.

It is in this twofold sense then that I want to be and remain a Catholic theologian and to defend the truth of the Catholic faith in Catholic depth and breadth. And there is no doubt that a number of those who describe themselves as Protestant or evangelical can be and are in fact catholic in this sense, particularly in Tübingen. There ought to be joy at this, even on the part of the institutional Church.

The Criterion of What Is Catholic

Does this affirmation of what is Catholic in time and space, depth and breadth, mean that you have to accept more or less *everything* that has been officially taught, ordered and observed in the course of twenty centuries? Is it such a total identification that is meant by the Vatican Congregation for the Doctrine of the Faith and the German Bishops Conference when they speak of the "complete," "full," "uncurtailed" truth of the Catholic faith?

Surely what is meant cannot be such a totalitarian conception of truth. For, even on the part of the institutional Church, it is now scarcely disputed that momentous and even theologically "justified" errors have occurred in the history of Catholic teaching and practice and have been corrected (most tacitly) up to a point even by the Popes. The list is immense and includes the excommunication of the Ecumenical Patriarch of Constantinople and of the Greek Church, prohibition of vernacular liturgy, condemnation of Galileo and the modern scientific worldview, condemnation of Chinese and Indian forms of divine worship and names of God, the maintenance of the medieval secular power of the Pope up to the First Vatican Council with the aid of all the secular and spiritual means of excommunication, condemnation of human rights and particularly freedom of conscience and religion, and discrimination against the Jewish people; finally, in the present century, the numerous condemnations of modern historical critical exegesis (with reference to the authenticity of the Books of the Bible, source criticism, historicity and literary genres) and condemnations in the dogmatic field, especially in connection with "modernism" (the theory of evolution, understanding of development of dogma); and, in very present times, Pius XII's cleaning-up measures (likewise dogmatically justified) leading to the dismissal of the most outstanding theologians of the pre-conciliar period such as M.D. Chenu, Yves Congar, Henri de Lubac, Pierre Teilhard de Chardin, who almost all became Council theologians under John XXIII.

Is it not obvious that a distinction must be made, precisely for the sake of what is truly Catholic? Not everything that has been officially taught and practiced in the Catholic Church is Catholic. Is it not true that catholicity would harden into "Catholicism" if that which has "become the Catholic reality" (the words are those of Joseph Cardinal Ratzinger of Munich) is simply accepted instead of being submitted to a criterion? And for the Catholic Christian too this criterion can be nothing but the Christian message, the *Gospel* in its ultimate concrete form, *Jesus Christ himself,* who for the Church and—despite all assertions to the contrary—also for me is the Son and Word of God. He is and remains the norm in the light of which every ecclesiastical authority—which is not disputed—must be judged: the norm by which the theologian must be tested and in the light of which s/he must continually justify her/himself in the spirit of self-criticism and true humility.

All this means that to be "Catholic" does not imply—for the sake of a supposed "fullness," "integrity," "completeness," "uncurtailedness"—a false humility obediently accepting *everything*, putting up with *everything*. That would be a fatal pooling of contradictions, a confusion of true and false.

Certainly Protestantism has often been reproached for accepting too little, for making a one-sided selection from the whole. But on the other hand, it is often impossible to avoid reproaching Catholicism for accepting too much:

a syncretistic accumulation of heterogeneous, distorted, and occasionally un-Christian, pagan elements. Which is worse: a sin by defect or a sin by excess?

Catholicity therefore must in every case be understood critically—critically according to the Gospel. To every Catholic "and" there must be added ever again the necessary protest of the "alone" from which alone the "and" is at all meaningful. Reforms—in practice and teaching—must remain possible. For the theologian, this means nothing other than the fact that the Catholic theologian in a genuine sense must be evangelically oriented and conversely that the evangelical theologian in a genuine sense must be oriented in a Catholic way. Admittedly, this makes the theological demarcations objectively and conceptually more complicated than they might seem to be in the light of official doctrinal documents which are often terribly simple and display little catholic depth and breadth. Why then do I remain a Catholic? Precisely because as such I can assert an "evangelical catholicity" concentrated and organized in the light of the Gospel, which is nothing but genuine ecumenicity. Being Catholic, then, means being ecumenical in the fullest sense.

But what of the Roman factor?

"Roman Catholic" is a late and misleading neologism. Once again, I have nothing against Rome. I mean that, precisely because I wanted to be a Catholic theologian, I could not tie my Catholic faith and Catholic theology simply to the ingrown Roman absolutist claims from the Middle Ages and later times. Certainly, there must be development in doctrine and practice, but only an *evolutio secundum evangelium*, or "a development in accordance with the Gospel." An *evolutio praeter evangelium*, or "a development apart from the Gospel," may be tolerated. But an *evolutio contra evangelium*, "a development contrary to the Gospel," must be resisted. Applied to the papacy, this means that I have always acknowledged and defended the pastoral primacy of the Bishops of Rome linked to Peter and the great Roman tradition as an element in Catholic tradition that is supported by the Gospel. But Roman legalism, centralism and triumphalism in teaching, morality and Church discipline, dominant especially from the eleventh century onward, but prepared long before then, are supported neither by the ancient Catholic tradition nor—still less—by the Gospel itself; they were also disavowed by the Second Vatican Council. On the contrary, these things were mainly responsible for the Schism with the East and with the Reformation churches. They represent the "Catholicism" about which the present controversy is being carried on in the name of the catholicity of the Catholic Church.

Are there some of our cardinals and bishops who do not want to see that in individual points of theory and practice their thinking is more Roman than Catholic? Perhaps my Protestant colleague, Walther von Löwenich, an authority on both Luther and modern Catholicism, has rightly seen this in the infallibility debate when he writes: "The essential question in the Küng case is not appropriately stated as 'Is Küng still a Catholic?' It should be, 'Will Catholicism struggle out of its dogmatic constriction into genuine catholicity?' "

Catholicity then is gift and task, indicative and imperative, origin and future. It is within this tension that I want to continue the pursuit of theology and as decisively as hitherto to make the message of Jesus Christ intelligible to people of the present time, while being ready to learn and to be corrected whenever it is a question of discussion between equal partners in a collegial spirit. I must insist, against all the repeated assertions to the contrary by the German Bishops, that I have never refused such a discussion even in regard to the Roman authorities, and that I have frequently had this kind of discussion both with representatives of the German Bishops Conference and with the local Bishop. But, for the sake of protecting human and Christian rights and for the sake of the freedom of theological science, I have had to resist throughout all the years an interrogation of an Inquisition according all rights to itself and practically none to the accused person. That much I owe to those also who have suffered—and, as it seems, will suffer in the future—under these inhumane and un-Christian measures.

Catholic Church, yes! Roman Inquisition, no!

I know that I am not alone in this controversy about true catholicity. I shall fight against any acquiescence together with the many people who have hiterto supported me. We must continue to work together for a truly Catholic Church that is bound by the Gospel. For this, it is worthwhile to remain a Catholic.

Translated by Edward Quinn and Leonard Swidler